MICHEL FOUCAULT'S ARCHAEOLOGY
OF SCIENTIFIC REASON

This book is an important introduction to and critical interpretation of the work of the major French thinker, Michel Foucault. Through comprehensive and detailed analyses of such important texts as *The history of madness in the age of reason, The birth of the clinic, The order of things,* and *The archaeology of knowledge,* Professor Gutting provides a lucid exposition of Foucault's "archaeological" approach to the history of thought, a method for uncovering the "unconscious" structures that set boundaries on the thinking of a given epoch.

The book also casts Foucault in a new light, relating his work to two major but neglected influences on him: Gaston Bachelard's philosophy of science and Georges Canguilhem's history of science. This perspective yields a new and valuable understanding of Foucault as a historian and philosopher of science, balancing and complementing the more common view that he was primarily a social critic and theorist.

An excellent guide for those first approaching Foucault's work, the book will also be a challenging interpretation and evaluation for those already familiar with his writings.

MODERN EUROPEAN PHILOSOPHY

Executive editor
RAYMOND GEUSS, COLUMBIA UNIVERSITY

Editorial board
HIDÉ ISHIGURO, BARNARD COLLEGE
ALAN MONTEFIORE, BALLIOL COLLEGE, OXFORD
MARY TILES, ROYAL INSTITUTE OF PHILOSOPHY

R. M. Chisholm, *Brentano and Intrinsic Value*
Raymond Geuss, *The Idea of a Critical Theory:*
Habermas and the Frankfurt School
Karel Lambert, *Meinong and the Principle of Independence*
Charles Taylor, *Hegel and Modern Society*
Mary Tiles, *Bachelard: Science and Objectivity*
Robert S. Tragesser, *Husserl and Realism in Logic and Mathematics*
Peter Winch, *Simone Weil: The Just Balance*

MICHEL FOUCAULT'S ARCHAEOLOGY OF SCIENTIFIC REASON

GARY GUTTING
University of Notre Dame

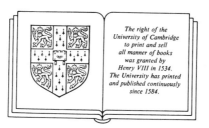

The right of the
University of Cambridge
to print and sell
all manner of books
was granted by
Henry VIII in 1534.
The University has printed
and published continuously
since 1584.

CAMBRIDGE UNIVERSITY PRESS

CAMBRIDGE

NEW YORK   PORT CHESTER

MELBOURNE   SYDNEY

Published by the Press Syndicate of the University of Cambridge
The Pitt Building, Trumpington Street, Cambridge CB2 1RP
40 West 20th Street, New York, NY 10011, USA
10 Stamford Road, Oakleigh, Melbourne 3166, Australia

© Cambridge University Press 1989

First published 1989
Reprinted 1990, 1991

Printed in the United States of America

Library of Congress Cataloging-in-Publication Data
Gutting, Gary.
Michel Foucault's archaeology of scientific reason / Gary Gutting.
p.   cm. – (Modern European philosophy)
ISBN 0–521–36619–4.   ISBN 0–521–36698–4 (pbk.)
1. Foucault, Michel – Contributions in archaeology of scientific
reason. 2. Science – Philosophy – History – 20th century. 3. Social
sciences – Philosophy – History – 20th century.   I. Title.
II. Series.
B2430.F724G87   1989
194–dc19   88–31881
CIP

British Library Cataloguing in Publication Data
Gutting, Gary
Michel Foucault's archaeology of scientific
reason. – (Modern European philosophy)
1. French philosophy, Foucault, Michel, 1926–1984
I. Title II. Series
194
ISBN 0 521 36619 4 hardback
ISBN 0 521 36698 4 paperback

Part of Chapter 1 was published as "Gaston Bachelard's philosophy of science"
in *International Studies in Philosophy of Science* 2 (1987) and is reprinted with
permission of Routlege and Kegan Paul. Part of Chapter 6 was included in
"Michel Foucault and the History of Reason," published in Ernan McMullin,
ed., *Construction and constraint: the shaping of scientific rationality*, 1988, and is
reprinted with permission of the University of Notre Dame Press.

To

ANASTASIA

τῇ καλλίστῃ

CONTENTS

Preface   *page* ix

Introduction   1

1 **Bachelard and Canguilhem**   9
  Bachelard's philosophy of science   12
    Reason and science   13
    Bachelard's model of scientific change   14
    The epistemological and metaphysical ramifications
    of Bachelard's model   22
  Canguilhem's history of science   32
    Canguilhem's conception of the history of science   32
    Canguilhem's conception of norms   45
    Foucault and the Bachelard–Canguilhem network   52

2 **Madness and mental illness**   55
  Early writings on mental illness   55
  Madness in the Classical Age   69
  Mental illness and the asylum   87
  The voice of madness   95
  The history of madness: methods and results   100

3 **Clinical medicine**   111
  Classical medicine   112
  A new medical consciousness   115
  The clinic as an institution   118

vii

	The linguistic structure of medical signs	120
	The probabilistic structure of medical cases	122
	Seeing and saying	124
	Anatomo-clinical medicine	127
	The birth of the clinic: methods and results	133
4	**The order of things: I. From resemblance to representation**	139
	The Renaissance episteme	140
	Classical order	146
	Classical signs and language	148
	Classical knowledge	155
	General grammar	157
	Natural history	162
	Analysis of wealth	169
	The common structure of the Classical domains	173
	Critical reactions	175
5	**The order of things: II. The rise and fall of man**	181
	The modern episteme	181
	Philosophy	184
	Modern empirical sciences	186
	Language and modern thought	195
	Man and the analytic of finitude	198
	The human sciences	208
	The order of things: methods and results	217
6	**The archaeology of knowledge**	227
	The elements of archaeology	231
	Statements	239
	Archaeology and the history of ideas	244
	Archaeology and the history of science	249
	Discourse and the nondiscursive	256
	Conclusion	260
7	**Reason and philosophy**	261
	Archaeological method and Foucault's philosophical project	262
	Is Foucault's critique of reason self-refuting?	272
	Conclusion	287
	Bibliography	289
	Index	304

PREFACE

Any study of Michel Foucault should anticipate two sorts of readers. On the one hand, there are those intrigued by what they have heard of his ideas and methods but frustrated by texts they find too difficult to penetrate. They turn to secondary literature to dispel their bemusement and confusion. On the other hand, there are those who have worked through at least some of his books with understanding and appreciation and are looking for further interpretative and critical perspectives. In writing this book, I have tried to keep both audiences in mind. I have put a very high premium on lucid and thorough explanations of Foucault's ideas, and my analyses offer coherent interpretations of each work as a whole, contrary to the tendency of many commentators to highlight only selected aspects of a given text. Because of this, I hope the book will be a useful resource for those making a first approach to Foucault's thought. For those already familiar with Foucault, it offers a new perspective that places his thought in the context of recent French history and philosophy of science, particularly the work of Gaston Bachelard and Georges Canguilhem. (It also provides an introduction to these two thinkers, who are not very well known in English-speaking countries.) This opens up a fresh and, I hope to show, fruitful way of understanding Foucault as a historian and philosopher of science, balancing and complementing the current standard construal of him as a social critic and theorist.

To date, most studies of Foucault have rightly taken the form of introductory surveys of the entire body of his work, aiming at a comprehensive preliminary understanding of his main claims, motivations, and methods. Here Alan Sheridan's *Foucault: The will to truth* probably remains the best single overall guide, although there is clearly a need for an updated and improved general introduction. More recently, there have appeared a number of studies with narrower interpretative and critical foci, most notably Dreyfus and Rabinow's *Michel Foucault: beyond structuralism and hermeneutics* and John Rajchman's *Michel Foucault and the freedom of philosophy*. These, like almost all more specialized work on Foucault over the last few years, are primarily concerned with the theme of the interconnection of power and knowledge that was Foucault's own primary emphasis during the 1970s. There are signs that the next wave of Foucault analysis will focus on the ethical direction his work took in the 1980s. By contrast, this book turns back to the earlier, explicitly archaeological period of Foucault's writings. I have chosen this emphasis not only because these writings have been relatively neglected in recent discussions but also because they are both difficult and important enough to warrant much closer scrutiny than they have yet received. Moreover, beyond their great intrinsic importance, they are crucial for an adequate understanding of Foucault's later development. As we shall see, some major elements of the later knowledge–power theme are implicit from the beginning of Foucault's work; and the archaeological approach to the history of thought remains a key element in the later genealogical method. Without downgrading the value and distinctiveness of the work after AK,[1] I want to call attention to the importance of the preceding archaeological period.

In addition to numerous specific points of interpretation and evaluation, my analysis of Foucault's archaeology will support three more general conclusions. First, archaeology is not an isolated method reflecting Foucault's idiosyncratic approach to the history of thought. Rather, it is rooted in the French tradition of history and philosophy of science and is specifically developed in the context of Gaston Bachelard's philosophy of science and

---

1. See list of abbreviations, p. xii.

through an extension and transformation of Georges Canguil-hem's history of science.

Second, Foucault's archaeology is essentially grounded in his-torical practice rather than philosophical theory. It is a method of historical analysis that was forged, pragmatically and piecemeal, to deal with specific problems posed by the history of thought. Foucault did not develop it as the corollary of fundamental philo-sophical views about language, meaning, and truth. This is not to deny that his historical work has a philosophical intent or that philosophical issues are frequently in the background of his dis-cussions. But his archaeological method originates primarily from concrete struggles for historical understanding, not from prior philosophical commitments. This understanding of archae-ology is closely linked to Foucault's radical reconception of the philosophical enterprise. He rejects the traditional goal of ulti-mate, fundamental Truth and instead construes philosophy as an instrument for realizing concrete and local objectives in the strug-gle for human liberation.

Third, Foucault's archaeology is not, as critics have often main-tained, an engine of universal skepticism or relativism, under-mining all pretensions to truth and objectivity. The project of archaeological analysis does not, in itself, question the objectivity or validity of a body of knowledge to which it is applied. There is no reason, for example, to think that an archaeology of modern physics or chemistry would have an epistemically subversive in-tent or effect. Moreover, as we shall see, even Foucault's analyses of the much more dubious medical and social scientific disci-plines typically allow them a substantial core of objective truth. Properly understood, archaeology is a technique for revealing how a discipline has developed norms of validity and objectivity, not for questioning the very possibility of any such norms. Ar-chaeology may, of course, find that some disciplines are far less scientific than their own self-understanding suggests. But we shall see that, even in such cases, it is designed as a careful scrutiny of the epistemic claims of a discipline, not as an a priori instrument for rejecting these claims.

The book begins with a brief introduction that formulates Fou-cault's fundamental historicophilosophical project and quickly surveys the whole of his work as carrying out this project. Chap-ter 1 provides some necessary background on Bachelard and Canguilhem and on Foucault's connection to them. We then turn to a detailed exegesis of the main books Foucault published through 1969 and assessments of their historical and philosophical significance. Chapter 2 deals with Foucault's study of the historical roots of modern psychology and psychiatry in FD. It begins with back- ground studies of his two earlier treatments of these disciplines, *Maladie mentale et personnalité* and the "Introduction" to Binswanger's *Dream and existence*. I am also concerned with developing an interpretation and evaluation of FD as a whole (not of just the greatly condensed English translation, *Madness and civilization*) and with showing how it sets the agenda for all of Foucault's earlier work. Chapter 3 deals with BC, both to offer a close analysis of its often dense text and to show its strong methodological ties to Canguilhem's approach to the history of science. Chapters 4 and 5 offer a detailed treatment of OT, providing both an overall interpretation and evaluation of its content and an explication of its full development of Foucault's archaeological method. In interpreting OT, my concern is not only to elucidate each element of its wide-ranging discussion but to show how all these elements fit together into a close though complex unity. I also show how the mature archaeological method of OT both derives from and transforms the approaches of Bachelard and Canguilhem, and I offer a critical assessment of its value as an approach to the history of thought. Chapter 6 turns to the explicit methodological account that Foucault puts forward in AK, paying particular attention to the relationship of this methodology to other approaches to the history of thought and to Foucault's own historical studies. Chapter 7 offers a concluding philosophical evaluation of Foucault's project of an archaeological history of reason.

Abbreviations

The following abbreviations are used in citing Foucault's writings. (Full references are given in the Bibliography.)

AK: *The archaeology of knowledge*
BC: *The birth of the clinic*
DP: *Discipline and punish*
FD: *Folie et déraison*
HS: *History of sexuality*
MC: *Madness and civilization*
MMP: *Maladie mentale et personnalité*

MMPsy: *Mental Illness and Psychology*
OT: *The order of things*
RE: "Introduction" to Binswanger's *Rêve et existence*

In general, citations from these works are from the English
translations listed in the Bibliography. Translations from RE,
from parts of FD not included in MC, and from parts of MMP
not included in MMPsy are mine. Translations from other works
by Foucault are mine except when the notes cite a published
English version.

Acknowledgments

I am grateful first of all to Karl Ameriks for our many conversations over the last several years about Foucault and much else.
He has been a continuing source of stimulating ideas and useful
information and offered characteristically judicious reactions to
the penultimate draft of this book. Thanks are also due to Steve
Watson for his helpful comments and suggestions; to Mary Tiles
and C. Hertogh, who read drafts of my chapter on Bachelard
and Canguilhem and provided valuable expert suggestions; and
to those who followed my seminars on Foucault at Notre Dame
and at the Free University of Amsterdam for their many helpful
questions and comments. I am especially appreciative of the
cheerful and excellent service provided by Margaret Jasciewicz
and her co-workers in the Notre Dame Arts and Letters Steno
Pool, particularly Nila Gerhold, Nancy Kegler, and Cheryl Reed.

On a more official level, I am happy to acknowledge support
for work on this book by the Notre Dame Institute for Scholarship in the Liberal Arts and by the National Science Foundation
(History and Philosophy of Science Division).

Finally, I am especially grateful to the members of my unfail-
ingly interesting and challenging family for a variety of forms of
support, encouragement, and tolerance: to Tasha, for her fresh-
ness, charm, and frequent reminders that there is more to life
than books and ideas; to Edward, for the intelligence, erudition,
and wit of his conversation; to Tom for always being so cheerful,
kind, and helpful; and, most of all, to my wife, Anastasia, whose
beauty and love are my constant joy.

INTRODUCTION

The work of Michel Foucault, now so abruptly and arbitrarily completed, can be fruitfully analyzed and evaluated from a wide range of contemporary intellectual standpoints. He can be regarded as a philosopher, a social historian, a literary analyst, a social and political critic; each of these perspectives focuses on something integral to his achievement. But his intellectual métier, through which he develops all his ideas about philosophy, literature, society, and politics, is the history of thought. With one exception, all his major books are histories of aspects of Western thought, and the exception (AK) is a methodological reflection on this historical work. Foucault's choice of title for his chair at the Collège de France was entirely appropriate: Professor of the History of Systems of Thought.

Foucault was not, however, interested in the history of thought merely for its own sake. His historical work was guided by a "philosophical *ethos*"[1] deriving from the Enlightenment values of human liberation and of autonomous human thought as an instrument of that liberation. Foucault's work is a search for truths that will make us free. But he develops this Enlightenment ideal in an

---

1. Michel Foucault, "What Is Enlightenment?" in Paul Rabinow, ed., *The Foucault reader* (New York: Pantheon, 1984), 45.

essentially self-critical mode, exhibiting an acute awareness of how specific employments of reasons, even bodies of scientific knowledge, can themselves constrain and oppress human beings. The project of Foucault's history of thought is, accordingly, two-fold: to show how particular domains of knowledge have constrained human freedom and to provide the intellectual resources for overcoming these constraints.

Foucault characterizes this project by comparing and contrasting it to Kant's eighteenth-century project for a critique of reason. According to Foucault, Kant's basic aim is implicit in his response to the *Berliner Monatschrift's* question, "What is enlightenment?" His famous answer was that enlightenment is man's release from his "inability to make use of his understanding without direction from another,"[2] an inability that was to be overcome by finding the courage to use one's own reason rather than submit it to books, pastors, physicians, and other external authorities. Kant felt that his own age was the beginning of reason's emergence as the autonomous force directing human life and so required a careful assessment of its precise scope and limits. As Foucault puts it:

> It is precisely at this moment that the critique is necessary, since its role is that of defining the conditions under which the use of reason is legitimate in order to determine what can be known, what must be done, and what may be hoped. Illegitimate uses of reason are what give rise to dogmatism and heteronomy, along with illusion; . . . It is when the legitimate use of reason has been clearly defined in its principles that its autonomy can be assured.[3]

Kant, however, thought that the limits of reason revealed by his critique derived from necessary a priori structures that defined the very possibility of our knowledge – that is, from "formal structures with universal value."[4] (We will see below, in our discussion of OT, how, according to Foucault, this connection of the limitations of knowledge to its possibility is characteristic of the modern conception of knowledge.) It is at this point that Foucault's project for a critique of reason differs from Kant's. Unlike Kant, he is not

2. I. Kant, "What Is Enlightenment?" translated by Lewis White Beck, in *On history* (New York: Bobbs-Merrill, 1963), 3.
3. Foucault, "What Is Enlightenment?" 38.
4. Ibid., 46.

concerned with determining the a priori, necessary conditions governing the exercise of reason but with reflection on what *seem* to be such conditions to reveal the extent to which they in fact have a contingent historical origin. Through such reflection – carried out by histories of thought – he aims at showing how we can free ourselves from ("transgress") the constraints of these conditions.[5] As a result, Foucault gives a new meaning to the project of a critique of reason.

> Criticism indeed consists of analyzing and reflecting upon limits. But if the Kantian question was that of knowing what limits knowledge has to renounce transgressing, it seems to me that the critical question today has been turned back into a positive one: in what is given to us as universal, necessary, obligatory, what place is occupied by whatever is singular, contingent, and the product of arbitrary constraints? The point, in brief, is to transform the critique conducted in the form of necessary limitation into a practical critique that takes the form of a possible transgression.[6]

Foucault's project of historical critique represents an important reconception of the cultural role of philosophy. He gives up the traditional philosophical goal of grounding theoretical and practical knowledge in an understanding of the essential, universal structures of thought and reality and instead applies the philosopher's analytic and synthetic skills to the task of uncovering and, when possible, dissolving contingent, historical constraints on thought. He thus abandons the venerable but empty pretension that philosophy provides a privileged access to fundamental truths.[7] But, at the same time, he offers a more concrete and effective approach to the equally venerable goal of liberating the human spirit.

Foucault's project also differs from Kant's in its point of application. Kant was primarily concerned with the scientific knowledge of nature, mathematics and physics, his idea being that an understanding of the conditions of possibility of these paradigms of knowledge would reveal the a priori structures of

5. This theme of transgression shows the influence of Georges Bataille on Foucault and is present as early as FD (Preface to the first edition, iii–v).
6. Foucault, "What Is Enlightenment?" 45.
7. In this sense, Foucault's view is skeptical. For a good discussion of Foucault as a skeptic, cf. John Rajchman, *Michel Foucault: the freedom of philosophy* (New York: Columbia University Press, 1985), 2–7.

knowledge as such. Foucault, by contrast, is concerned with the much more dubious disciplines ("the human sciences") that try to provide knowledge of human beings. This is because he sees these disciplines, rather than the natural sciences, as the primary source of contemporary constraints on human freedom. We can, accordingly, characterize his fundamental intellectual project as a philosophical critique of the human sciences, carried out by a history of thought in the service of human liberation.

Foucault's critique of the human sciences is, in every case, a matter of questioning key aspects of their contemporary self-understanding. For example, contemporary psychology and psychiatry regard themselves as scientifically objective disciplines that have discovered the true nature of madness as "mental illness." They further see themselves as employing their knowledge of mental illnesses for the purely humanitarian purpose of curing those who suffer from them. In his first major book, FD, Foucault traces the historical origins of psychology and psychiatry with a view to showing, first, that there is no privileged status to the modern conception of madness as mental illness. Second, he tries to show that the mad are regarded as threats to the moral order of modern society and that their "medical" treatment has been more a matter of social control than of compassionate relief.

In Foucault's second book, BC, he moves from "mental illness" to physical illness. Like psychiatry, modern medicine sees itself as based on a body of objective, scientific knowledge (e.g., that of pathological anatomy). Moreover, it thinks it has achieved this knowledge simply by, for the first time, looking at the human body and its diseases with a clear and unbiased empirical eye. Foucault, however, sets out to show that modern medicine is no more a matter of pure observation than was, for example, the medicine of the seventeenth and the eighteenth centuries. In both cases, medical knowledge was based not on a pure experience, free of interpretation, but on a very specific way of perceiving bodies and diseases, structured by a grid of a priori conceptions.

FD and BC were studies of particular human sciences. Moreover, they primarily dealt with knowledge of deviations (madness, illness) from "normal" human states. In OT (in many ways his major work), Foucault provided a comprehensive, though often very schematic, account of the entire body of modern positive knowledge of human beings. Here his central claim is that all such knowledge is based on a particular conception of human beings (a conception he labels *man*). The distinctive feature of man, in this sense, is to be both an object in the world and the knowing subject through which there exists a world of objects. Although modern thinkers tend to take this conception of ourselves as definitive of human reality once and for all, Foucault maintains that it is just one historical construal of it – and one that is presently passing away. Overall, OT can be regarded as a critique of the concept of man carried out in three stages. First, Foucault shows that the concept had no role at all in the Classical Age that preceded our modern period. Second, he analyzes modern philosophical efforts to develop a coherent understanding of man and exhibits their failure. Finally, he analyzes the more successful efforts of the human sciences to attain a knowledge of man and shows that they themselves are based on disciplines that undermine the concept of man. Foucault concludes that the age of thought dominated by this particular conception of human reality is nearing its end and that, accordingly, we are in a position to break free of the constraints on our freedom that it imposes.

In the course of developing his critique of the human sciences, Foucault became increasingly sensitive to questions about the methods of historical analysis he was using. Specifically, he came to see himself as employing a distinctive method of analysis that he called *archaeological*. The use of *archaeology* as a methodological metaphor goes back at least to Merleau-Ponty, and Foucault initially uses it in a very casual and vague way.[8] By the time he wrote BC, he was sufficiently taken with it (though still not entirely clear about its meaning) to subtitle the book "An archaeology of medical perception [régard]". In the book following OT – AK – Foucault offered an extended reflection on the archaeological method he had developed in his preceding studies.

8. Cf., for example, M. Merleau-Ponty, "Phenomenology and Psychoanalysis," in Alden Fisher, ed., *Essential writings: Merleau-Ponty* (New York: Harcourt, Brace, & World, 1969), 86. Here Merleau-Ponty characterizes psychoanalysis as an archaeology. Earlier, Cavaillès (referring to Fink's 1933 *Kantstudien* article), refers to phenomenology as an archaeology. (I owe these references to my colleague, Steve Watson.) Foucault's own first use of the term seems to be in MMP, where he says that Freudian "neurosis is a spontaneous archaeology of the libido" (26). His first use of it to refer to an approach to the history of thought is in the Preface to the first edition of FD, where, speaking of the end of reason's dialogue with madness in the Classical Age, he says that he wants to write "the archaeology of this silence" (FD, ii).

AK clearly marks the end of one major stage of Foucault's work. After its publication in 1969, he remained relatively silent for six years. DP, published in 1975, resumes his critique of the human sciences but now in a mode that places far more emphasis than his previous work on social and institutional mechanisms of power. Here Foucault's primary concern is to show how bodies of knowledge – particularly the modern social sciences – are inextricably interwoven with techniques of social control. They are not, he maintains, autonomous intellectual achievements applied, à la Bacon, as instruments of social power. Rather, their very constitution as knowledge depends essentially on (although it is not reducible to) mechanisms of power. In DP, for example, Foucault details the essential dependence of criminology on the development of prisons in the nineteenth century, and he suggests similar ties between other social sciences and such controlling social structures as schools, military camps, and factories. Similarly, in the first volume of HS he argues that the "sciences of sexuality" developed in the nineteenth and twentieth centuries are integral parts of another aspect of modern society's control of its members. Roughly, the disciplinary techniques associated with "disciplines" such as criminology and pedagogy control by making men objects, whereas the sciences of sexuality make them self-monitoring subjects.

The theme of the essential connection of knowledge with power develops fully and explicitly what was suggested at numerous points in Foucault's earlier work. What is distinctive in DP and HS is Foucault's new conception of the nature of power. He rejects the standard view that power is a purely negative, repressive social force that is challenged and overcome by the liberating light of truth. According to Foucault, power, although frequently destructive and always dangerous, is also a creative source of positive values (including those of truth and knowledge). He further rejects the common picture of social and political power as flowing from a single dominant center (e.g., the ruling class, the monarch). Instead, he sees a society as shot through with a multiplicity of power relations, interacting but mutually irreducible.

In order to analyze the development of bodies of knowledge out of systems of power, Foucault employs a new historical method that he calls *genealogy*. Genealogy does not replace archaeology, which is still needed to uncover the discursive rules that constitute bodies of knowledge. But genealogy goes beyond archaeology by explaining (through the connections with power) changes in the history of discourse that are merely described by archaeology.

As Foucault researched and wrote the later volumes of his history of sexuality, his conception of the project broadened considerably. Instead of just looking at the emergence of the modern notion of the self as subject, he proposed to trace the Western concept of the self from the ancient Greeks on. Moreover, he began to combine this historical project with the ethical one of constructing alternatives to modern moral codes. Two volumes on Greek and Roman views of sexual ethics (*The use of pleasure* and *The care of the self*) appeared in 1984 just before his death. Another volume (*Les aveux de la chair*), centering on the Christian practice of confession, may appear posthumously.

The focus of this study will be the earlier period of Foucault's work, beginning with the somewhat confused emergence of an archaeological approach in FD, through its eventual crystallization in BC and especially OT, to the explicit reflective formulation of AK. As essential background to an understanding of Foucault's archaeology, we begin with a discussion of the work of Gaston Bachelard and Georges Canguilhem.

1

BACHELARD AND CANGUILHEM

Foucault himself emphasized the importance of Bachelard and Canguilhem not only for French thought in general but also for his own intellectual orientation. In an essay on Canguilhem, he proposes a fundamental division within post-World War II French philosophy between a "philosophy of experience, of meaning, of the subject and a philosophy of knowledge [*savoir*], of rationality, and of the concept."[1] The former he associates with the existential phenomenology of Sartre and Merleau-Ponty, the latter with the history and philosophy of science of Cavaillès, Koyré, and especially Bachelard and Canguilhem. Foucault notes that this division can be traced back well into the nineteenth century, beginning with the opposition between Maine de Brian and Comte and continuing in the differences separating Lachelier and Courturat as well as Bergson and Poincaré. In the twentieth century, the division is reflected in the two different ways French thinkers appropriated the thought of Husserl after his Paris lectures in 1929. On the one hand, there was Sartre's existential reading (in *The transcendence of the ego*); on the other, there was

1. Michel Foucault, "La vie: l'expérience et la science," *Revue de métaphysique et de morale* 70 (1985), 4. An earlier version of this paper was published in English as the introduction to the English translation of Georges Canguilhem, *On the normal and the pathological*, (Dordrecht: Reidel, 1978).

9

Cavaillès's "formal" reading in *Méthode axiomatique* and *La formation de la théorie des ensembles*. Whereas Sartre moves Husserl's thought forward to the concerns of Heidegger's *Being and time*, Cavaillès brings it back to its origins in the philosophy of mathematics. After World War II, the philosophy of the subject was inextricably tied to phenomenology in the work of Sartre and Merleau-Ponty. However, the philosophy of the concept was developed by Bachelard and Canguilhem in essential independence of Husserl's work. According to Foucault, "these two forms of thought have constituted in France two frameworks that have remained, at least for a time, quite profoundly heterogeneous."[2]

From 1945 to the late 1950s, existential philosophy, along with Marxism as a social and political outlook, dominated French thought. During this period, the central concern (which culminated in Sartre's *Critique of dialectical reason*) was to develop a synthesis of existential phenomenology and Marxism. But, according to Foucault, by the end of the 1950s, existential phenomenology began to founder on the problems of language and the unconscious, and structuralism presented itself as a superior alternative. "It was clear that phenomenology was no match for structural analysis in accounting for the effects of meaning that could be produced by a structure of the linguistic type, in which the subject (in the phenomenological sense) did not intervene to confer meaning." Further, "the unconscious could not feature in any discussion of a phenomenological kind. . . . the phenomenological subject was disqualified by psychoanalysis, as it had been by linguistic theory."[3] As a result, the efforts of the 1940s and 1950s to unite Marxism and phenomenology were replaced by efforts to connect Marxism with various forms of structuralism (particularly, Lacan's structuralist Freudianism). "With phenomenology disqualified . . ., there was simply a succession of fiancées, each flirting with Marxism in turn" in the effort to produce a "Freudian-structuralist-Marxism."[4] This remained the dominant theme of French thought until the end of the 1960s.

However, according to Foucault, this was the line of development only for those on the dominant side of the basic division in French thought – that is, for those who worked in terms of the

2. Ibid.
3. Gerard Raulet, "Structuralism and Post-Structuralism: an Interview with Michel Foucault," *Telos*, 1983, 198.
4. Ibid.

categories of experience, meaning, and subjectivity. "There were also people who did not follow [this] movement. I am thinking of those who were interested in the history of science. . . . Particularly around Canguilhem, an extremely influential figure in the French University – the young French University. Many of his students were neither Marxists, nor Freudians, nor structuralists. And here I am speaking of myself."[5]

By Foucault's own account, then, his intellectual development did not fit the pattern followed by many in France during the 1960s precisely because he was connected to what he calls the "network" of thought then represented by Canguilhem.[6] This is not to say that Foucault did not try to come to grips with Marxist, Freudian, and structuralist thought; these were some of his major concerns. But it is essential to realize that his reaction to these dominant movements is based on a fundamental orientation toward the history of science that is strongly influenced by Canguilhem (and, through him, Bachelard).

The centrality of this influence is particularly apparent in light of Foucault's specification of the Bachelard–Canguilhem "network" as the primary French locus of the historical critique of reason that he sees as the main concern of his own work. He notes that in Germany this critique has been carried out in the context of "a historical and political reflection on society" from "the post-Hegelians to the Frankfurt School and Lukàcs, by way of Feuerbach, Marx, Nietzsche, and Max Weber." But "in France, it is the history of science which has above all been the basis for raising the philosophical question of what enlightenment is." Specifically, "the work of Koyré, Bachelard, Cavaillès, and Canguilhem" poses questions "to a rationality that claims to be universal even while it develops in a contingent manner."[7] In this way it examines "a reason whose structural autonomy carried with it the history of dogmatisms and despotisms – a reason that, as a result, produces emancipation only on the condition that it succeeds in freeing itself from itself."[8] As we saw in the Introduction, this is equally a characterization of Foucault's own approach to the history of reason.

It is apparent, then, that Foucault himself situates his work

5. Ibid.
6. Foucault, "La vie." The French term Foucault uses is *filiation*.
7. Ibid., 6.
8. Ibid.

within the tradition of French history and philosophy of science
from Comte to Bachelard and Canguilhem. Canguilhem, especially through his "history of concepts" and his concern with the
status of norms in science and its history, was the most immediate and the strongest influence on Foucault's historical work. But
Bachelard's philosophical view of science and, especially, of scientific change was also a major presence in Foucault's intellectual
environment. Because of this – and also because their work is
not very well known outside of France[9] – I offer here an outline
of the main themes of the history and philosophy of science of
Bachelard and Canguilhem.

BACHELARD'S PHILOSOPHY OF SCIENCE

Gaston Bachelard developed his philosophy of science in a series
of books published from 1927 to 1953.[10] In addition to its impor-

9. Bachelard's works on literature and poetic imagination are fairly well-known
   among English-speaking literary theorists. Mary Tiles, *Bachelard: science and
   objectivity*, (Cambridge: Cambridge University Press, 1984) is a very interesting and intelligent effort to find inspiration in Bachelard for an approach to
   current problems of analytic philosophy of science. It is not intended, however, as a general guide to Bachelard's philosophy of science in its own terms.
   Only one of Canguilhem's books has been translated into English, and his
   work has so far received little attention from Anglo-American historians and
   philosophers of science. Dominique Lecourt, a student of Canguilhem, has
   written a number of essays on Bachelard, Canguilhem, and Foucault that
   have been translated and published together under the title, *Marxism and
   epistemology: Bachelard, Canguilhem, Foucault*, translated by Ben Brewster (London: NLB, 1975). Lecourt places Foucault in the same "tradition" as Bachelard and Canguilhem but does little to develop the point as a means of
   interpreting his work. He does offer valuable expositions and interesting
   criticisms (from a Marxist standpoint) of Bachelard and Canguilhem.
10. References to Bachelard's texts will be given internally in accord with the
    following scheme of abbreviations:
    AR: *L'activité rationaliste de la physique contemporaine* (PUF, 1951).
    CA: *Essai sur la connaissance approchée* (Vrin, 1927).
    FES: *La formation de l'esprit scientifique* (Vrin, 1938).
    MR: *Le matérialisme rationnel* (PUF, 1953).
    NES: *Le nouvel esprit scientifique* (PUF, 1934). References will be to the
             English translation by Arthur Goldhammer, *The New Scientific
             Spirit* (Boston: Beacon Press, 1984).
    PN: *La philosophie du non* (PUF, 1940). References will be to the En-
             glish translation by G. C. Waterston, *The Philosophy of No* (New
             York: Orion Press, 1969).
    RA: *Le rationalisme appliqué* (PUF, 1949).
    VIR: *La valeur inductive de la relativité* (Vrin, 1929).
    Except for NES and PN, translations of Bachelard's texts are mine.

tance for understanding Foucault (as well as other recent French thinkers such as Louis Althusser, Georges Canguilhem, and Michel Serres), Bachelard's work often suggests interesting approaches to problems that are central for Anglo-American philosophy of science. In presenting this survey of his thought, I will emphasize what is crucial as background to Foucault but also note connections with recent Anglo-American issues.

Reason and science

According to Bachelard, reason is best known by reflection on science, and science is best known by reflection on its history. The first thesis derives from his conviction that the structures of reason are apparent not in abstract principles but in the concrete employments of reason. Norms of rationality are constituted in the very process of applying our thoughts to particular problems, and science has been the primary locus of success in such applications. The proof of the second thesis – that science is best known through its history – lies in the repeated refutation of a priori philosophical ideals of rationality by historical scientific developments. Descartes, for example, held that science must be grounded in clear and distinct intuitions of the essential properties of matter. This view is refuted by the fact that matter, as described by twentieth-century physics and chemistry, is simply not available to our intellectual intuition. We know it only through the indirections of hypothetico-deductive inference from data that are themselves mediated by complex instruments (NES, 138–45 and Chapter 6). Similarly, Kant's formulation of a transcendental, a priori analytic of principles that regulate all employments of reason collapsed with the triumph of theories (relativity and quantum mechanics) based on the denial of such Kantian principles as the permanence of substance, which require a continuity of energy inconsistent with quantization (PN, Chapter 3). What initially seem to be a priori constraints on thought as such turn out to be contingent conditions derived from philosophers' inability to think beyond the framework of present science.

There are, then, no viable accounts of rationality except those derived from the historical developments of scientific reason. To understand reason, philosophy must "go to the school of science." Here, as elsewhere (e g., the development of metaphysical theories), the achievements of science are the dynamics behind all philosophical understanding. "Science in effect creates philosophy" (NES, 3). The rationality that philosophy tries to discover in the history of science is no more fixed and monolithic than that history itself. As we shall see shortly, Bachelard finds sharp breaks in the history of science and corresponding changes in the conception of reason. Moreover, Bachelard reminds us that there is, strictly speaking, no such thing as the history of science, only various histories of different regions of scientific work. Correspondingly, philosophy cannot hope to uncover a single, unified conception of rationality from its reflection on the history of science; it will find only various "regions of rationality" ("*les régions rationelles*") (RA, Chapter 7). Bachelard, for example, analyzes (in *Le rationalisme appliqué*) the rationalities implicit in nineteenth-century theories of electricity and of mechanics. He agrees that the history of science tends to the integration of diverse regions of rationality but sees no place for a "science in general" to which would correspond a "general rationality." Bachelard was particularly concerned with the new rationality that he saw in the achievements of twentieth-century physical science, especially relativity theory and the physics and chemistry of quanta.

Bachelard's model of scientific change

Because of his demand that the philosopher of science work from the historical development of the sciences, the center of Bachelard's philosophy of science is his model of scientific change. This model, which also provides his account of the nature of scientific progress, is built around four key epistemological categories: epistemological breaks, epistemological obstacles, epistemological profiles, and epistemological acts.

Bachelard employs the concept of an epistemological break in two contexts. First, he uses it to characterize the way in which scientific knowledge splits off from and even contradicts common-sense experiences and beliefs. This sense of "break" is fundamental for Bachelard, since it constitutes science as a distinctive cognitive realm: "Scientific progress always reveals a break [*rupture*], constant breaks, between ordinary [*commune*] knowledge and scientific knowledge" (MR, 207). Bachelard illustrates this claim with several examples that we can use to elucidate the key features of epistemological breaks. He finds one simple example in a chemistry text's comment that glass is very similar to wurtzite (zinc sulfide). The comparison is one that would never occur to common sense, since it is not based on any overt resemblance of the two substances but on the fact that they have analogous crystalline structures. Thus, science breaks with ordinary experience by placing the objects of experience under new categories that reveal properties and relations not available to ordinary sense perception.

But we should not think of scientific breaks as merely a matter of discovering new aspects of ordinary objects, of taking up where everyday experience leaves off, as a telescope reveals stars not visible to the naked eye. New, scientific concepts are required to give an adequate account of even familiar facts. This is very nicely illustrated by the case of Lamarck's futile efforts to use his exceptional observational abilities to develop an account of combustion in opposition to Lavoisier's. His approach was to note carefully the sequence of color changes a piece of white paper undergoes when burned. On the basis of such observations, Lamarck interpreted combustion as a process whereby the "violence" of the fire "unmasks" the fundamental, underlying color of the paper (black) by stripping away successive chromatic layers. Bachelard argues that Lamarck's idea here is not merely wrong in the ordinary way of an incorrect scientific hypothesis. Rather, it is essentially anachronistic because it is based on immediate phenomenal experiences that Lavoisier had already shown to be inadequate for the task of understanding combustion. "The time for direct, natural observation in the realm of chemistry had passed" (MR, 219).

A final example shows how science may break with common sense even when employing models based on its language and concepts. This is the case of Bohr's "water drop" model of the atomic nucleus. Via this model, Bohr pictured the protons and neutrons of the nucleus as forming a drop of water, the "temperature" (internal energy) of which increased when a neutron was added and which partially "evaporated" when a particle was emitted from the nucleus. This model was an excellent aid to understanding the process of fission, but its use of ordinary concepts must not mislead us. As Bachelard puts it, such words as *water drop, temperature,* and *evaporation* occur only in quotation marks. In fact, the words are tacitly redefined so that they express concepts that "are totally different . . . from the concepts of common knowledge" (MR, 216). (Imagine, Bachelard says, the stupidity of asking a physicist to make a thermometer to measure the "temperature" of the nucleus.)

This last example also illustrates Bachelard's second sort of epistemological breaks: those that occur between two *scientific* conceptualizations. If nuclear "temperature" is a very different concept from ordinary phenomenal temperature, it is likewise very different from the classical conception of temperature as the mean kinetic energy of a collection of molecules. This illustrates how science develops not only by breaks with ordinary experience but also by breaks with previous scientific theories. For Bachelard, the most striking and important such breaks came with relativity and quantum theory, which he saw as initiating a "new scientific spirit." This "new spirit" involved not only radically new conceptions of nature but also new conceptions of scientific method (e.g., new criteria of explanatory adequacy). Bachelard's detailed treatments of this topic (in, e.g., *La valeur inductive de la relativité* and *Le nouvel esprit scientifique*) preceded by two or three decades similar discussions by Anglo-American historians and philosophers of science such as Kuhn and Feyerabend.

The language of epistemological "breaks" suggests that there is something to be broken, a barrier that must be shattered. Bachelard follows out this suggestion with his notion of an *epistemological obstacle*. An epistemological obstacle is any concept or method that prevents an epistemological break. Obstacles are residues from previous ways of thinking that, whatever value they had in the past, have begun to block the path of inquiry. Common sense is, of course, a major source of epistemological obstacles. Thus, the animism of primitive common sense, which inclined people to explain the world on analogy with vital processes (sex, digestion, etc.) was an obstacle to the development of a mechanistic physics. Likewise, the still strong commonsense idea that phenomena must be the attributes of an underlying substance blocked the rejection of the ether as the locus of electromagnetic waves. More generally, Bachelard regards the commonsense mind's reliance on images as a breeding ground for epistemological obstacles. Images may have heuristic use in science, but they have no explanatory force, and if they do their job properly, they are eventually eliminated from scientific thought. Thus, of Bohr's planetary model of the atom, Bachelard says: "The diagram of the atom provided by Bohr . . . has . . . acted as a good image: there is nothing left of it" (PN, 119). But epistemological obstacles may also arise from successful scientific work that has outlived its value. The most striking such cases occur when the concepts and principles of an established theory lead us to regard new proposals as obviously absurd – for example, the counterintuitive feel of quantum mechanics' rejection of classical determinism. But previously successful scientific methods can also become epistemological obstacles. For example, the emphasis on direct observation that led in the seventeenth century to major breaks with Aristotelian science became an obstacle to eighteenth-century developments of atomic theories. Finally, traditional philosophy, with its tendency to canonize as necessary truths the contingent features of one historical period of thought, is another major source of epistemological obstacles.

The attitudes that constitute given concepts and methods as epistemological obstacles are not explicitly formulated by those they constrain but rather operate at the level of implicit assumptions or cognitive and perceptual habits. Consequently, Bachelard proposed to develop a set of techniques designed to bring them to our full reflective awareness. He spoke of these techniques as effecting a "psychoanalysis" of reason. Bachelard's use of this term signals his aim of unearthing unconscious or semiconscious structures of thought, but it does not express a commitment to the details of Freudian theory.[11]

Closely related to the concepts of epistemological obstacles and psychoanalysis of reason is the idea of an epistemological profile. This is an analysis of a given individual's understanding of a scientific concept, an analysis that reveals the degree to which the understanding involves elements from various stages in the concept's historical development. These stages correspond primarily to various philosophical embodiments of past scientific ideas (as well as to various commonsense notions). Thus, Bache-

---

11. For a discussion of the relation of Bachelard's psychoanalysis of epistemological obstacles to Freudian psychoanalysis, see George Canguilhem, "Gaston Bachelard, Psychanalyste dans la cité scientifique?" *Il Protagora* 24 (1984), 19–26. Bachelard's idea that what was once an integral part of science can later become an impediment to its development undermines the sharp distinction, so prominent in many Anglo-American discussions, between internal and external history of science. For him, what at one point is internal to the rational development of science may, at a later time, be an external obstacle to this development.

lard (PN, 36–38) provides the profile of his own concept of mass, which he finds to be dominated by the classical rationalist conception (mass as the primitive term of eighteenth-century mechanics). It also has a very strong empiricist or positivist component (mass defined operationally as what is measured on scales). There are smaller, but still significant, contributions corresponding to the child's naive understanding of mass as a desirable quantity of matter and of the highly abstract and rationalized conceptions of relativity theory and quantum mechanics. A parallel profile of Bachelard's understanding of energy (PN, 38–43) shows a similar domination by the rationalist conception of the eighteenth century but less influence of the empiricist conception and more of the child's naive notion.

Obviously, an epistemological profile provides a record of the epistemological obstacles hindering the scientific thought of a given individual. But Bachelard does not make the scientistic move of rejecting all positive significance for those elements of the profile that are not fully adequate to the achievements of contemporary science. Rather, particularly in his later work, he comes to see the full range of the elements of epistemological profiles – including the philosophical and common-sense components – as valid on various levels of human life and experience. Scientific inadequacy does not entail complete invalidity. Instead, Bachelard concludes that the complexity of an epistemological profile shows that "a single philosophy cannot explain everything" and that "it is necessary to group all the philosophies to obtain the complete notional spectrum of a particular piece of knowledge" (PN, 42). Bachelard's full appreciation of the nonscientific ("poetic") dimension of human experience is developed in a series of books beginning with *The psychoanalysis of fire*. On one level, this book simply provides a detailed analysis of the epistemological obstacles connected with our images of fire. (One example is the "violence of fire" that we noted in Lamarck's thinking about combustion.) But Bachelard's reflections lead him to an appreciation of poetic images and experience for their own sakes. He continues to resist "the ontological temptation of beauty";[12] that is, he is steadfast in rejecting any view ("naive realism") that would make the contents of ordinary, subjective experience as real (or more real) than scientific

12. Cf. Roch C. Smith, *Gaston Bachelard* (Boston: Twayne Publishers, 1982), 77.

objects. But he sees the subjective realm that feeds the poetic spirit as intrinsically valuable and a necessary complement to scientific knowledge.

The concept of an *epistomological act* counterbalances that of an epistemological obstacle. Whereas epistemological obstacles impede scientific progress through the inertia of old ideas, "the notion of epistemological acts corresponds to the leaps [*saccades*] of scientific genius that introduce unexpected impulses into the course of scientific development" (AR, 25). An epistemological act is not, however, just a change; it has a positive value that represents an improvement in our scientific accounts. There are, accordingly, different values that must be accorded to different episodes in the history of science. Consequently, Bachelard holds that writing history of science is different from writing political or social history. In the latter case, "the ideal is, rightly, an *objective* narration of the facts. This ideal requires that the historian *not judge;* and, if the historian imparts the values of his own time in order to assess the values of a past time, then we are right to accuse him of accepting 'the myth of progress' " (AR, 24). But in the case of the history of the natural sciences, progress is no myth. Present science represents an unquestionable advance over its past, and it is entirely appropriate for the historian of science to use the standards and values of the present to judge the past. Application of these standards results in a sharp division of the scientific past into "*l'histoire périmée*" (the history of "outdated" science) and "*l'histoire sanctionnée*" (the history of science judged valid by current standards). More broadly, following F. K. Richtmyer, Bachelard distinguishes between the *story* of science – an account of past scientific achievements that have contributed to our present body of knowledge – and mere *history* of science, which includes efforts that have no positive place in the genesis of current science (AR, 27). Bachelard also speaks of an account of science that "starts from the certainties of the present and discovers in the past progressive formations of the truth" as "recurrent history" (*l'histoire récurrente*).

Georges Canguilhem points out[13] that this Bachelardian writing of the history of the past on the basis of the present is not equivalent to the now generally disdained "Whiggish" approach

13. G. Canguilhem, *Etudes d'histoire et de philosophie des sciences* (Vrin, 1970, 197–98); *Idéologie et rationalité* (Vrin, 1983), 21–23.

to the history of science. For one thing, Bachelardian history does not try to understand past science in terms of present concepts. It realizes the need to explicate the past in its own terms. For another, there is no assumption of the immutable adequacy of present science. Precisely because they are scientific, the present achievements by which we evaluate the past may themselves be surpassed or corrected by future scientific development. Our evaluation of the past in terms of the present is, in Canguilhem's words, not the application of "a universal touchstone" but "a selective projection of light on the past."[14]

But, for Bachelard, even though all scientific results are open to revision and some can be definitively rejected, others must be accepted as permanently valid achievements. Thus, he says that phlogiston theory is "outdated [*périmée*] because it rests on a fundamental error." Historians who deal with it are working "in the paleontology of a vanished scientific spirit" (AR, 25). By contrast, Black's work on caloric, even though most of it has long been jettisoned, did yield the permanent achievement of the concept of specific heat. "The notion of *specific heat* – we can assert with equanimity – is a notion that is *forever* a scientific notion. . . . One may smile at the dogmatism of a rationalist philosopher who writes 'forever' regarding a scholastic truth. But there are concepts so indispensable in a scientific culture that we cannot conceive being led to abandon them" (AR, 26).

How is this idea of unalterable progress consistent with Bachelard's insistence that all scientific results are open to revision? How can an achievement be "permanent" and at the same time open to correction in the wake of an epistemological break? Bachelard's response is that an epistemological break is not merely the rejection of past science but also a preservation, via reformulation, of old ideas in a new and broader context of thought. Specifically, past results are replaced by generalizations that reject them as unconditionally correct but preserve them as correct under certain restricted conditions. Bachelard finds a model here in the development of non-Euclidean geometry. This development refutes the claim that the Euclidean postulates express the sole truth about geometry but at the same time presents these postulates as defining one exemplification of a more general class of geometries (i.e., Euclidean geometry is the

14. Canguilhem, *Idéologie et rationalité*, 22.

particular geometry possessed by a space of zero curvature). In the same way, "Newton's astronomy can . . . be seen to be a special case of Einstein's 'pan-astronomy' " (NES, 45). This is so not merely because, to a certain approximation, Newtonian calculations yield the same numbers as Einsteinian calculations but also because key Newtonian concepts such as mass and velocity can be shown to be special simple cases of the corresponding Einsteinian concepts. Bachelard characterizes this process of replacement by generalization as "dialectical," not in the Hegelian sense of a synthesis of opposites but in the sense of a process of conceptual expansion whereby what previously appeared to be contraries (e.g., Euclidean and Lobachevskian geometries) are seen as complementary possibilities. Earlier concepts are not mysteriously "sublated" into a higher unity but are rectified (corrected) on the basis of superior successor concepts that allow us to explain precisely the extent to which they are applicable.[15]

This account of scientific change allows Bachelard to reject the *continuity* of science and still accept its *progress*. Science develops by a series of epistemological breaks that make it impossible to regard its history as a linear accumulation of truths within a single conceptual framework. The conceptual framework of science at one stage will be rejected as erroneous at later stages. Nonetheless, some of its results may be permanent scientific achievements in the sense that they will be preserved as special cases within all subsequent scientific frameworks. Each successive framework will represent progress over its predecessors in that it attains a more general perspective from which the range of validity of previous perspectives can be assessed.

Bachelard's picture of science as discontinuous but progressive involves an essential role for two complementary factors that are usually excluded from the history of science; errors and norms. The former are generally thought of as unfortunate, contingent deviations from the path of science, due to scientifically extraneous factors such as prejudice, inattention, and ignorance. Strictly speaking, the scientist as such (like the mathematician of *Republic* I) does not make mistakes. The history of science is the history

15. Bachelard's references to geometry are not just metaphorical. He sees the dialectical rectification of scientific concepts as essentially connected to the mathematical nature of scientific thought. Cf. Mary Tiles, op. cit., Chapter 3, and C. M. P. M. Hertogh, *Bachelard en Canguilhem: epistemologische discontinuiteit en het medisch normbergrip* (Amsterdam: VU Uitgeverij, 1986), Chapter 2.

of scientific truth, in which errors have no essential role. For Bachelard, however, even a permanent scientific achievement such as Newton's mechanics may be judged an error (i.e., in need of correction) from the more general viewpoint of a later theory. Such errors are essential stages in the development of science and are, as we have seen, preserved in rectified form by subsequent theories. Similarly, scientific norms are generally regarded as outside the historical process of scientific development, since they are thought of as atemporal, universally valid principles of reason. Bachelard however sees norms as formed in the very process of the historical development of science. Norms are products of science's rational activity and can be superseded at later times by other norms that prove themselves more adequate. In this way, Bachelard's model of scientific change fulfills his program of treating reason as a genuinely historical phenomenon.

Bachelard's approach to scientific change promises solutions to some of the fundamental problems of post-Kuhnian philosophy of science. For example, by suggesting that we can maintain the progressiveness of science while denying the continuity of its development, he offers a way of reconciling historical evidence of radical shifts in paradigm with the rationality of science. Similarly, his treatment of norms suggests that this rationality can itself be regarded as fundamentally historical. However, Bachelard's account of these matters needs further development, particularly with regard to the "dialectical" process whereby past scientific concepts emerge as special cases of present scientific concepts. In precisely what sense, for example, is Newtonian mass a "special case" of relativistic mass? More generally, what are the general conditions under which one concept may be said to be a special case of another? A plausible account of these matters requires a more careful analysis of the nature of concepts and of the meanings they express than Bachelard offers.[16]

The epistemological and metaphysical ramifications of Bachelard's model of scientific change

Bachelard's philosophy of scientific change involves, via its presuppositions and consequences, more general epistemological

16. One promising direction for such an analysis is suggested by the work of Wilfrid Sellars. Cf. his *Science and metaphysics*, 128–34, and "Conceptual Change" in his *Essays in philosophy and its history* (Dordrecht: Reidel, 1975).

and metaphysical positions. These positions derive from his reflections on the methodological and ontological results of actual scientific practice. Bachelard dismisses as groundless speculations any purely philosophical theories about how we know and what there is. The nature of knowledge and of reality can be known only by reflection on the successful applications of reason to the understanding of our world. (This view of epistemology and metaphysics is, of course, just a generalization of the considerations noted above that led Bachelard to insist on approaching the philosophy of science through the history of science.) It is important to realize that Bachelard's subordination of philosophy to science is not an instance of positivistic scientism. He does not think – as does, for example, Quine with his notion of naturalized epistemology – that philosophy itself is part of science. Philosophy for Bachelard is a reflection on sciences but its methods and results do not share the empirical character of scientific disciplines.

What, in any case, does Bachelard's reflection on science yield as to the general nature of knowledge? Where does he stand as an epistemologist? Since he explicitly proclaims his epistemology to be "non-Cartesian" (NES, Chapter 6), we can profitably proceed by contrasting his position with that of Descartes.

Bachelard accepts Descartes's view that knowledge arises from a critically methodical questioning of accepted beliefs, but he rejects Descartes's claim that to attain knowledge this questioning must terminate in indubitable intuitive certainties.[17] Cartesian foundationalism is entirely implausible relative to Bachelard's view of science's history as a series of epistemological breaks. What reason do we have to think that the basis of our science will prove any firmer than did that of our forebears? But, beyond this, Bachelard argues that there are no grounds for according Cartesian intellectual intuitions (or any other sort of claim to direct intuitive knowledge) the privileged certainty that Descartes does. His critique of intuition centers on the two poles of an intuitive experience: its subject and its object.

With respect to the latter, the object of a foundational intuition must be analyzable into a set of simple elements, each known fully and unambiguously. To the extent that the objects of our experience contain hidden complexities, our judgments about them are subject to correction in the light of more pene-

17. Cf. Tiles, 28–33.

trating analyses. This is why Descartes, in particular, required that clear and distinct perceptions effect a reduction of their objects to "simple natures." (Similarly, foundationalists in the modern empiricist tradition take unanalyzable sense data as the ultimate objects of experience.) Bachelard's criticism of this aspect of foundationalism is that even the apparently most simple objects of our intuition have later proved to have complex hidden structures. Their apparently intrinsic simplicity was really only the result of an ultimately misleading simplification. Specifically, Bachelard sees major breaks in the history of science as due to the discovery of hidden complexities in objects that had been regarded as simple intuitive givens. One famous example is Einstein's analysis of time and simultaneity. Another less known but very striking example is the twentieth-century study of hydrogen through the analysis of its atomic spectrum (cf. NES, 148–150). Here physicists did at first proceed in accord with the Cartesian ideal. They began with the simple case of the hydrogen atom (a single proton orbited by a single electron) and tried to show how the empirical formula that described its spectrum (the Balmer formula) could be generalized to arrive at formulas describing the spectra of more complex atoms. In this way, it seemed that knowledge of complex cases could be developed from knowledge of the simple case. But in fact the development was in exactly the opposite direction. "In order to give a detailed account of the spectroscopic data, the more complicated spectrum (here that of the alkaline metals) had to be treated first" (NES, 154–55). For example, the fine structure of spectral lines (i.e., the doubling noted in what at first seem to be single lines) was found first in the spectra of more complex atoms, and only because it was noted there, did scientists look for it in the spectrum of hydrogen. Similarly, the role of the angular momentum of the nucleus (and of the orbiting electrons) was discovered only by paying attention to the more complex spectra.

In sum, according to Bachelard, the Cartesian approach of beginning with the simplest case turned out to be a "positivism of the first glance" (NES, 154) that emphasized the most apparent features of the hydrogen atom over those that are in fact central to an understanding of it. As it turned out, the spectrum of hydrogen could be properly understood only by noting its similarity to complex cases where its essential characteristics were more clearly present. Bachelard sums up the anti-Cartesian attitude of modern science toward the simple as follows:

But even here, Bachelard may still be giving priority to consensus, since he immediately goes on to contrast rational systems of truths that are codified into books "provided with the guarantee of the scientific community" with the errors found in books that are "most often characterized by a detestable originality" (RA, 59). It seems that, in the end, he does not provide an entirely clear and cogent account of the normative grounds of scientific objectivity.

Correlative to Bachelard's critique of foundationalism is his rejection of realism. The correlation is apparent from the definition of realism he offers in an early book: "Realism [is] . . . any doctrine that maintains the organization of impressions on the level of the impressions themselves, that places the general after the particular, as a simplification of the particular, that consequently believes in the prolix richness of the individual sensation and in the systematic impoverishment of abstractive thought" (VIR, 206). Thus understood, realism asserts the primacy and indispensability of the objects of everyday sense experience. It is the view, held by philosophers ranging from phenomenologists to Whiteheadians to ordinary language analysts, that the things we see, hear, and touch are the concrete ("really real") realities for which science supplies merely partial and abstract accounts. When scientists say that a gas (e.g., the air we breathe) is a collection of molecules, this is only a manner of speaking. Talk of molecules is one way of elucidating some important aspects of the behavior of air, but there is no question of claiming that air is really nothing but a collection of molecules, that scientific talk of molecules can take the ontological place of our everyday talk about air.

Bachelard sees realism in this sense as conflicting with his thesis that the history of science advances by a series of epistemological breaks. For the realist, there are no epistemological breaks because every scientific discovery is just the addition of another truth about the familiar objects given to ordinary experience. Science never takes us beyond the fundamental conceptual framework that we acquire when we learn our natural language. Accordingly, Bachelard's first way of criticizing realism is identical with his case for the reality of epistemological breaks. Another, closely related line of criticism is his argument from the guiding role of theory over observation in the development of scientific knowledge. Bachelard's point here is strikingly illustrated by his reflections on how a modern scientist would approach Descartes's project (in the Second Mediation) of studying the nature of a piece of wax. Descartes, of course, used the wax example against a form of realism that rejects the need for intellectual understanding to interpret the givens of the senses. But this is just an antiempiricist account of the nature of our experience of material objects; it is not a rejection of the realist thesis (which Descartes accepts) that such objects are as they are given in this experience properly understood.

Bachelard argues that Descartes's approach to the wax is fundamentally different from that of the modern scientist. Whereas Descartes describes a piece of wax as it is in its natural state, "just taken from the hive," a modern scientist would "start with . . . chemically pure wax produced by careful purification techniques" (NES, 167). Then, instead of observing the wax under various conditions in which we might find it in our daily experience (rolled between the fingers, softened by the sun), the scientist would submit it to a series of carefully controlled manipulations designed to put it in a state that will allow the observation of its characteristic features. Thus, he would "melt this wax in a crucible and resolidify it in a slow, methodical way. In this manner he can obtain a wax 'droplet' whose shape and surface composition can be precisely controlled" (NES, 168). Next, he might proceed to study the surface of this carefully prepared droplet by exposing it to X rays: "Thanks to the slow cooking of the ball of wax, the surface molecules will be oriented in a precise way relative to the surface of the drop. This orientation will determine the diffraction pattern of the X-rays and yield spectrograms similar to those obtained . . . for crystals" (NES, 168). On the basis of established results with crystals, the scientist will expect these spectrograms to provide explanations of many of the wax's surface properties, such as smoothness, adherence, and oiliness. Bachelard goes on to suggest how further techniques might be employed to determine the molecular structure of the wax at deeper levels. But the essential point should be already clear: Scientific observation consists in the systematic manipulation of an object on the basis of a theoretical preunderstanding of it. The scientist treats the object as he does because an already accepted theory tells him that this is how to reveal the object's secrets. The very process of scientific observation is based on a theoretical redescription of the object that characterizes it in terms of very different categories (e.g., "chemically pure sample," "orientation of surface molecules") from those of untutored experience. "For science, then, the qualities of reality are functions of our rational methods. . . . 'Objective meditation' [in contrast to Descartes's "subjective meditation" on the wax] in the laboratory commits us to a path of progressive objectification that gives reality to both a new form of experience and a new form of thought" (NES, 171). In this process, the familiar sensory objects enshrined by realism are left far behind.

It seems clear that what Bachelard here calls realism is a variety of what current analytic philosophers of science call antirealism. (Either terminology is possible since the view is realistic about the objects of ordinary experience and antirealistic about the theoretical postulations of science.) Similarly, Bachelard's own position is very similar to what is now called scientific realism. In particular, he vigorously defends the reality of the entities postulated by explanatory scientific theories and even maintains that it is these entities rather than the objects of ordinary sense experience that are the concrete realities of the physical world.[19] Moreover, Bachelard's approach offers a way of defending scientific realism that has important advantages over some more recent defenses. For one thing, it does not present realism as merely the result of a peremptory demand for further, theoretical causes of phenomena that are already adequately accounted for by empirical generalizations. Like Wilfrid Sellars, Bachelard bases his case for realism on the inadequacy of the "manifest framework" of everyday observation language and the corresponding explanatory superiority of theoretical frameworks. Further, whereas many recent versions of realism find themselves in tension with historical accounts (à la Kuhn) of radical changes in scientific concepts, Bachelard's realism is built on a model of scientific development that allows such changes. Specifically, his notion of *l'histoire sanctionée* provides a way of reconciling the scientific progress required by realist accounts with historical discontinuity.

However, while Bachelard provides a valuable approach to the defense of scientific realism – that is, of the ontological superior-

19. Bachelard's rejection of what he calls "realism" also includes some features that are not part of the current notion of scientific realism – for example, his opposition to the "*chosisme*" that gives ontological priority to substances rather than processes. Cf. NSS, 42.

ity of the framework of theoretical science – he is not willing to accept a full-blooded metaphysical realism. That is, he is not willing to assert the mind-independent existence of scientific entities. Instead, he proposes what he calls "applied rationalism" (*le rationalisme appliqué*). The term "rationalism" emphasizes, first, the active role of the mind in the construction of the concepts needed to describe adequately the objects of science. Secondly, it emphasizes Bachelard's claim that, contrary to a widespread empiricist misconception, it is (theoretical) ideas rather than sense experiences that give us objects in their full concreteness: "Ideas reveal details and make specific features [*spécifications*] appear. It is through ideas that we see the particular in all its richness; thus, they go beyond sensations, which grasp only the general."[20] So, for Bachelard, theoretical conceptions are not abstractions from the full reality of objects but the way of reaching this reality beyond the vagueness and incompleteness of our sense experience.

We must not, however, think of Bachelard as an idealist who gives absolute priority to thought. He rejects an idealist constitution of reality from the pure thought of a *cogito*. On the contrary, he holds that, if we began with mere thought itself (after, for example, a Cartesian "destruction of the world" through methodic doubt), then any world that thought posited would be an entirely arbitrary construction. Idealism must reduce either to a skepticism that restricts reality to thought or to a "creationism" that makes the world a mere caprice of thought. Bachelard presents his version of rationalism as a middle ground between these two extremes. We arrive at truth neither by skeptically destroying the world nor by mentally creating it. Rather, truth results from reason's revision (*rectification*) of the world. "Between the two poles of a destroyed world and a constructed world, we propose simply to slip in [*glisser*] a rectified world" (RA, 51). Accordingly, Bachelard's rationalism is *applied* in the sense that for it any application of concepts by reason must be to an object that has already been conceptualized: "Rationalism is a philosophy that continues; it is never truly a philosophy that begins" (RA, 54). The objects of our knowledge are "already there," not as autonomous givens but as the results of previous applications of reason.

20. Gaston Bachelard, *L'histoire des sciences dans l'enseignment*, Publications de l'enseignement scientifique, no. 2, 1933, 159.

Bachelard's conception of an *applied* rationalism is also designed to highlight the role of scientific instruments in the constitution of scientific reality. The mind's rectification of the world is mediated by the techniques of experimental manipulation that are an integral part of modern scientific theories. Indeed, Bachelard speaks of scientific instruments as "theories materialized" (NES, 13). It is through this instrumental materialization that theoretical concepts overcome the abstraction of the merely mental and provide truths more concrete than those of ordinary experience. This is how Bachelard dissolves the paradox we may feel in his claim that the objects of theory are more concrete than those of sensation. (He alludes to this paradox by speaking of the scientific object as an "abstract-concrete" object.) Science replaces ordinary experiences with its own theoretically informed experience. It moves us from the "phenomenology" that describes the objects of ordinary experiences to what Bachelard calls a "phenomeno-technics," which produces objects by the application of scientific instruments. "Science *realizes* its objects; it never finds them ready-made. Phenomeno-technics *extends* phenomenology. A concept has become scientific to the extent that it has become technical, that it is accompanied by a technique of realization" (FES, 61). Accordingly, Bachelard rejects "the classic division that separated a theory from its application" and asserts rather "the necessity of incorporating conditions of application into the very essence of the theory" (FES, 61). It is through the technical application of a theory's abstract rational structures that there appears the concrete scientific object.

Bachelard sees his applied rationalism as a viable ontological middle ground between idealism and realism and between empiricism and classical rationalism. It accepts idealism's emphasis on the mind's active role, regarding any particular object as constructed by the application of theory. But, at the same time, it accepts the realist's emphasis on the transcendence of the object, agreeing that any particular act of theoretical construction operates on an object already given to it. What from one (relatively idealist) point of view is the mind's rectification of a concept is, from another (relatively realist) point of view, a better approximation to reality (cf. CA, 279). Similarly, applied rationalism tries to do justice to both classical rationalism's emphasis on the guiding role of theory and empiricism's emphasis on the need to put theory to the test of experience. "Scientific culture is animated by a subtle [*fine*] dialectic that constantly goes from theory to experience in order to come back from experience to the fundamental organization of [theoretical] principles" (AR, 16). Bachelard's retreat from metaphysical realism is less impressive than his defense of scientific realism. His attempt to combine realistic and idealistic views of objects seems to be unstable. In order to avoid idealism, Bachelard maintains that any operation of the mind is a transformation of an object pregiven to it. But, unless he is willing to fall back into metaphysical realism, he must agree that any pregiven object itself must be the result of a previous "constitution" by mental activity. If so, his position reduces to a form of idealism. Consequently, it seems that Bachelard's position collapses into either idealism or metaphysical realism and does not in fact offer a viable third alternative.

CANGUILHEM'S HISTORY OF SCIENCE

Canguilhem was Bachelard's successor as director of the Institut d'Histoire des Sciences et des Techniques at the University of Paris. Whereas Bachelard was primarily a philosopher of science who based his conclusions on historical studies, Canguilhem is primarily a historian of science, though one extremely sensitive to the philosophical presuppositions and implications of his work. Although Canguilhem definitely operates from the context of Bachelard's philosophy of science, there are a number of key points at which he criticizes and modifies Bachelard's views. To some extent, their differences reflect the fact that, whereas Bachelard took physics and chemistry as his models of scientific rationality, Canguilhem focuses primarily on biology and medicine.

Canguilhem's conception of the history of science

Canguilhem's project as a historian of science is to write the history of concepts, not – to cite some major alternatives – the history of terms, the history of phenomena, or even the history of theories. A history of terms reflects the naive and all-too-common idea that there is some historical significance in finding people who, for example, spoke of mass before Newton, of atoms before Dalton, of evolution before Darwin. Such history is misled by superficial similarities in language and ignores the really important question of whether two scientists had the same understanding of a given aspect of nature. A history centered on phenomena is concerned with who first observed or accurately described a given natural process or structure, without taking account that the crucial factor is not what was observed but the interpretation involved in the observation. Thus, Priestley may have discovered oxygen in the sense of being the first to produce it in a laboratory and describe its phenomenal features accurately. But such a "discovery" is of little significance for Canguilhem's history of concepts, since Priestley failed in the decisive matter of providing an adequate scientific understanding of oxygen, which he incorrectly interpreted as dephlogisticated air. The decisive achievement was Lavoisier's understanding of oxygen as a chemical element.

It might seem that Canguilhem's rejection of history of science as the history of the discovery of phenomena corresponds simply to a rejection of the positivists' sharp distinction of theory and observation. He is, we may think, drawing the obvious consequence of recognizing that there are no scientifically interesting observed facts apart from their theoretical interpretations. This would suggest that Canguilhem's is in fact a history of theories. Why then does he insist that his primary concern is with concepts rather than theories?

To understand Canguilhem's view here, we need to distinguish – in a way that Anglo-American philosophers of science typically do not – between interpretation and theory. Many recent analytic philosophers of science have emphasized that scientific observation does not present us with pure, uninterpreted data; all scientific data are given already interpreted. Canguilhem would agree with this point, which was, after all, emphasized by Bachelard long before Hanson and Kuhn. But the typical Anglo-American discussion of this topic also assumes that the interpretation of data is a matter of reading them in terms of a theory; that is, in terms of a set of scientific generalizations put forward to explain the phenomena under investigation. Interpretation is held to derive from theoretical commitments. Aristotelians saw the motion of a heavy body swinging from a chain as a constrained fall because of their theory that falling bodies seek their natural place. Galileo saw it as the nearly periodic movement of a pendulum because of his theoretical principle of inertia.[21] On this view, the concepts whereby data are interpreted derive from the theories whereby they are explained. It is not surprising that some philosophers holding this view (Feyerabend, for example) took the further step of maintaining that the entire meaning of a concept or term is given by the role it plays in the statements of theory. This led to the puzzling conclusion that any revisions in theory entailed changes in the meaning of scientific concepts.

For Canguilhem, however, it is essential to separate the concepts that interpret data from the theories that explain them. A concept provides us with the initial understanding of a phenomenon that allows us to formulate in a scientifically useful way the question of how to explain it. Theories provide a variety of (often competing) ways of answering the explanatory question. Thus, Galileo introduced a new way of conceiving the motion of falling bodies. But in order to explain the motion so conceived, he, Descartes, and finally Newton introduced a series of different theories. Accordingly, Canguilhem can make sense of the same concept playing a role in very different theories – of, as he says, concepts that are "theoretically polyvalent" (FCR, 6).[22] This in turn allows him to write historical accounts of the formation and transformation of concepts that operate at a different – and more fundamental – level than accounts of the succession of explanatory theories.

Canguilhem's conception of history of science as history of concepts is well illustrated by his own work on the formation of the concept of the reflex. As he sees it, the development of the concept of bodily reflex movement was a major innovation, paral-

21. Cf. Thomas Kuhn, *The structure of scientific revolutions*, 2d ed. (Chicago: University of Chicago Press, 1970), 118–19.
22. References to Canguilhem's works will be given internally in accord with the following scheme of abbreviations:
CV: *La Connaissance de la vie*, 2d ed. (Vrin, 1975).
E: *Etudes d'histoire et de philosophie des sciences*, 2d ed. (Vrin, 1970).
FCR: *La formation du concept de reflex aux XVIIe et XVIIIe siecles*, 2d ed. (Vrin, 1977).
IR;   *Idéologie et rationalité* (Vrin, 1977).
NP: *Le Normal et le pathologique* (Canguilhem's thesis, *Essai sur quelques problèmes concernant le normale et le pathologique*, first published in 1943, along with "Nouvelles reflections sur le normal et le pathologique") (PUF, 1966). Citations will be from the English translation *On the Normal and the Pathological* (Dordrecht: Reidel, 1978).
Except for NP, all translations are mine.

lel to the Copernican revolution in astronomy. Earlier physiology, from Aristotle and Galen on, had postulated a "single principle of command and control" (the heart for Aristotle, the brain for Galen) for all bodily movements. By contrast, reflexes are movements that occur independently of the organ of central control: "The Copernican revolution in the physiology of movement is the dissociation of the notions of the brain and of the sensory-motor center, the discovery of eccentric centers, the formation of the concept of the reflex" (FCR, 127).

Standard history attributes this revolutionary development to Descartes. Thus, a recent standard reference work says:

> The concept of the reflex . . . embraces in a single theory the physiological description of complex behaviour and the explanation of how simple involuntary activities, such as the knee jerk, are regulated. All these elements of the concept as a key to psychology, animal behavior and involuntary motions are in René Descartes' (1596–1650) *Traité de l'Homme*.[23]

Canguilhem agrees that Descartes described and tried to explain the phenomena (e.g., the withdrawal of an arm or leg from a fire) that we call "reflex movements." But he insists that he did not formulate the concept of the reflex: "In Descartes' work . . . we find neither the term nor the concept of the reflex" (FCR, 52). One reason this is so is that a distinguishing characteristic of reflex movement is the fact that "it does not proceed directly from . . . a central seat" such as the heart or the brain (FCR, 41). But, according to Descartes, a movement such as the withdrawal of a limb from fire does proceed directly from a central seat; it is produced by the movement of the animal spirits from the brain (and ultimately from the heart, which is for Descartes the first source of all bodily movement). On Descartes's account there is no place for movements originating from "eccentric" centers. Further, the idea of *reflex* motion (as the terminological analogy with the reflection of light suggests) implies that the two movements, from the sense organs to the response center and back again, are of the same kind. But this is by no means so for Descartes, for whom "the excitation of the senses and the contraction of the muscle are two movements with no analogical rela-

---

23. *Dictionary of the history of science* (Princeton, N.J.: Princeton University Press, 1981), 366.

tion" (FCR, 41). The first Descartes conceives as a pulling on the chain of nerve fibers connecting the surface of the body to the brain, analogous to pulling the cord that rings a bell. The second he conceives as a pushing of the animal spirits through the tubes containing the nerves, analogous to pumping air through an organ pipe. In both cases, Descartes employs a mechanical account of the motion, but the two mechanisms are entirely different. Canguilhem maintains that Descartes's views were in fact a major obstacle to the formation of the concept of the reflex, precisely because they did not allow for the sort of "reflected" motion, the same in both directions, that is required by reflex action (FCR, 51).

One source of the mistaken belief that Descartes introduced the concept of the reflex is a confusion of the identification or description of a phenomenon with its proper conceptual interpretation. But the misattribution also derives from a confusion of concept and theory. In modern physiology, the concept of the reflex has been a central element in mechanistic theories of the organism – that is, theories that treat living things as merely complex versions of inanimate physical systems. Descartes, of course, is famous as an early proponent of mechanistic biology. Accordingly, it was easy for historians who regarded the course of science as a succession of theories to assume that Descartes's description of reflex action in the context of his mechanistic theory was equivalent to the introduction of the concept of reflex movement. This, however, ignores the essential independence of concepts from even what come to be their canonical theoretical embodiments. In fact, according to Canguilhem, the concept of the reflex was first introduced in the distinctly nonmechanistic physiological theory of Thomas Willis, a seventeenth-century English physician.

Willis explained bodily processes in terms of the chemistry of combustion and a vitalistic notion of the animal soul. His accounts were therefore far removed from the Cartesian mechanism that seems the natural locus of reflex movement. Nonetheless, Willis was led, as Descartes was not, to the two central elements of the concept of the reflex. First, he clearly distinguished the cerebellum, as the center of involuntary movement, from the cerebrum (or brain proper), as the center of rational thought and voluntary action. This effected the crucial decentering of reflex movement. Second, he conceived of reflex movement as a genuinely symmetrical process of back-and-forth motion by the animal spirits, explicitly employing the term *motus reflexus* in analogy to the reflection of light. Consequently, Canguilhem concludes that, "concerning the reflex, we find in Willis the thing, the word, and the notion" (FCR, 68). Eighteenth-century uses and developments of the concept of the reflex (by, e.g., Astruc, Unzer, and Prochaska) likewise placed it in the context of nonmechanistic approaches to physiology. It is only in the late nineteenth century that "the majority of physiologists tend to understand [the reflex] as an elementary and rigid mechanism" (E, 302). Later work (e.g., that of Sherrington), although thoroughly excluding any aspect of final causality from the concept of the reflex, has rejected extreme mechanistic interpretations of it (E, 304). In sum, the concept of the reflex has, since its introduction by Willis two hundred years ago, functioned effectively in a wide variety of theoretical contexts.

Canguilhem places great emphasis on the point that his history of scientific concepts does not itself pretend to have scientific status. This is in contrast with a number of other influential conceptions of the history of science. There is, for example, the essentially positivist conception, articulated by Dijksterhuis (and earlier by Comte's disciple, Pierre Lafitte), of history of science as the "laboratory" of epistemology (cf. E, 13). Here the idea is that the events and results of science's past are simply given to historians as already constituted objects. Their function is to scrutinize these data – Lafitte spoke of the historian's "mental microscope" – and use them to evaluate epistemological accounts of science.

Two other examples of history of science modeled on science itself are the "externalist" and "internalist" approaches so much discussed by Anglo-American historians of science. The externalist uses the techniques of psychology or the social sciences to relate scientific developments to economic, social, political, or religious conditions. The internalist ignores such conditions in favor of the internal logic of a science's development, but he is still interested in employing the facts about this development to evaluate, in a broadly scientific way, generalizations about the nature of science. This, we might add, is particularly true of internalist history – for example, that of Kuhn, Lakatos, and Laudan – designed to illumine the philosophy of science. Here historians view themselves as experimenters in Dijksterhuis' laboratory, using the data of history to test methodological principles and models of scientific development.

According to Canguilhem, what is common to all these scientific approaches to the history of science is their failure to see history itself as passing normative judgments about the science it studies. Consequently, to the model of history of science as a laboratory, he opposes the model of history of science as a law court in which "judgments are made regarding the past of knowledge, or the knowledge of the past" (E, 13). On such a model, history of science is not a scientific discipline precisely because its explicitly normative intent excludes the value-free orientation characteristic of a scientific analysis.

But in just what sense does Canguilhem see history of science as evaluating (judging) the past of science? Here he invokes Bachelard's distinction of *l'histoire périmée* and *l'histoire sanctionnée*, according to which past science is evaluated as outdated or validated on the basis of its relation to the results of current science. Thus, the historian's judgments are based on norms derived from an epistemological analysis informed (à la Bachelard) by current science. "It is epistemology that is called upon to furnish to history the principle for judgment, and epistemology provides this judgment from its understanding of the latest language spoken . . . by science" (E, 13).

Canguilhem also expresses the nonscientific nature of history of science in terms of the difference between its object and the object of science. "The object in the history of science has nothing in common with the object of science" (E, 17). Essentially, this is because the object of history of science has a historical character, whereas "science is science of an object . . . which does not have a history" (E, 16). In this context, an object's "having a history" is not a matter of its merely having existed and changed over time. Rather, an object is historical (has a history) when it is regarded as essentially part of a process of historical development *that is not finished.* As historical, the object is essentially incomplete and hence not given in its full reality. The objects of sciences (even of "historical" sciences such as geology or evolutionary biology) are not historical in this sense because science treats them – along with any history they may have – as givens completely available for analysis.[24] The objects of the history of science are rather treated as only partially given, not fully deter-

<hr>

24. Thus Canguilhem would presumably view "scientific" approaches to the history of science as not genuinely historical, since, in treating events as data, they take them out of their historical context.

mined. As a result, the value and even the meaning of science's past may alter with its future progress. In this regard, the work of historians of science is very similar to that of critics of art and literature.

Canguilhem regards his conception of the history of science as eliminating one major concern of many historians of science: the search for precursors of major scientific discoveries. A precursor, according to his wry definition, is "someone of whom we know only after that he came before."[25] In speaking of precursors, Canguilhem has particularly in mind the claim, frequently made by historians, that major scientific innovations by, for example, Copernicus and Darwin were essentially anticipated by much earlier thinkers (e.g., Aristarchus, Diderot). Sometimes, in fact, it seems that the historian's goal is to find ever earlier precursors for any important scientific work. As Canguilhem points out, if this search for precursors is taken to the limit, then science ceases to have a history; all scientific achievements occurred in some initial golden age (E, 21). In any case, he argues that the "discovery" of a precursor is usually based on a failure to recognize fundamental conceptual differences that underlie superficially similar formulations. Those, for example, who think that Réaumur or Maupertuis were precursors of Mendel's work on heredity do not understand the distinctive nature of Mendel's concept of an independent hereditary character (E, 22). Only under the most stringent conditions does Canguilhem allow any talk of scientists from different historical periods having pursued the same line of research or having made the same discovery. Unless, he says, we have

> explicitly established that two researchers are asking the same question and have the same research goal, that their guiding concepts have the same signification and draw their meaning from the same system of concepts, it is artificial, arbitrary, and inadequate . . . to say that two scientific authors stand in a logical relation of beginning to completion or of anticipation to realization. (E, 22)

But, although Canguilhem is firmly opposed to what, following J. T. Clark (cf. E, 20), he calls "the virus of the precursor,"

25. Reported from a class lecture by J-J. Salomon, "Georges Canguilhem ou la modernité," *Revue de métaphysique et de morale* 90 (1985), 53.

this does not mean that he denies the need to understand the influence of earlier scientific work on later.[26] Because science is a part of human culture, its discoveries are conditioned by the (explicit and implicit) education of those who make them (E, 235). Here Canguilhem speaks very positively of understanding scientists' work in terms of what they have learned from their "predecessors" and argues that failing to do this leads to the sort of empiricist or positivist history of science that denies that genuine historicity of science. Accordingly, we should not misunderstand Canguilhem's rejection of the search for scientists' precursors in different historical periods as a refusal to consider the undeniably important influence of their predecessors in their own historicocultural contexts. An adequate history of scientific concepts will have to pay detailed attention to such influences, as Canguilhem himself does on many pages of his history of the concept of the reflex.

Canguilhem's conception of the history of science has obvious strong affinities to Bachelard's history and philosophy of science. To cite two major examples, his focus on conceptual innovation corresponds to Bachelard's picture of science as a series of revolutionary breaks, and he understands the evaluative function of history of science in terms of Bachelard's contrast between *l'histoire périmée* and *l'histoire sanctionnée*. However, there are also a number of important ways in which Canguilhem refines, enriches, and even corrects ("rectifies") Bachelard's ideas. Even on the central point of epistemological breaks, Canguilhem offers a more nuanced view than Bachelard's, emphasizing the need to recognize continuities through even major breaks in the history of science.

> Often . . . the effect of a break is presented as global, affecting the totality of a scientific work. But we need to know how to uncover, even in the work of a single historical figure, successive breaks and partial breaks. In a theoretical fabric, certain threads can be entirely new, while others are taken from earlier weavings. The Copernican and Galilean revolutions also involved the preservation of a heritage. (E., 25)

---

26. But cf. NP, 84, for what seems to be an example of Canguilhem himself falling victim to the virus.

Likewise, with regard to *l'histoire périmée* versus *l'histoire sanctionnée*, Canguilhem's distinction of concepts from theoretical context helps clarify the way in which a single piece of scientific work (e.g., Black's discovery of specific heat) can be simultaneously *sanctionnée* (in terms of the concept introduced) and *périmée* (in terms of the theoretical context of the introduction). Canguilhem also effects an implicit correction of Bachelard's concept of an epistemological obstacle. For Bachelard, the concept has an entirely negative connotation, referring merely to what blocks the path of inquiry and hence needs to be removed. Canguilhem, however, allows that what are impediments in one respect may at the same time be in other ways important sources of scientific progress. Such, for example, is the case in the history of biology with the much abused doctrine of vitalism.[27] Although Canguilhem agrees that many decisive advances have required a mechanistic viewpoint, he nonetheless insists that vitalism has played the positive role of keeping biologists aware of the distinctive features of the organisms they are trying to understand. Canguilhem admits that "classical vitalism" was entirely wrong in its claim that organisms were exceptions to the laws of physics and chemistry. "One cannot defend the originality of biological phenomena . . . by setting up, within the domain of physics and chemistry, enclaves of indeterminism, zones of dissidence, centers of heresy" (CV, 95). In the sense that vitalism tried to reject the application of physics and chemistry to organisms, it was an obstacle to scientific progress. But, in another sense, vitalism was – and remains – a salutary reminder that, even if physico-chemical laws are fully applicable to organisms, vital phenomena still have distinctive features that exclude any facile reduction of them to inanimate systems. During the eighteenth century, for example, vitalists were, according to Canguilhem, "prudent positivists" or "Newtonians" who refused to engage in either materialist or animistic speculations about the metaphysical nature of life and instead called for fidelity to the specific phenomena of the biological realm.

27. Bachelard, in a discussion of animist obstacles to scientific progress, explicitly sets aside the questions of the role of vitalism in the life sciences, saying he is only concerned with obstacles to progress in physics and chemistry (NES, 149).

Vitalism was simply the recognition of life as an original order of phenomena and hence a recognition of the specificity of biological knowledge. . . . [The vitalists'] vital principle, their *vis vitalis, vis insita, vis nervosa* were so many names that they gave to their inability to accept either pure mechanism or the action of the soul [animism] as explanations of the phenomena of life. (FCR, 164–65)

A specific positive contribution of vitalism was to the development of the concept of the reflex: "Vitalism was more suited than mechanism to accustom the thought of biologists to the decentralization of the functions of sensori-motor coordination" (FCR, 171–72).

Canguilhem's distinction of concept and theory is helpful for understanding the dual status of vitalism. On the one hand, vitalism is often an epistemological obstacle to the development of the best theoretical system of explaining biological phenomena. On the other hand, it keeps biologists' concepts open to the uniqueness of the phenomena they are designed to understand and thus warns them against the reductionistic pretentions of successful mechanistic theories.

Given the ambivalence he sees in some epistemological obstacles, it is not surprising that Canguilhem gives less weight than Bachelard to the distinction between science and nonscience. For Bachelard this distinction is fundamental, since he sees the history of science as a constant struggle of scientific reason to break away from nonscientific (especially imaginative and philosophical) constraints on thought. Canguilhem's uneasiness with the idea of a sharp break between the scientific and the nonscientific first appears in some comments about the application of Bachelard's ideas to the history of the reflex. At the end of his study of this topic, he asks the Bachelardian question: "What sort of history, after all, have we been studying? A history of scientific thought or of prescientific thought?" (FCR, 159). His answer is that Bachelard's dichotomy is not particularly applicable here, since the concept of the reflex was formed during a period of transition from prescientific to scientific thinking. More to the point, he suggests, is Bachelard's closely related distinction between everyday experience (*l'expérience commune*) and scientific experience (*l'expérience scientifique*). But even this distinction, Canguilhem notes, is a relative one. In physiology, for example, the work of Legallois seems to involve scientific experience in comparison to the everyday experience employed by Whytt, but when compared to the work of Pflüger or Sherrington, that of Legallois seems based on everyday rather than scientific experience (FCR, 161). In the end, Canguilhem concludes that the most we can say is that work on the reflex at later times (e.g., around 1850) was *more scientific* than at other times (e.g., around 1800), where the "more" is due to the fact that the concept of the reflex is more fully integrated into experimental techniques and employed in the explanation of a wider variety of phenomena.

Canguilhem's early hesitations about the significance of a sharp distinction between the scientific and the nonscientific eventually led him to the important intermediate concept of a *scientific ideology*. As he explicitly acknowledges (IR, 9), his work on this topic is influenced by that of his pupils, Louis Althusser and Michel Foucault.

Canguilhem notes that the term *ideology* originally referred to "the science of the genesis of ideas" that, during the eighteenth century, Cabanis and Destrutt de Tracy proposed as a basis for "treating ideas as natural phenomena" understood in relation to their natural environment. The liberal political views of these "ideologists" brought them into conflict with Napoleon's imperial ambitions, and, in the ensuing controversy, Napoleon and his supporters portrayed them as unrealistic metaphysicians who were trying to cut reality to fit their theories. Marx picked up on this abusive use of "ideology" and gave the term its canonical meaning as "any system of ideas produced as the effect of a situation doomed from the start to misunderstand its real connection to reality [*son rapport réel au réel*]" (IR, 36).

Marx himself draws a sharp contrast between science (i.e., his own scientific economics) and ideology, so that for him the notion of a *scientific ideology* would seem to be a "logical monster" (IR, 36). But Canguilhem notes that, in *The German ideology*, Marx does not include "bourgeois sciences" such as Newtonian mechanics or classical electrodynamics in the list of ideologies, although he does emphasize, against Feuerbach, their essential debt – for both goals and methods – to capitalist business and industry (IR, 37). This suggests that, even from a Marxist viewpoint, there is room for activities that are genuinely scientific – that is, yield objective knowledge – even though they are molded by the sort of forces that produce ideologies. To give Canguilhem's thought here an expression he does not use, we might say that even Marx needs to allow for the existence of "ideological sciences."[28]

But Canguilhem thinks we must also introduce the further category of a *scientific ideology*, an ideology (hence not a body of objective knowledge) that has nonetheless an essential orientation to science. Such an ideology has two main characteristics. First, it takes some existing science as its model of knowledge; hence it has pretentions to a scientific status defined by the standards of science contemporary to it. Second, however, a scientific ideology makes claims about reality that go far beyond the capacity of contemporary science to establish; hence its pretentions are merely pretentions and its claims scientifically presumptuous. Scientific ideologies are not ideologies of scientists – that is, ideologies deriving from scientists' efforts to determine the place of their science in relation to other forms of culture. They are rather ideologies of philosophers, deriving from "discussions with scientific pretentions carried out by men who are still, regarding the subject under discussion, only presumptive or presumptuous scientists" (IR, 44).

As examples of scientific ideology, Canguilhem cites Maupertuis's work on genetics in his *Vénus physique* and Herbert Spencer's evolutionary theory. Both cases represent the double relation that scientific ideology bears to genuine science. On the one hand, it points "laterally" toward a science contemporary to it that serves as its model; on the other hand, it points forward toward a future science that will replace the ideology's pretentions with genuine results. Maupertuis's genetic speculations were modeled on his own successful work in mechanics and the calculus of probabilities and were superseded by Mendel's scientific theory of hereditary characteristics. Spencer presented his "law of evolution" as a generalization of the principles of Von Baer's embryology, and his work was eventually displaced by Darwin's scientific theory of evolution through natural selection.

Although the pretentions of scientific ideologies may well present obstacles to the progress of science, Canguilhem also em-

28. Canguilhem notes (IR, 38) that Marx himself admits that Greek art, for example, has a permanent value despite its relativity to particular social conditions. "Can Marxism," he asks, "refuse to Greek geometry what Marx accorded to Greek art?" As we will see in Chapter 6, Foucault also recognizes sciences with ideological content (AK, 184–86).

phasizes their positive role. This derives from the fact that the progress of science "requires . . . a certain priority [*antériorité*] of intellectual adventure over rationalization, presumptuous surpassing, in view of the demands of life and action, of what has been properly verified as knowledge" (IR, 38). Scientific ideologies provide this needed dimension of intellectual adventure that is, strictly speaking, not entirely responsible. Accordingly, Canguilhem concludes that a scientific ideology can be "at the same time an obstacle and a condition of possibility . . . for the constitution of science" (IR, 38). So scientific ideologies appear as a major example of the ambivalence of epistemological obstacles.

Canguilhem notes that scientific ideologies will be of no interest to those who think that the history of science is simply the continual accumulation of truths. But for those, like Bachelard and himself, who see the history of science as a never completed "purification" (IR, 44) of errors, they are an essential concern. Although it is always necessary to distinguish genuine science from scientific ideology, the two are in fact intertwined in the history of science, and an adequate understanding of the progress of science requires an understanding of both. Bachelard's distinction of what is outdated and what is validated in the scientific past is still sound, but it does not justify the historian in mining only the scientific gold and ignoring the ideological dross (IR, 45). This reinforces the rejection of a sharp distinction between internal and external history of science, which, as we saw (note 11 above), was already implicit in Bachelard's account of epistemological obstacles.

Canguilhem's conception of norms

Our discussion of Canguilhem's conception of the history of science shows that for him it is an essentially normative discipline. But so far we have said almost nothing about his views on the nature of norms and evaluation. That is a crucial issue, particularly given the difficulties that we have seen Bachelard has understanding and grounding normative judgments. Moreover, Canguilhem has devoted a substantial portion of his historical and philosophical effort to an analysis of norms and the normal, and, as we shall see, the status of norms is an important issue for Foucault. So it will be valuable for us to take a close look at this key aspect of Canguilhem's work.

Canguilhem's thesis for his doctoral degree in medicine, published in 1943, was an "Essay on Some Problems Concerning the Normal and the Pathological." Here Canguilhem undertakes a substantial historical analysis and philosophical criticism of a thesis put forward by F.–J. V. Broussais in the early nineteenth century and later taken up by Auguste Comte and Claude Bernard. According to this thesis (*Broussais's Principle*), pathological states (diseases) are merely quantitative modifications of normal (healthy) states. Illness is nothing more than an excess or defect of some factor requisite for health. As Claude Bernard put it:

> Health and disease are not two essentially different modes. . . . They should not be made into distinct principles, entities which fight over the living organism and make it the theatre of their contest. These are obsolete medical ideas. In reality, between these two modes of being, there are only differences of degree: exaggeration, disproportion, discordance of normal phenomena constitute the diseased state. There is no case where disease would have produced new conditions, a complete change of scene, some new and special products. (Cited, NP, 33)

To cite some simple examples: Diabetes is due to an excess of sugar in the urine, leukemia to an excess of white blood cells, anemia to a lack of red blood cells. Given Broussais's Principle, there is no essential difference between physiology (the study of normal bodily functions) and pathology (the study of diseases as deviations from the norm).

Canguilhem criticizes Broussais's Principle on both conceptual and empirical grounds. Conceptually, he claims that its defense frequently involves a confusion of *continuity* and *homogeneity* – that is, a failure to realize that just because one state can be derived from another by a continuous series of quantitative changes, it does not follow that the two states do not differ qualitatively. Empirically, he argues that many diseases, particularly if they are understood in their full complexity, are in fact not produced by an excess or defect of some constituent of a healthy body. In this regard, he offers a thorough discussion of the nature and etiology of diabetes (NP, 37–40).

More important for our purposes, Canguilhem also outlines his own view of health and disease, the normal and the pathological, as qualitatively different states of the organism. At the heart of this view is his claim that biological norms are posited by the organism itself. Certain states and modes of functioning have a special value from the organism's point of view, even though other states and modes of functioning are equally possible and perhaps even more common. Here Canguilhem thinks there is an important contrast between modern physics and biology. Aristotelian mechanics distinguished between normal (natural) and pathological (violent) motions. This polarity of motions was rejected by Galileo and Descartes in favor of a principle of inertia that "made the distinction between natural and violent movements absurd, as inertia is precisely an indifference with respect to directions and variations in movement" (NP, 71). By contrast, life, the object of biology, "is far removed from such an indifference to the conditions which are made for it" (71). For example, when an organism fails to excrete digestive wastes, which then congest or poison it, "this is all indeed according to law (physical, chemical, etc.) but none of this follows the norm, which is the activity of the organism itself" (NP, 71). It is biologically absurd to make no distinction in principle between states that enhance an organism's functioning in its environment and those that impede or eliminate it.

Accordingly, Canguilhem insists on a qualitative distinction between health and disease, a distinction understood in terms of values established by the very nature of the organism. However, he does not think of health (the normal state) as life in accord with norms and of disease as merely life in violation of these norms. To *any* state of an organism there corresponds a certain mode of living, and this mode of living defines norms appropriate to it. Hence, any state of an organism, even a pathological one, is governed by norms; that is, there is a standard pattern of behavior appropriate for an organism in the state. In what then consists the uniqueness and the superiority of states that are healthy? According to Canguilhem, it is the fact that in a healthy state the organism is capable of adjusting to new situations by instituting new norms.

> Being healthy means being not only normal in a given situation but also normative in this and other eventual situations. What characterizes health is the possibility of transcending the norm, which defines the momentary normal, the possibility of tolerating infractions of the habitual norm and instituting new norms in new situations. (NP, 115)

Thus, the loss of a kidney is pathological, even though, in most cases, the organism continues to function just as it did with two. The pathology consists in the fact that the range of circumstances in which the organism can maintain normal functions has been significantly reduced. Thus, "disease is characterized by the fact that it is a reduction in the margin of tolerance for the environment's inconsistencies" (NP, 116). This point is particularly supported by the fact that, typically,

> we are more concerned about the disease any given disease may plunge us into than about the disease itself. . . . Measles is nothing, but it's bronchial pneumonia that we dread. Syphilis is so feared only after it strikes the nervous system. Diabetes is not so serious if it is just glycoria [presence of carbohydrates in the urine]. But coma? gangrene? what will happen if surgery is necessary? (NP, 117)

In sum, an organism is healthy when it is not only capable of surviving in its current circumstances (by functioning in accord with norms appropriate to those circumstances) but also capable of surviving in a significant range of alternative circumstances (by functioning according to new norms appropriate to the new circumstances).

A crucial point follows from this account of biological norms. The concept of such norms "cannot be reduced to an objective concept determinable by scientific methods" (NP, 138). Physiology does, of course, describe and explain the states that we call normal and healthy. But the appellations "normal" and "healthy" are not applied on the basis of physiological results. They are applied in virtue of the meaning of the states in question for the organism itself. Similarly for pathology's concern with disease. When physiologists study healthy states and pathologists diseased ones, the states so characterized are given to them on the basis of nonscientific judgments grounded in the life experience of the organism. As Canguilhem says, it is the patient who calls the doctor (NP, 134).[29] That is, all the apparatus of scientific medicine is oriented toward norms (health, the avoidance of disease) that are defined independently of and prior to objective scientific analysis. Of course, a physician may tell a patient that he is sick even

---

29. Except, he says, for the case of mental illness, a remark for which Foucault's FD can be regarded as providing an elaborate commentary.

when the patient feels healthy. But this is only because medical science has discovered causal connections between the patient's present "healthy" state and one that the patient would judge unhealthy. At root, the norms that concern medical science are not objective facts that it discovers. "One does not scientifically dictate norms to life" (NP, 134). Rather, norms are constituted by organisms themselves – by life itself.

In view of this, Canguilhem says that medical norms have a "subjective" origin and that in consequence "there is no objective pathology" (NP, 134). This does not mean, of course, that the descriptions and explanations offered by the pathologist (or the physiologist) are not rigorously scientific and fully objective. But the precise characterization of the states described and explained *as* healthy or diseased does not derive from objective scientific analysis but from the organism's experience of the state.

Although Canguilhem insists on the "subjective" nature of organic norms, it is important to realize that he regards them as rooted not in the whims or idiosyncrasies of the individual organism but in its essential nature as the sort of organism it is. As he comments in his "New Reflections on the Normal and the Pathological," published twenty years after his thesis, "the vital needs and norms of a lizard or a stickleback in their natural habitat are expressed in the very fact that these animals are very natural living beings in this habitat" (NP, 158). He even speaks in this connection of an "innate model" for the behavior of an organism (NP, 155–56). Although biological norms are not objective in the sense of conclusions from neutral scientific investigation, they are nonetheless firmly rooted in the biological reality of the organisms they regulate. They are subjective only in the sense that they derive from the organism's lived experience of this reality.

Another point worth noting is that, for Canguilhem, although the abnormal (or pathological) is grammatically and logically subsequent to the normal, it is existentially prior. This is because "rule begins to be rule only in making rules and this function of correction arises from infraction itself" (NP, 147). Merely healthy persons do not think of themselves as such. The concept of health is formed only as a contrast to an experience of disease or of the threat of disease. "Health," in the phrase of René Leriche, "is life lived in the silence of the organs," a silence that has no need to articulate a concept of itself (cited, NP, 149).

But can we move from this account of biological norms to an understanding of the norms that apply to social groups and to the norms of that very special social group, the community of scientific researchers? According to Canguilhem the status of social norms is very different from that of biological norms. He agrees that societies mimic the norms of organisms and that, in the case of archaic and so-called primitive societies, social norms expressed in dominating traditions may have the kind of inevitable force that biological norms do. But this is not so for the sort of societies that we live in. In order to treat a society as an organism with respect to norms, we must "be able to speak of a society's needs and norms as one speaks of an organism's vital needs and norms, that is, unambiguously" (NP, 158). In other words, there has to be a fixed set of norms applicable to the society as a whole, defining its essential purpose as a society. But, says Canguilhem, in societies like ours, "one of the tasks of the entire social organization consists in informing itself of its possible purposes," a fact that "seems to show clearly that, strictly speaking, [such a society] has no intrinsic finality" (NP, 155). The very fact that individuals question the de facto needs and norms of their society shows, in Canguilhem's view, "that these needs and norms are not those of the whole society" (NP, 158). Reflection on such challenges should lead us "to understand to what extent social need is not immanent, to what extent the social norm is not internal, and, finally, to what extent the society, seat of restrained dissent or latent antagonisms, is far from setting itself up as a whole" that could determine unequivocally authoritative norms (NP, 158).

In fact it seems that, for Canguilhem, it is not only the fact of dissent by individuals that undermines the authority of social norms. Even a universal consensus regarding standards would not in itself give them genuinely normative status. This, at least, is Canguilhem's position with regard to the case most important for us, the norms of the scientific community. This position becomes clear in his critical evaluation of Thomas Kuhn's notions of paradigm and of normal science. The terms *paradigm* and *normal science* suggest, as they should, the idea of norms regulating scientific activity. But, according to Canguilhem, Kuhn understands them in a way that deprives them of any genuinely regulatory function. This is because he accords his paradigms and normal sciences "only an empirical mode of existence as cultural facts." More fully, for Kuhn,

> the paradigm is the result of a choice by those who use it. The normal is what is common, over a given period, to a collectivity of specialists in a university or other academic institution. We think we are dealing with concepts of a philosophical critique, only to find ourselves on the level of social psychology. (IR, 23)

So the consensus about a paradigm that provides the basis for Kuhnian normal science is only a de facto psychological agreement with no normative force. Here Canguilhem's critique of Kuhn is very similar to that of Popper, Lakatos, and their followers.

Canguilhem contrasts what he sees as Kuhn's merely psychological notion of normal science with the norms of Bachelard's history and philosophy of science.[30] The latter, he says, have more than a psychological status since they are standards for the correction (*rectification, normalisation*) of the errors of the past (IR, 23). But in another discussion Canguilhem raises an objection to Bachelard that is very similar to his criticism of Kuhn. He begins by recalling Bachelard's emphasis on the psychological origins of epistemological obstacles to scientific progress and on the need for a "psychoanalysis of knowledge" to overcome them. He then asks:

> But does not an enterprise that consists, by its author's own admission, in searching, through the psychoanalysis of epistemological obstacles, for the psychological conditions of the progress of science run the risk of disqualifying science's claim to objectivity? Psychologism does not have a good press. (E, 204–205)

Bachelard's response, of course, is that the process of rectification of past errors eliminates the merely contingent psychological elements in favor of genuine norms. By progressively eliminating errors on particular issues, "the task of depsychologization is carried out" (RA, 48; cited, E, 205). But Canguilhem is not at all sure

---

30. In my view this psychological interpretation of normal science is not an accurate reading of Kuhn. For an alternative reading, see my Introduction to G. Gutting, ed., *Paradigms and revolutions* (Notre Dame, Indiana: University of Notre Dame Press, 1980).

this is an adequate response. How precisely do norms derive from the process of rectification? As we have seen, Bachelard invokes his concept of "corationalism," whereby a scientific claim is supported not just by an individual inclination to accept it but by the logical force that its proof will exercise on *any* rational mind. He also speaks of the "intellectual surveillance of the self," whereby the self, divided into the "existing I" of the *cogito* and the "surexisting I" of the *cogitamus* internalizes epistemic values. Canguilhem finds all this ingenious but not finally convincing. He notes that throughout "Bachelard continues to employ the vocabulary of individual and interpersonal psychology" (E, 205). He speaks of "normative psychism" and "normative psychology." But, Canguilhem asks, if we describe scientific norms in this way, haven't we in fact proposed a "psychologism of normalization" – that is, reduced norms to contingent psychological factors? The most Canguilhem is willing to grant is that "Bachelard is totally clear about the difficulty of thoroughly constituting the vocabulary of a rationalist epistemology without referring to an ontological theory of reason or to a transcendental theory of categories" (E. 206).

So it seems that, in the end, Canguilhem finds in Bachelard no more than in Kuhn an adequate account of the basis for social norms. Even for the privileged special case of the norms of scientific communities, neither adequately grounds the authority of norms. Nor does Canguilhem himself anywhere provide the needed middle ground between psychologism and transcendentalism. Although biological norms are for him firmly rooted in the life of the organism, social norms, even those of Canguilhem's normative history of science, remain without an adequate foundation.

Foucault and the Bachelard–Canguilhem network

In many important respects, Foucault's view of science is Bachelardian. He accepts, for example, the essential historicity of scientific conceptions as well as the understanding of this historicity in terms of a discontinuous series of breaks. Indeed, all the talk of *"rupture," "coupure," "mutation,"* and so on, that Foucault and others (e.g., Althusser) made so fashionable in the 1960s derives directly from Bachelard. Foucault further implicitly accepts the basic negative epistemological and metaphysical theses – for ex-

ample, the rejections of a sharp theory/observation distinction
and of naive realism – associated with Bachelard's account of
science. He also shares Bachelard's emphasis on the need to treat
questions of scientific rationality in "regional" terms, eschewing
grandly global theories for specific studies of particular disciplinary and chronological domains. Similarly, Foucault's historical
studies share what he himself appreciatively noted[31] as Bachelard's penchant for focusing on obscure and neglected works
and figures as a way of challenging orthodox views in the history
of science. But there are even deeper affinities between Foucault and
Bachelard. Foucault's fundamental critical project of showing
the contingent nature of what present themselves as necessary, a
priori limits on knowledge corresponds to Bachelard's insistence
that philosophical a prioris derive from our inability or unwillingness to think beyond the categories of current (or recently past)
science. Similarly, Foucault's basic idea of an archaeological uncovering of the "deep structures" of knowledge is closely related
to Bachelard's idea of a "psychoanalysis" of knowledge. Indeed,
Foucault himself characterized his work as primarily aimed at
the elucidation of the unconscious of our knowledge.[32]

Furthermore, on a number of points where Foucault would
disagree with Bachelard, his disagreement mirrors that of Canguilhem. In AK, for example, he follows Canguilhem in emphasizing the various ways that continuities can persist across epistemological breaks. He likewise rejects Bachelard's entirely negative
construal of "unconscious" factors in scientific thought as epistemological obstacles. Also, Foucault sympathizes with Canguilhem's move away from Bachelard's insistence on a sharp distinction between science and nonscience.

Positively, Foucault's work in the history of science is strongly
influenced by Canguilhem's history of concepts. This is not surprising, since Canguilhem was not only one of his teachers at the
Ecole Normale Supérieure but also the director of his doctoral

31. "Gaston Bachelard, le philosophie et son ombre: 'pieger sa propre culture',"
Figaro littéraire, Sept. 30, 1972, p. 16.
32. Cf. for example, an interview with J-P. El Kabbach, "Foucault repond à
Sartre," Quinzaine littéraire, Mar. 1–15, 1968, in which Foucault says: "I have
tried to disengage an autonomous domain that would be that of the unconscious of science, the unconscious of knowledge [savoir], which would have its
own rules, just as the unconscious of the human individual also has its rules
and determinations" (21).

thesis, FD. (Although most of the thesis seems to have been written while Foucault was teaching outside France, the preface to FD explicitly notes the close reading and commentary Canguilhem gave the manuscript.) In any case, as we shall see, Foucault's historical analyses consistently reflect Canguilhem's emphasis on concepts over theories and on the vanity of superficial pursuits of "precursors." It would be clearly wrong to identify Foucault's archaeological method with Canguilhem's history of concepts. But it is equally clear that this sort of history is one important aspect of archaeological analysis and sometimes (as in BC) the dominant one.

None of the above is meant to suggest that Foucault was a mere disciple of Bachelard and Canguilhem. His work developed from his own distinctive agenda and embraced many topics and concerns far removed from their domain of the history and philosophy of science. Moreover, even where the influence of Bachelard and Canguilhem is particularly strong, Foucault extends, adapts, and transforms their idea and methods. But it remains true that understanding his relation to these two thinkers is a significant aid in understanding the methodology he developed for writing the history of reason. Accordingly, in the following chapters, my comments on the methodological aspects of FD, BC, and OT will often take the form of reflections on Foucault's connections with Bachelard and Canguilhem. And my discussion of AK in Chapter 6 will provide the occasion for some final conclusions about Foucault's place in the Bachelard–Canguilhem network. Here – as well as in Chapter 7 – I will also raise the issue of Foucault's position on the crucial issue of normativity.

2

MADNESS AND MENTAL ILLNESS

Early writings on mental illness

Foucault's first publications appeared in 1954: a monograph entitled *Maladie mentale et personnalité* (MMP) and a long (120 pages) introduction to the French translation of Ludwig Binswanger's *Traum und Existenz* (RE). These two works were the culmination of his studies in philosophy and psychology at the Ecole Normale Supérieure and provide essential background for understanding his major work on madness, *Folie et déraison,* published seven years later. They also reflect the strong influence of existential phenomenology and of Marxism on his early work.

MMP appeared again in 1962 in a second edition, retitled *Maladie mentale et la psychologie* (MMPsy). The first part is essentially the same in the two editions, but the second part has been radically rewritten in the second edition, in accord with the views Foucault put forward in *Folie et déraison* (FD). Thus, comparing the two editions provides a sense of the development of Foucault's thought from 1954 to 1961 and is very important for understanding his viewpoint in FD. Unfortunately, matters have been very confused by the presentation of the English translation, which is in fact of the 1962 second edition but which gives the copyright date of the original being translated as 1954. This has misled some commentators into thinking that Foucault held already in 1954 views that he in fact developed later. The confusion about translation – along with the replacement in France of the first edition by the second – has also led to a lack of awareness of Foucault's important and interesting early views on the nature and explanation of mental illness. I will begin with an analysis of the 1954 texts (MMP and RE) and then move to a discussion of the 1962 text (MMPsy) as a transition to FD.

Foucault's goal in MMP is to see what sense there is in our talk of mental "illnesses" and just how such disorders are related to organic illness. His initial proposal is that it is a mistake to "give the same meaning to the notions of illness, symptoms, and etiology in mental pathology and in organic pathology" (1–2, 2) and that to understand mental illness we must abandon the "abstract metapsychology" that assumes that "organic disturbances and personality changes . . . possess the same type of structure" (2, 2).[1] Consequently, he proposes to analyze the phenomenon of mental illness in its own terms, with no reliance on organic analogies, and determine its specific character and origin.

> Placing our credit in man himself and not in the abstractions of illness, we must analyze the specificity of mental illness, seek the concrete forms it can take in the psychological life of an individual, and then determine the conditions that have made these diverse aspects possible and restore the whole of the causal system that has grounded them. (16–17)[2]

According to Foucault, mental pathology needs to be understood on successively more concrete and significant levels. On a first level, mental illness appears as a regression in the process of human evolution:

> The illness . . ., going back to the earlier phases of evolution . . . eliminates recent acquisitions and rediscovers forms of behavior

---

1. The first page reference is to MMP; the second is to the corresponding passage in the English translation of MMPsy. Translations of passages that appear only in MMP are mine.
2. In the second edition, this passage rather concludes: "Seek the concrete forms that psychology has managed to attribute to it, then determine the conditions that have made possible this strange status of madness, a mental illness that cannot be reduced to any illness" (MMPsy, 13).

that have normally been surpassed. The illness is the process throughout which the web of evolution is unraveled. (22, 18)

This aspect of mental illness is most familiar through Freud's account of neuroses as involving fixations at various stages (e.g., oral, anal) of infantile sexuality. But Foucault maintains that all forms of mental illness exhibit a regressive replacement of late, more complex behavior patterns by early, simpler ones. He accepts the idea of evolutionary regression as the basis for a structural description of mental illness but denies it an explanatory role. He does this first because, in his view, there is never in fact a literal return to an "archaic personality": "We must accept the specificity of the morbid phenomenon: the pathological structure of the psyche is not a return to origins: it is strictly original" (31, 25–6). The disturbed personality contains regressive elements, but it has its own unique overall structure. Further, Foucault notes that regressive analysis is not explanatory because it cannot tell us why a particular person becomes mentally ill at a particular time. "From the point of view of evolution, [mental] illness has no other status than that of a general potentiality" (34–35, 28). He concludes that our effort to understand mental illness must move from the level of general categories of evolutionary development to the level of personal life histories of mentally ill people.

Foucault thinks that moving to this level of personal history reveals the function of regressions to archaic modes of behavior. They serve to defend the personality against anxiety generated by present conflicts (e.g., between desire for something and guilt over the desire). The patient reverts to an earlier (e.g., infantile) mode of behavior as a way of escaping from ("derealizing") present conflicts. Unfortunately, however, the behavior resorted to for escape is the very behavior that is historically tied to the anxiety being fled. Consequently, the patient finds himself trapped in a "circularity that makes him defend himself against anxiety with mechanisms that . . . serve merely to augment that anxiety . . ." (50, 41). An understanding of mental illness requires a knowledge (sought, e.g., by Freudian psychoanalysis) of the factors in individuals' psychological histories that have led them to such ill-fated regressive defenses against anxiety.

But Foucault maintains that individual history itself cannot be understood without reference to yet another level of understanding: that of the patient's lived experience. The objective facts of personal history (of, e.g., the Oedipal situation) may be the same for various individuals. This raises the question:

Why, in a given situation, does one individual encounter a surmountable conflict and another a contradiction within which he is enclosed in a pathological way? Why is the same Oedipal ambiguity overcome by one individual while, in another, it sets off a long sequence of pathological mechanisms? (51, 42)

According to Foucault, the answer lies in the special meaning given to the facts of an individual's history by his organization of them into a world of concrete, lived experience. Accordingly, we need an understanding of the experience of mental illness from the inside, a "phenomenology of mental illness" (56, 46).

In MMP, Foucault sketches this phenomenology in terms of the standard division of noetic analysis (of the "sick consciousness") and noematic analysis (of the "pathological world"). The former focuses on the various ways in which the mentally ill are aware of themselves as different from other, "normal" people. Thus, a patient may perceive his or her illness as merely an organic matter, as in hypochondria, or as "the explosion of a new existence that profoundly alters the meaning of his life" (58, 48), as in obsessions or manias, or as another world inhabited in addition to the ordinary one, as in hallucinatory psychoses. Finally, in the most extreme forms of mental illness (the worst forms of schizophrenia and dementia), "the patient is engulfed in the world of his illness" and experiences the ordinary world as merely a "distant, veiled reality" (59, 49). Foucault's noematic analysis of mental illness is based primarily on the work of Eugene Minkowski and distinguishes disturbances in patients' experiences of time, space, the cultural and social worlds, and even of their own bodies.

In terms of this phenomenological approach, Foucault, citing Binswanger, says that mental illness involves two key elements. First, the world of the mentally ill is a private one, opaque to the perspectives and attitudes of other people. But this privacy, though it represents the ill person's attempt to flee the real, objective world, does not in fact bring freedom from it. On the contrary, precisely because the mentally ill fail to engage with the shared, intersubjective meanings of the real world, they experience this world merely as a series of causally determining external events. Hence, the second element of mental illness is that a person suffering from it "abandons himself to events. . ... One sees the mark of disintegration that abandons the subject to the world as to an external fate." So, paradoxically, mental illness "is both a retreat into the worst of subjectivities and a fall into the worst of objectivities" (69, 56).

Foucault provides a much fuller development of the basis of his understanding of mental illness on the level of lived experience in his "Introduction" to the French translation of Binswanger's *Traum und Existenz*. This essay (twice as long as Binswanger's piece) is far more than an introduction to someone else's work. It is, in fact, Foucault's critical synthesis of ideas from a variety of major thinkers (including Freud, Husserl, Heidegger, Binswanger, Bachelard, and Sartre) into a general existential view of human reality. Foucault characterizes his view as an "anthropology of the imagination," since he sees the essential features of human reality expressed in our imaginative life, particularly dreams.

He begins with a criticism of Freud's method of dream interpretation, which he faults for treating dreams merely as pointers to external factors (e.g., traumatic past events, unconscious desires) and ignoring the intrinsic meaning they have in their own right. "The language of the dream is analyzed only in its semantic function; Freudian analysis leaves in the dark its morphological and syntactic structures" (RE, 19). This is a mistake since "the imaginary world has its own laws, its specific structures; the image is something more than the immediate fulfillment of meaning; it has its thickness" (RE, 20). Foucault suggests that the root of Freud's error here is his failure to distinguish between a symbol as a mere indication of something else and a symbol as an expression of meaning – the distinction Husserl draws (in his *Logical investigations*) between index and signification. The former – for example, the tracks by which a hunter recognizes the presence of a rabbit – functions only in virtue of "an actual situation that does, has, or will exist." The latter – for example, the word *rabbit* – "need not, in order to be significant, be based on any objective situation" (RE, 31–32). Freud in effect treats dreams as merely indices and not as significations. As a result, he thinks their meaning is exhausted in their references to unconscious memories and desires and fails to see them as expressions of human existence as such. Thus, Freud's analysis of a crucial dream of his patient "Dora" revealed only symbols of repressed heterosexual and homosexual love and failed to recognize the dream's essential meaning as an expression of Dora's resolve to break off psychoanalytic treatment and to assume a new, independent mode of existence. Such analysis failed to discover what Freud himself sometimes suspected: that "the dream was not content to symbolize and express in images the history of past experiences [but rather] encompassed the entire existence of the subject. . ." (RE, 76). Binswanger, however, explicitly recognizes the dreaming subject itself "as the foundation of all the possible meanings of the dream: and, to this extent, [the dream] is not the reappearance of an earlier form or an archaic style of the personality; it reveals itself as the process and the totality of existence itself" (RE, 79–80). As such, dreams do not merely point to the past; they also evoke the future the subject is creating for itself: "The dream cannot have as its subject the quasi-objective subject of past history; its constituting moment can be only this existence that makes itself in the course of time, this existence in its movement toward the future" (RE, 83).

Although dreams thus represent an individual's world, "the world that belongs to me by announcing my own solitude," their essential structures reveal the fundamental dimensions – freedom, values, destiny, death – of human existence as such. "If in sleep consciousness slumbers, in the dream existence awakens" (RE, 70). Following Binswanger, Foucault sketches the dream's essential existential meanings in terms of the "spatiality" of the dream world, which he regards as defining "the trajectory of existence itself" (RE, 86). Specifically, he distinguishes three dimensions of "oneiric space," each defined by a pair of polar categories and each correlated with the mode of human experience expressed by a particular literary genre. Thus, he correlates the dimension of the near and the far with epic experiences of travel and return, that of the obscure and the clear with lyrical experiences of confusion and enlightenment, that of the vertical, up/down axis with experiences of tragic exaltation and fall. Foucault regards this last dimension as the fundamental one. It is only in this dimension, which founds human temporality, authenticity, and historicity, that "we abandon the anthropological level of reflection that analyzes man as man, within his human world, for an ontological reflection that concerns [his] mode of being and existence as presence to the world" (RE, 105).

Foucault next turns to the relation between dreaming and imagining. His account of the imagination is developed through critiques of Sartre and Bachelard. On a classical view (e.g., Hume's), an image is merely a diminished perception, presenting an object in a positive but less "lively" way. Sartre, by contrast, views the image as "negating" its object by positing it as unreal. Foucault, however, rejects the assumption, common to both the classical and the Sartrean accounts, that the image is defined through its relation – positive or negative – to its object. He agrees with Sartre that, when I imagine an object, "its absence surrounds and circumscribes the movement of my imagination" (RE, 108). But he argues that this absence is "already there" before the act of imagination (through e.g., feelings of regret or nostalgia) and is not the essence of this act. The essence of imagination is rather a derealizing of the imaginary *subject:* "To imagine Pierre after he has been absent for a year is not a matter of my introducing him in the mode of unreality . . . it is first a matter of my derealizing myself, absenting myself from this world in which it is not possible for me to meet Pierre" (RE, 108).

Not only does the imagining subject absent itself from the world that lacks the imagined object; it also enters – Foucault even says it becomes – a world in which the object exists. Imagination is a free projection of myself into a world that I constitute and pervade and that, consequently, expresses my existence. So understood, imagining has precisely the same essential structure as dreaming; both are projections of the self into a world expressing its existence. Indeed, Foucault maintains, contrary to the usual view of dreaming as a special form of imagining, that imagination is just a waking dream.

Nor, according to Foucault, should we think of the world of imagination as something separated off from the real world of perception, an isolated and insulated domain of existential solitude. On the contrary, imagination is essentially involved in even our perceptual experiences. Even when Pierre is present, "I am required to imagine him" (RE, 114) – that is, I experience him not as merely present here and now but as moving along a trajectory through which I am projecting my existence into its future. Accordingly, for Foucault, "the imaginary is not a mode of unreality but a mode of actuality, a manner of taking presence 'on the diagonal' in order to call primitive dimensions [of existence] forth from it" (RE, 116).

We see, then, how Foucault develops his account of dreaming – and of imagining as a form of dreaming – into a general existential account of human reality. He goes on to maintain that a proper understanding of imagination leads to an existential grasp of the significance of mental illness. Here his key move is the displacement of the image from the central role it is usually given. Bachelard, for example, whom Foucault has followed in emphasizing the dynamic, vectorial role of imagination in perception, regards the movement of the imagination as culminating in the image. Foucault, however, says that the image is the death of imagination and that imagining requires the destruction of images:

> The image constitutes a ruse on the part of consciousness whereby it tries to avoid further imagining. . . .. And, if it is true that [imagination] moves through a universe of images, [this is only] to the extent that it breaks them, destroys them, consumes them: it is by essence iconoclastic. (RE, 119, 120)

What Foucault has in mind here is this: Imagining is a dynamic and creative process whereby I freely project a world of my own beyond what is present to me. An image, however, is a static representation that destroys the movement of the imagination, disrupts the dream world I have created, and returns me to the merely present world. (True, the object of which I form an image may not be part of the present world, but, as Sartre's analysis has shown, what I experience through the image is precisely the present world as lacking this object.) Accordingly, "to have an image is to give up imagining" (RE, 117).

Foucault uses this opposition of the image to imagining to characterize the essential nature of mental illness. The world of the mentally ill is a morbid one that paralyzes and stifles those who inhabit it precisely because it is a world of dominating images that allow no space for the free flight of imagination. The goal of psychotherapy is to break through the patient's images in order to liberate his imagination.

Foucault also sees this opposition as relevant to the (Heideggerian) distinction of anthropological from ontological reflection. The former treats human reality solely in terms of images, whereas the latter operates on the level of free imagination. In this connection, Foucault speaks of the move from images to imagination as a "transcendental reduction of the imagination" and claims that such a reduction is concretely carried out in Binswanger's *Traum und Existenz* (RE, 124).

Finally, Foucault notes that there is yet another aspect of the life of the imagination, beyond its liberating move from the world of images to the world of dreams. For, although imagination as dream constitutes the world of my personal existence, it does not bring me into the real, objective world of human history. For this to happen, he says, imagination must go beyond dreaming to *expression* – that is, a realization of itself in the objective world via, for example, artistic creation or ethical action. On the level of expression, there is a return to the image. But it is an image transformed, one that is no longer an "image of something" but an "image addressed to someone" (RE, 125–26). Here the image functions not as a replacement of an absent object but as the means of expression for the imagination, the vehicle of its creative "style." For example, in the realm of literary creation, which seems to be both the model and the primary example of Foucault's existential account, metaphor (the primary vehicle of imagination) is first of all a way of destroying images. It breaks away from language that merely represents (mirrors) reality. But once language is freed from the image in this sense, it goes on to create new images that are not tied to a representative function but have their own intrinsic fullness and weight as the author's free expression. Foucault concludes that even more fundamental than the anthropology of imagination he has outlined in this essay is an anthropology of expression, which remains to be developed.

The importance of the phenomenological/existential level of analysis for Foucault is obvious from the complexity and detail in which he develops it. There is no doubt that the young Foucault was strongly influenced by Husserl, Sartre, Merleau-Ponty, and especially Heidegger.[3] (And, as we shall see, this influence is still a significant presence in FD.) However, from the first, Foucault's interest was mixed with caution. Even in the highly existential introduction to Binswanger, Foucault is careful at the outset to qualify his allegiance to Heidegger and Binswanger. He merely

3. For a good discussion of Heidegger's influence on Foucault's early writings, cf. H. Dreyfus's Foreword to the University of California Press edition of *Mental illness and psychology.*

says that "it seems to us worth the trouble to follow, *for the moment*, the path of this reflection" (RE, 12, my emphasis). Similarly, he explicitly warns that the "concrete encounter with existence . . . [and] the status that must in the end be accorded the ontological condition of existence pose problems, [which] we postpone approaching until another occasion" (RE, 13–14). The reservations about the existential approach suggested by these passages are made explicit in the last part of MMP. Here Foucault notes that though mental illness manifests itself on the three, successively deeper, levels of "organic evolution, psychological history, [and] the situation of man in the world," none of these levels of analysis reveals the conditions that explain the occurrence of mental illness: "the roots of the pathological deviation, as such, are to be found elsewhere" (MMP, 60). Specifically, "it is not possible to account for pathological experiences without referring to social structures; nor to explain the psychological dimensions of mental illness . . . without seeing the human environment of the mentally ill as their real condition" (MMP, 83). Here Foucault's analysis takes a distinctly Marxist direction. The conflicts psychiatrists discover in individuals' life histories derive, he says, from "contradictions" in existing social relations that are themselves determined by "present economic conditions in the form of conflict, exploitation, imperialist wars, and class struggles" (MMP, 86). Foucault rejects the three levels of analysis that he has discussed, including "existential anthropology," as "mythical explanations" of mental illness and concludes that "in reality, it is only in history that one is able to discover the conditions for the possibility of psychological structures" (MMP, 90).

Given this view, Foucault next asks what account we can give of the mechanisms whereby "real" social contradictions are transformed into the psychological conflicts at the root of mental illness. He suggests that the key is Pavlov's physiology of the reflexes, which tells us how stimuli from the external environment trigger various responses in the nervous system. In particular, he argues that mental illness derives from a "generalized defense reaction" of a nervous system overwhelmed by its environment. Normally, individuals are able to react to conflicts in their social environment (e.g., between family and work obligations) by *differentiated* reactions – that is, "individualized reaction[s] to each term or to each phase of a conflictual situation." However, "when . . . the conflict presents itself with a contradictory character that is so absolute, or when the individual's possibilities are so restricted that differentiation cannot occur, then the individual can defend himself only by putting himself out of play, only by responding with a generalized inhibition" (MMP, 101–102). Such generalized inhibition gives rise – in accord with Pavlov's principles – to all the phenomena of mental illness.

Foucault insists that this appeal to Pavlovian reflex theory is not a materialist reduction of psychology to physiology. Even though mental illness is triggered by disorders in physiological functions, nonphysiological social conflicts remain as necessary conditions. Mental illness is still a disturbance of the personality that derives from conflicts in the social world. But social and psychological conflicts do not of themselves produce mental illness. This occurs only when social and psychological conflicts become physiological conflicts. Thus, Foucault sees his account of the etiology of mental illness as not reducing the psychological to the organic but unifying the two in the account of mental illness: "It is necessary to abandon the antithesis between psychogenesis and organogenesis"; as a result, "mental pathology finds itself united with organic pathology" (MMP, 106).

The irreducibly social nature of Foucault's account of mental illness is apparent in his insistence that the reality of mental illness is proof of the inadequacy of bourgeois society.

> The mentally ill demonstrate that bourgeois society, because of the very conflicts that make their illness possible, is not the measure of the real man, . . . that it constantly puts into conflict the unitary idea that it has created of man and the contradictory status that it gives to him. The mentally ill are the apotheosis of this conflict. And if, by the myth of mental alienation, they are pushed back to the outer limits of the city, this is so as not to see in them the scandalous expression of the contradictions that have made their illness possible. . . . (MMP, 104)

The last point in the above quotation is one that Foucault makes earlier in a passage that strikingly anticipates FD: "Our society does not wish to recognize itself in the ill individual whom it rejects or locks up: as it diagnoses the illness, it excludes the patient" (75, 63).

Finally, Foucault draws from his analysis some conclusions about psychotherapy. One key point concerns the inadequacy of psychoanalysis, which regards the patient's conflicts as entirely due to events in his personal psychological history and ignores their roots in the objective contradictions of his social world. "Psychoanalysis psychologizes the real in order to derealize it: it forces the subject to regard his conflict as the disordered law of his own heart, in order to avoid seeing there the contradictions of the order of the world" (MMP, 109). In contrast, Foucault proposes the use of therapies "that offer the patient concrete means of going beyond the conflict-situation, of modifying his environment or of responding in a differentiated (i.e., adapted) way to the contradictions of his conditions of existence" (MMP, 109).

The second edition of *Maladie mentale et personnalité*, retitled *Maladie mentale et psychologie*, appeared just after the publication of *Folie et déraison*. This edition is significantly different from the first in three ways, each representing a distinctive new feature of the approach to the historical understanding of mental disorders that Foucault develops in FD.[4] The most obvious difference is a shift away from Marxist principles and categories. Thus, Foucault simply omits the entire attempt (Chapter VI of the first edition) to employ Pavlov's physiology of the reflex as a materialist vehicle for transforming social contradictions into psychological conflicts. Further, in his description of the social conditions of mental illness, he often backs away from Marxist terminology. For example, where he had previously referred (MMP, 87), in a comment on Freud's view on the origin of war, to "capitalism" as having an experience that derives from "contradictions in social relations," he now (MMPsy, 83) speaks merely of the experience of "our culture" and omits any mention of contradictions in social relations. Similarly a mention of "imperialist wars" (MMP, 86) is omitted in a list of causes of social relations that determine a "culture" (replacing the first edition's "economy") (MMPsy, 82). This is not to say that Foucault abandons all Marxist concepts and terminology (even in the passage last cited he continues to speak of exploitation and class struggle). But there is a definite move away from the routine employment of Marxist categories that suggests an increasingly critical attitude on Foucault's part. Overall – and this is borne out by FD – Foucault seems to retain much of the Marxist dissatisfaction with bour-

4. For a detailed catalogue and analysis of the differences between the two editions, see Pierre Macherey, "Aux sources de 'L'histoire de la folie': une rectification et ses limites," *Critique*, 43 (1986), 752–74.

geois society but has become much less confident of orthodox Marxist analyses of and remedies for its defects.

Another major way in which the second edition differs from the first is in its switch from a focus on mental illness, an object of psychology, to psychology itself. This switch is reflected first of all in the new title but even more importantly in the new account of how mental illness develops from a social milieu. In the first edition, Foucault is content to accept from psychology the basic category of mental illness. He wants to understand the meaning of this category and is convinced that the nature and origins of mental illness in a given society will be a function of the character of that society. But he does not question modern psychology's fundamental claim that mental illness represents an intrinsic defect in those who suffer from it. His approach is similar to Canguilhem's toward organic pathology: Just as the nature of an organism defines norms in terms of which certain physical conditions are pathological, so does the nature of a given society define norms in terms of which certain personality traits are pathological. But in the radically rewritten Part II of the second edition, Foucault moves to the idea that the category of mental illness is a construction of a psychology and psychiatry in the service of our society's attempt to control (by excluding and silencing) those who do not conform to its basic values. On this new view, mental illness is not, as Foucault assumes in the first edition, something that will be found, in different forms, in any society. There are, no doubt, in all societies, individuals whose deviant behavior warrants the appellation "mad." But the characterization of such people as "mentally ill" – that is, suffering from some psychic analogue of disease – is the peculiar invention of a period of Western culture beginning at the end of the eighteenth century and continuing to the present. Admittedly, madness will always involve serious deviations from the ruling norms of society. But other societies – for example, those of medieval and Renaissance Europe – tolerated and even accepted the importance of the mad's deviations. Our society, however, refuses the mad even a marginal place and instead claims – on the allegedly scientific authority of psychology and psychiatry – that madness has no status beyond that of an objective mental deficiency. In his second edition, Foucault questions this claim as well as the authority in whose name it is made. What is present in the development of our psychology and psychiatry "is not the gradual discovery of the true nature of madness, but simply the sedimentation of what the history of the West has made of it for the last three hundred years" (MMPsy, 69).

This shift leads to an important change in the nature of the social criticism involved in Foucault's discussion of mental illness. In the first edition, the criticism is aimed at certain essential defects in the structure of a given society – "social contradictions," as he is apt to call them. On this view, the presence of mental illness is the result of a historical necessity rooted in the evolution of social institutions. In the second edition, as in FD, Foucault is critical of contingent historical developments – for example, that of "scientific" psychology – within our society that are not inevitable consequences of the social infrastructure. Consequently, his criticism suggests the possibility of reform in treatment of the mad within the existing structures of society. By contrast, the first edition seems to see no possibilities except revolutionary transformation of society or else the madman's acceptance of (adaption to) the norms of his society.

The third major difference between the first and the second editions is less obvious but more surprising. It is implicit in an extremely interesting modification Foucault introduces in a text, cited above, characterizing various levels of understanding mental illness as "mythical explanations." In the first edition, Foucault includes, as we noted, the levels of evolutionary development, individual history, and existential anthropology in this characterization (MMP, 89). But in the second edition (MMPsy, 84), he pointedly omits existential anthropology from the list of "mythical explanations." Further, whereas the first edition goes on to say merely that the real explanation of mental illness is to be found in history, the second edition says that the key to avoiding the mythical explanations is to treat "these various aspects of mental illness as ontological forms" (MMPsy, 84). Since the second edition retains the idea that the real explanation of mental illness must be historical, the implication seems to be that Foucault is envisaging some sort of historical application of existential analysis. This idea is further supported by Foucault's subsequent talk (in the title of the second edition's Chapter V) of "the historical constitution of mental illness." And, in fact, FD places great emphasis on the effort to understand the "experience" of madness during various historical periods. So it seems that in moving away from Marxist historical analysis, Foucault was also trying to develop a way of extending the techniques of existential analysis to understand how people of past historical periods constituted the world of their experience. This impression is confirmed by Foucault's comment in a 1983 interview: "At the time I was working on my book about the history of madness. . . . I was divided between existential psychology and phenomenology, and my research was an attempt to discover the extent these could be defined in historical terms."[5]

We see, then, that in writing FD Foucault abandoned the project of providing a Marxist explanation of mental illness for a much more ambitious and original project: that of explaining the contingent historical origin of modern psychology and psychiatry (along with their concept of mental illness) through a historical understanding of past ages' experiences of madness. We now turn to Foucault's carrying out of this project, his history of madness.

Madness in the Classical Age

Foucault's view of the history of madness is in one key respect similar to Bachelard's view of the history of science. He sees it as split at different points by sharp changes or breaks in the way people experienced and treated the mad. One such break occurred in the middle of the seventeenth century when large numbers of citizens (madmen and others) were confined in detention centers such as the Hôpital Général in Paris. This break begins what Foucault calls the "Classical experience" of madness, an experience that defines the European attitude toward madness until the end of the eighteenth century. (The term *Classical* derives from the fact that in France this period is generally called "*l'Age Classique.*") He locates another break in the history of madness at the end of the eighteenth century, right around the time of the French Revolution; this break initiates a new way of experiencing madness that corresponds to our modern psychological view of madness as "mental illness." Foucault's overall strategy in FD is to present the Classical experience of madness in some detail as a basis for understanding the new, modern experience of madness that dominates the nineteenth and twentieth centuries.

5. "An Interview with Michel Foucault" (by Charles Ruas), printed as a "Postscript" to Ruas's translation of Foucault's *Raymond Roussel: death and the labyrinth: the world of Raymond Roussel* (Garden City, N.Y.: Doubleday and Company, 1986), 174.

It is important to understand what Foucault means in speaking of an age's "experience" of madness. For one thing, he does not mean that people of the age were aware of certain intrinsic characteristics of the mad that other ages did not notice. Rather, an age's experience of madness is its distinctive way of viewing madness, its manner of "constituting" madness as an object. Moreover, this constitution is not merely a mental interpretation. It is essentially connected to the institutions and practices an age uses to deal with the mad. For example, Foucault maintains, as we shall see, that the Classical practice of confining the mad "did not play merely a negative role of exclusion but also a positive organizational role. Its practices and rules constituted a domain of experience that had its own unity, coherence, and function" (FD, 102). FD's project of an existential analysis of the historical experience of madness thus continues (though in a very different key) Foucault's earlier theme of madness as the product of "real" social factors.

To provide some background for his treatment of the experience of madness in the Classical Age, Foucault starts with a brief discussion of madness in the Renaissance. Adopting a strikingly existential tone, he says that the Renaissance experience of madness was an "experience of nothingness" (FD, 16).[6] The Middle Ages' experience of nothingness had focused on physical death, especially represented by the leprosy that consumed so many bodies. But for the Renaissance, "death's annihilation is no longer anything because it was already everything, because life itself was only futility, vain words, a squabble of cap and bells. The head that will become a skull is already empty" (FD, 19; MC, 16). This move from death to madness as the quintessence of human loss also meant that the nothingness of existence was "no longer considered an external final term, both threat and conclu-

6. References are to the first edition (1961), *Folie et déraison: l'histoire de la folie à l'âge classique*. The second edition (1972) (with a new preface and two further articles appended) is titled *L'histoire de la folie à l'âge classique*. It was reprinted in 1976 without the appendices. The English translation, titled *Madness and Civilization* (MC), is primarily of Foucault's 1964 abridgment of FD, with some material added (by Foucault) from the complete version. *Madness and civilization* translates less than half of FD. (Translations of passages of FD not available in MC are my own.) Foucault himself offers a lucid summary of the main themes of FD in Chapter 5 of MMPsy. Cf. also the very helpful exposition, from a sociological viewpoint, in Chapter 9 of P. Hirst and P. Woolley, *Social relations and human activities* (London: Tavistock, 1982), and J. Russ's "profile" of FD, *Histoire de la folie: Michel Foucault* (Paris: Hatier, 1979).

sion; it is experienced from within as the continuous and constant form of existence" (FD, 20; MC, 16).

The distinctive Renaissance experience of madness took, on Foucault's account, two importantly different forms. In one (which he finds dominant in Renaissance painters such as Brueghel and Dürer), madness appears as something that "communicated with the great tragic powers of the world." Here madness is man's animality breaking loose from conventional bonds and leading him to a secret knowledge, a hidden wisdom that means his destruction: "The animal that haunts his nightmares . . . is his own nature, which will lay bare hell's pitiless truths" (FD, 27; MC, 23). By contrast, the second Renaissance form of madness (which Foucault finds particularly in humanist writers, such as Erasmus and Brant) "is not linked to the world and its subterranean forms, but rather to man, to his weakness, dreams, and illusions" (FD, 29; MC, 26). Madness in this sense is expressed not in dramatic images of power and horror but in the ironic thrusts of moral satire. In sum, Foucault sees in the Renaissance "an opposition between a cosmic experience of madness in the nearness of [its] fascinating forms and a critical experience of this same madness in the impassable distance of irony" (FD, 32).

Although this twofold experience of madness is clearly present at the beginning of the sixteenth century, within a hundred years the cosmic experience almost entirely disappears and only the critical experience remains. Foucault sees this as a particularly important development since it represents a suppression of madness as an autonomous and positive form of human experience. This suppression has persisted, he says, with a few striking exceptions, from the later Renaissance through the Classical Age down to the present. The result has been that, apart from such isolated "lightning flashes" such as Nietzsche's last messages and Van Gogh's final paintings, madness has been encountered only as one or another sort of negation of reason. It is no longer a tragic confrontation with a preternatural world but only a deviation from the life of reason.

However, this tamed madness has, according to Foucault, been itself regarded in very different ways. During the later Renaissance, it is domesticated and takes its place as an integral if clearly subordinated part of the human world, like the jester at a royal court. Here reason and madness speak to one another, like Lear and his fool. They are in "a perpetually reversible relation in virtue of which every folly [*folie*] has its reason that judges and masters it, and every reason has its folly in which it finds its derisory truth" (FD, 36).[7] Foucault sees this relation expressed, for example, in the ironic literary themes (influenced by Christianity) of the folly of wisdom and the wisdom of folly. Later Renaissance madness is part of one world with reason, in dialogue with it; it is reason's essential mocking counterpart, with a place and perspective of its own that is acknowledged by reason itself.

Foucault finds particular evidence of this special relationship of madness and reason in the Renaissance phenomenon of the "ship of fools," which sent the mad traveling from city to city on the canals and rivers of Northern Europe. Their voyages separated them from the "normal" life of reasonable men (and consignment to the waters was a symbolic gesture of purification). But the fact that the mad were periodically dropped off at new towns showed that, though at the margins of Renaissance life, they were not sharply excluded from it.

With the advent of the Classical Age, the relationship of reason and madness is, according to Foucault, fundamentally transformed. The focal point of this transformation is the "Great Confinement," whereby, for example, within the space of just a few months during 1656, over 1 percent of the population of Paris was compelled to live under state supervision in one or another division of the Hôpital Général. Foucault maintains that, in the middle of the seventeenth century, similar developments occurred all over Europe. Everywhere significant parts of the population were isolated in state-controlled houses of confinement.

Those confined were, to our eyes, a heterogeneous group, including not only the mad but also the sick, the poor, the promiscuous, blasphemers, rebellious children, irresponsible parents, etc. Their most obvious common characteristic, Foucault notes, was merely that they were idle; through unwillingness or through lack of ability or opportunity, they did no work in society. Corresponding to this, the immediate and explicit motive for their confinement was economic and political. In the mid-seventeenth century, a crisis in the Spanish economy had pro-

7. On the ambiguity in French between *folie* meaning "madness" and *folie* meaning "folly," see Alan Sheridan, *Michel Foucault: The will to truth* (London: Tavistock, 1980), 16–17.

duced, throughout Western Europe, "reduction of wages, unemployment, scarcity of coin" (FD, 80; MC, 49). Confinement was, according to Foucault, first of all, a way, in difficult economic times, of controlling the threat of violence from the unemployed. Further, even when prosperity returned, confinement seemed to promise the economic benefit of providing an inexpensive, closely controlled source of labor. Thus, confinement provided "cheap manpower in periods of full employment and high salaries; and, in periods of unemployment, reabsorption of the idle and social protection against agitation and uprisings" (FD, 82; MC, 51).

But Foucault maintains that confinement was much more than just an (ultimately unsuccessful) economic and political expedient. Besides being an act of physical exclusion carried out for the sake of specific goals of public policy, it also produced (and expressed) a radically new experience of those who were confined and, in particular, a new experience of madness.

He says that a first key feature of this new experience of madness lies precisely in the fact that the mad are included as one particular group in the more general category of those confined. We have already noted that all those confined shared the economic failing of idleness. But there is another general categorization of those confined that is, in Foucault's view, much more important for an understanding of the Classical Age's experience of madness. This is the category of *unreason* (*déraison*). Every group confined deviated in some way from the Classical Age's norms of rational behavior. Each corresponded to a mode of existence that rejected the defining standards of "the age of reason." Thus, madness was regarded as one variety of unreason.

In this respect, the Classical experience of madness is not deeply different from that of the later Renaissance (except that madness is no longer the only inverse of reason). But Foucault cites a second key feature of the Classical experience of madness that sharply distinguishes it from that of the Renaissance. Just as the Great Confinement physically excluded the mad from the shared life of the community, so did the Classical experience of madness regard it as conceptually excluded from the life of reason. Foucault sees this strikingly illustrated in Descartes's attitude toward madness in the First Meditation, when he is considering various possible grounds for doubting his beliefs. The possibilities that his senses deceive him and that he is dreaming both allow, in

Descartes's view, for some residual truths. The former possibility does not call into question overwhelmingly obvious sense perceptions (that he is now in front of a fire, holding a piece of paper, etc.); the latter depends on "simple natures" from which images are formed and which, even in a dream, may be objects of mathematical knowledge. So in both cases, Descartes argues that, even if his senses are in some respects unreliable or if he is dreaming, some truths remain certain. But, in the case of madness, he does not similarly argue that, even if he is mad, some truths remain. Rather, he says, in effect, that "I who am thinking am not able to be mad" (FD, 55). By this Descartes means, according to Foucault, that his very project of pursuing the rational path of methodic doubt excludes the possibility that he is mad. The fact that he is engaged in attentive, reflective thought shows that he has chosen reason over unreason. "Dreams or illusions are overcome in the very structure of truth; but madness is excluded by the doubting subject [itself]" (FD, 55).[8]

According to Foucault, Descartes's attitude here is typical of the Classical Age. Madness is no longer, as in the Renaissance, the ever-present foil of reason, continually engaging it in challenging dialogue. Rather, it has been excluded ab initio from the life of reason. Physical confinement mirrors conceptual exclusion.

Foucault identifies a third key aspect of the Classical experience of madness as that of moral condemnation. As a species of idleness – like all forms of unreason – madness is a violation of the fundamental ethical consciousness of bourgeois society. For this society, work is the instrument of redemption and hence "idleness is the fault *par excellence*" (FD, 88; MC, 56). The madman is not an outsider because he "comes from the world of the irrational and bears its stigmata; rather, he is an outsider because he crosses the frontiers of bourgeois order of his own accord and alienates himself outside the sacred limits of its ethics" (FD, 90; MC, 58). As an object of moral censure, madness is no longer regarded as a tragic fate (as in the early Renaissance) nor as a

8. For a criticism of Foucault's interpretation of Descartes, see Jacques Derrida, "Cogito et l'histoire de la folie," *Revue de métaphysique et de morale* 3–4 (1964), 460–94. This is reprinted in Derrida's *Ecriture et la différence* (Editions du Seuil, 1967), which has been translated by Alan Bass as *Writing and difference* (University of Chicago Press, 1978). Foucault responds to Derrida in "Mon corps, ce papier, ce feu," *Paideia*, September, 1971. The essay is also included in the 1972 edition of FD and is translated by G. P. Bennington in *Oxford Literary Review* 4 (1979), 5–28.

psychological infirmity requiring medical treatment (as in modern psychiatry). It is, rather, an originary choice of unreason over reason.

Closely tied to the moral condemnation of madness is Foucault's fourth key feature of the Classical experience: a perception of madness as an object requiring administrative control. Earlier societies had, of course, punished moral faults under the civil law. But, according to Foucault, it was only with the Classical Age that a system for total public control of "the disorders of hearts" was developed. For the first time, "men were confined in cities of pure morality, where the law that should reign in all hearts was to be applied without compromise, without concession, in the rigorous form of physical constraint." In this bourgeois society, "morality presented itself to be administered like trade or economy" (FD, 92; MC, 60–61).

The features of the Classical experience of madness discussed so far are also features of the Classical experience of unreason in general. Everything we have said about the physical confinement, conceptual exclusion, moral condemnation, and administrative control of the mad could also be said about the poor, the promiscuous, and other confined groups. The next step is to locate the specific difference that sets madness off from the other varieties of unreason. According to Foucault, this difference resides in the animality that was attributed to the mad. Put simply, the Classical Age regarded the mad as people in whom the animal aspect of human nature was dominant. But we must be careful to understand the precise conception of animality that is involved here. It is not, Foucault says, animality as a dark inverse of reason but rather as something wholly outside the rational order. At the same time, however, he notes that it is not an animality that expresses some power beyond man (like the cosmic force of the early Renaissance view). Rather, the animality of madness is simply the human being at his zero degree, bereft of reason. As such it represents humanity in its most impoverished, most abject state.

Foucault points out that, in contrast to later views, the animality ascribed to the mad by the Classical Age is not regarded as a sign that they are sick. On the contrary, it was "common knowledge" that the animality of the mad made them healthier than others, impervious, for example, to the rigors of heat and cold. Again in contrast to later views, this animality is not associated with a mechanistic determinism that destroys freedom. It is regarded not only as the result of a free choice but as itself "an area of unforseeable freedom where frenzy is unchained" (FD, 187; MC, 76, emphasis omitted). In this connection, Foucault also points out that the animality of the mad is not regarded as part of the plentitude of nature but as an antinature, the locus of a frenzy that threatens to undermine the natural order. This attitude, he says, led to a lack of emphasis on medical treatment of madness, since such treatment was a matter of operating on its object through natural causal mechanisms. He agrees that there was some medical attention given the mad during the Classical Age but holds that it was mostly a matter of residual medieval practices. Similarly, he says that, although madness was regarded as a moral defect, the ordinary techniques of moral correction (exhortation, confession and repentence) were not applied to it. This was because the mad were thought to be so immersed in their animality that there was no question of their responding to such techniques. They could only be disciplined – that is, brutally coerced to obey.

The essential animality of the madman explains, according to Foucault, a striking difference in the treatment of madness in contrast to other forms of unreason. Ordinarily, unreason was treated as a scandal to be hidden from public awareness in houses of confinement. There were, however, regular public exhibitions of the mad, fixed times when the general population was allowed and encouraged to visit the houses of confinement and observe the bizarre antics of madmen. Foucault explains this in terms of the religious significance that the Classical Age saw in the animality of the mad. This animality represented the lowest depths to which man's sinful nature could bring him. The exhibition of the mad showed men "how close to animality their Fall could bring them; and at the same time how far divine mercy could extend when it consented to save men" (FD, 193; MC, 81).

The above description of the Classical experience of madness is not complete. It covers only what Foucault calls the "critical" and the "practical" consciousness of madness (FD, 201–204). The former is reason's reflective and morally disapproving awareness of madness as its opposite, the latter reason's choice, in the light of group norms, to exclude madness. Together these two comprise what we might call (though Foucault does not use the term) an *evaluative* awareness of madness, an awareness that embodies reason's concrete rejection of madness as a form of unreason. We have not yet discussed what we might call the Classical Age's *cognitive* awareness of madness, its awareness of madness as an object of knowledge rather than as an object of rejection. Here Foucault also distinguishes two forms of awareness: an immediate recognition (*reconnaissance*) and a body of objective knowledge (*connaissance*). He calls the former an "enunciative" consciousness and the latter an "analytic" consciousness (FD, 205–206). He emphasizes, anticipating his later insistence on the intimate ties between knowledge and power, that the distinction between (what I am calling) the evaluative and the cognitive awareness of madness is not a distinction between the practical and the theoretical. The two forms of evaluative consciousness are grounded in theoretical conceptions of madness and the two forms of cognitive consciousness are informed by society's practices for dealing with the mad. But the theory that is inchoately present in evaluative consciousness is explicitly formulated and developed as a body of positive knowledge in cognitive consciousness.

According to Foucault, the Classical Age recognizes (*reconnait*) madness through its twofold relation to reason – that is, first, as a deviation from the norms of reason and, second, as an object available for reason's scientific knowledge (in, e.g., medicine). Such a dual apprehension of madness is found in previous epochs, but Foucault thinks the Classical Age is distinctive in weaving the two modes of recognition together so closely that they cannot be distinguished. There is no effective distinction between "the moral negativity of the madman" and "the positivity of what can be known about him" (FD, 225). The result is that there is no longer (as there clearly was in the early Renaissance) a distinction between the "powers of reason" and the "powers of the insane." The reason for this seems to be that the moral judgment that madness is an unacceptable deviation from reason provides all the objective content of any scientific knowledge of madness. Consequently, Classical madness is, in Foucault's view, *simply* unreason. More fully, reason provides the only positive element in the recognition of madness; what distinguishes madness as such is simply the fact that it misuses (and in that sense negates) reason. Thus the structure of the Classical recognition of madness reflects the purely negative view that we saw in the Classical evaluative consciousness of it.

With regard to Classical knowledge ("analytic consciousness") of madness, Foucault finds the situation more complex. He notes that accounts of madness were developed as part of the theory of illness in general. The typical approach (characteristic of Classical thought) was to offer complex classifications of the varieties of madness. (Chapter 3 discusses in some detail the application of this approach to bodily illness.) Since Classical thinkers viewed illness as an essentially positive phenomenon (here Foucault cites the view of Boissier de Sauvages as typical), there was a tension between the Classical Age's efforts to develop a body of knowledge about madness and the criteria whereby it recognized it. However, he maintains that this tension never became critical, primarily because none of the numerous efforts to provide classificatory schemes for madness had any lasting effect on Classical thought. Each scheme (from Plater's in 1609 through Weickhard's in 1790, including that of Linnaeus, the greatest classifier of all) disappeared almost as soon as it was put forward and had no lasting effect.

Foucault cites a number of reasons for this failure: the conceptual inadequacy of all the schemes offered, the persistence of a pre-Classical classification (based more on experience than on conceptual analysis), and the development of the medicine of vapors, which classified diseases on the basis of medical therapy rather than nosological theory. But he thinks the deepest reason for the failure was simply the fact that the treatment of madness as a positive phenomenon was inconsistent with the Classical Age's fundamental view of it as negative. The classification schemes failed because they conflicted with the basic structures defining the possibility of the Classical experience of madness.

In turning to the Classical Age's cognitive consciousness of madness, Foucault has moved from reading its experience of madness in practices and institutions for controlling the mad to reading this experience in the writings of "sages and philosophers" and of "physicians and scientists." He notes that the Classical Age was remarkable (in contrast, for example, with our own) in the extent to which it accepted a wide gap between its evaluative and its cognitive consciousness of madness. In particular, the economic, social, and political policies that centered on confinement made no appeal to medical or other "scientific" accounts of madness. Nonetheless, Foucault maintains that the Classical Age's evaluative and cognitive consciousness of madness share a fundamental structure. "These two do-mains, so rigorously separated, do not fail to exhibit, on close examination, the most precise structural analogies. . . . As sepa-rated as they are, there is nothing of importance in the first that is not matched [*équilibré*] in the second" (FD, 211–12).

However, Foucault thinks that this common structure is more readily discernible through analysis of the cognitive conscious-ness. What is seen only in partial glimpses in a study of the evaluative domain appears full blown in a study of the cognitive. Accordingly, Foucault expects that in disengaging the Classical Age's positive knowledge of madness he will also reveal explicitly the "common experience" of madness that underlies both do-mains. "This unique experience, which resides both here and there, which supports and justifies the practice of confinement and the cycle of knowledge – it is this that constitutes the classical experience of madness" (FD, 212).

This effort to find a common structure that underlies both the scientific knowledge and the institutional practices of an age is in effect Foucault's first use of his archaeological method. (How-ever, except for one sentence in the Preface (FD, ii) he does not use the term *archaeology*.) Later works, culminating in the explic-itly methodological reflections of *The archaeology of knowledge*, will modify and refine the method. Eventually, for example, Fou-cault will abandon the idea that archaeology illuminates some sort of fundamental experience and will instead construe it as dealing with objective conditions for the possibility of linguistic acts. Also, he will think much more carefully about the relation of archaeological structures to institutions and practices. But the fact remains that his study, in Part II of FD, of the structure of the Classical experience of madness represents Foucault's first development of what he later calls the archaeological approach to the history of thought.

In taking this archaeological approach, Foucault abandons the effort, pursued so far in his treatment of the Classical knowledge of madness, to describe "the evolution of theoretical concepts on the surface of a [body of] knowledge." Now, rather, "by cutting into the historical thickness of an experience, we will try to recap-ture the movement by which a knowledge of madness finally became possible" (FD, 252). As our discussion so far has sug-gested and as we shall see more fully, this possibility could not be fully realized within the context of the Classical experience of

madness. Its realization required, first, a break with the Classical
view of madness as essentially negative and, second, the development of the modern conception of madness as mental illness.
Foucault's archaeology of Classical madness provides the basis
for his development of these ideas.

Foucault presents this new level of his inquiry as one that requires close attention to detail. "We must now proceed slowly and
detail by detail. . . , with the respect of a historian" (FD, 252). His
goal, he says, is to discover in this detail the "constituting forms of
madness," an expression that shows that, even in embarking on
this new archaeological path, he still has in mind his project of
developing a historical version of existential analysis.

Foucault's archaeology of Classical madness begins by noting
that the Classical Age regarded madness as an affliction not of
the mind or soul alone but of the whole person: "When someone
in the 17th or 18th century speaks of madness, he is not, strictly,
speaking of 'illness of the mind' but rather of something where
the body and the soul are *together* in question" (FD, 259–60). It is,
he says, only in the nineteenth century that medicine takes up a
dualistic view of mind and body and begins to raise questions
about the relation of matter and the immaterial, the nature of
the soul, and so on. Even though Descartes's two-substances view
of man was put forward at the beginning of the Classical Age, it
did not become a major influence on medical thought and practice until much later.

Foucault maintains that, in the context of this holistic view of
madness, Classical medicine gave a central role to *passion* (here
following Descartes's opinion that passion is the point of union
of mind and body). He notes that passion and madness had been
closely associated long before the Classical Age. Thus, the Greek
and Latin moralists saw passions as temporary and attenuated
forms of madness. But, for the Classical Age, Foucault maintains
that the relation was reversed; instead of understanding passion
in terms of madness, it saw passion as the root cause of madness.
Moreover, the passion behind madness is self-destructive in a
fundamental sense. For the madness to which it gives rise threatens the mind-body unity in which passion itself is grounded.

Here Foucault finds two main lines of development. On the
one hand, madness may lead to "a movement of the nerves and
muscles so violent that nothing in the sequence of images, ideas,
or volitions seems to correspond to it" (FD, 280; MC, 91, transla-

tion modified). On the other hand, "madness can, in the body's repose or inertia, generate and then maintain an agitation of the soul . . ., as is the case in melancholia, where external objects do not produce the same impression on the sufferer's mind as on that of a healthy man" (FD, 280; MC, 92). In either case, there is a dissociation between mental activity and bodily movements that threatens even though it does not abolish the unity of soul and body. Most importantly, there is a dissociation between the madman's experiences and the bodily organs that put him into contact with the external world. This gives rise to delusions and hallucinations.

Thus at the core of classical madness is the experience of the unreal, of "chimeras, of hallucinations, and of error – the cycle of nonbeing" (FD, 282; MC, 93). The next step in Foucault's archaeology is an examination of this experience.

An initial important point is that the unreality of madness is not that of mere imagination, even the most fantastic. Rather, "madness will begin only in the act which gives the value of truth to the image" (MC, 94; FD, 282) – that is, with the acceptance of what is imagined as real. On the basis of such an acceptance, the mad construct entire systems of reasoning. This clarifies Foucault's point, encountered earlier, that Classical madness is essentially unreason. It is the employment of reason to derive (what may well be rigorously valid) conclusions from delusory premises. (Here we might recall G. K. Chesterton's characterization of the madman as one who has lost everything *except* his reason.) This is the precise sense in which Foucault maintains that madness is nothing more than a negation of reason. Its positive content is entirely that of the methods of reason, but its employment of these methods is an essential misuse of them in the service of a delusion. "The ultimate language of madness is that of reason, but the language of reason enveloped in the prestige of the image" (FD, 284; MC, 95). The language of reason so misused is what Foucault calls the "language of delirium."

The above analysis not only confirms and further explicates the idea that Classical madness is unreason. It also leads Foucault to the crucial point that Classical madness is essentially linguistic. "Madness, in the classical sense, does not designate so much a specific change in the mind or in the body, as the existence, under the body's alteration, under the oddity of conduct and conversation, of *a delirious discourse*" (FD, 287–88; MC, 99). Foucault finds this point strikingly illustrated by the fact that Classical authors frequently classify vertigo as a type of madness but seldom so classify hysterical convulsions. The reason, he maintains, is that vertigo "involves the delirious affirmation that the world is really 'turning around'," whereas "it is often impossible to find in hysterical convulsions the unity of a language" (FD, 288; MC, 100). Thus, for the Classical Age, madness is not in its deepest reality the garbled and incoherent experience that its often foolish and frenzied manifestations suggest. It is, on the contrary, a highly structured experience, and "language is [its] first and last structure, its constituted form; on language are based all the cycles in which madness articulates its nature" (FD, 288; MC, 100). Further, the linguistic character of madness fits in well with its association with the union of mind and body, since the delirious discourse of the mad is "both the silent language by which the mind speaks to itself in the truth proper to it, and the visible articulation in the movements of the body" (FD, 288; MC, 100).

But no matter how "rational," in the sense of logically structured, Classical madness may be, Foucault holds that it remains a manifestation of unreason because all its rationality is based on the fundamental error of taking dreams and delusions for realities. Further, as we have seen earlier, the Classical Age does not regard this error as an involuntary mistake but as something *chosen* by the mad. "The madman, in the 17th and 18th centuries, is not so much the victim of an illusion, of a hallucination, of his senses, or of a movement of his mind. He is not *abused,* he *deceives himself*" (FD, 292; MC, 104).

Next Foucault inquires as to the precise nature of the deception the madman has brought on himself. He notes that the characterization (often found in Classical writers) of the mad as blind as particularly apt. This is because blindness is able to express both "that night of quasi-sleep which surrounds the images of madness" and the "ill-founded beliefs, mistaken judgments, . . . that whole background of errors [that is] inseparable from madness" (FD, 294; MC, 106). Saying that the mad are blind catches both the dreamlike obscurity and the falsity of their delirium.

Finally, Foucault points out that for the Classical Age the reason of the mad is blind not because it is cut off from light but because it is dazzled by an excess of light. "The madman sees the daylight, the same daylight as the man of reason . . .; but seeing the same daylight and nothing in it, he sees it as void, as night, as nothing. . . . Which means that he does not see at all. And believing he sees, he admits as realities the hallucinations of his imagination and all the multitudinous population of night" (FD, 296; MC, 108).[9] He points out that this understanding of the blindness of the mad fits in well with the famous Classical conception of reason as a "natural light." In keeping with his fundamental idea that reason is the entire positive content of Classical madness, madness is not a matter of being cut off from the light of reason but of being dazzled by focusing on the light alone and not on the reality it reveals.

Foucault emphasizes that this talk of light and dazzlement is no mere passing metaphor. Rather, it derives from "the great cosmology which animates all classical culture" (FD, 296; MC, 109). The fundamental law of this cosmology is "the circle of night and day" in which there is an alternation of light and darkness that "excludes all dialectic and all reconciliation . . .; everything must be either waking or dream, truth or darkness." This "law prescribes an inevitable order, a serene division which makes truth possible and confines it forever" (FD, 297; MC, 110). Thus, according to Foucault, at the root of all Classical thought lies a sharp division between the lucid order of reason and truth and the dark confusion of unreason and falsity. Madness, however, transgresses this division by creating a rational order of falsehoods. As such, it is an essential negation of Classical reason and a threat to its defining structure. This is why Classical reason can, on Foucault's account, accord madness no rights, can enter no dialogue with it. The only possible relation of Classical reason to madness is one of rigorous exclusion.

Foucault sees the above analysis as deepening our understanding of the starting point in his study of Classical madness, the historical fact of the Great Confinement. Whatever the immediate political and economic motives of this physical exclusion of the mad, he maintains that we must ultimately understand it as an expression of madness's incompatibility with the basic cosmology governing Classical thought. The Great Confinement was

9. Compare Edmund Burke: "Extreme light . . . obliterates all objects, so as in its effects exactly to resemble darkness," *A philosophical enquiry into the origin of our ideas of the sublime and the beautiful*, 1757; cited by Lawrence Alloway, "The American Sublime," *Living Arts*, June, 1963, 18.

not just another event in the flow of history but an expression of the fundamental structures of Classical reason.

We are now in a position to present an overview of Foucault's complex analysis of the Classical Age's experience of madness. He distinguishes four different types of consciousness of madness. Two are evaluative: the critical, involving a moral judgment of madness; and the practical, involving society's choice of how to treat the mad. Two are cognitive: the recognition of madness in terms of criteria expressing its relation to reason and the knowledge of madness through objective, systematic inquiry. The Classical Age's evaluative consciousness of madness was expressed in the physical exclusion of the mad through social and economic policies such as the Great Confinement. Foucault's reflection on this physical exclusion yields four key characteristics of the Classical evaluative consciousness of madness: (1) the placing of madness in the general category of unreason, along with a number of other groups of idle citizens; (2) the conceptual exclusion of madness from the life of reason; (3) the moral condemnation of madness; and (4) the administrative control of the mad. These are also features of the Classical consciousness of unreason in general. For the Classical evaluative consciousness, the distinguishing feature of madness was a specific sort of animality. With regard to the Classical cognitive consciousness of madness, Foucault finds that madness is recognized merely as a deviation from reason and hence has no positive content of its own. This made it strictly impossible for the Classical Age to develop a body of knowledge about madness, although there were numerous attempts to do so.

Foucault maintains that all four of the above forms of the Classical consciousness of madness share a common underlying structure, a structure that he delineates in what we can now recognize as his first attempt at an archaeological analysis of thought. The main stages in this analysis are: (1) a characterization of madness as a phenomenon of *mind–body unity;* (2) a correlative grounding of madness in *passion;* (3) a recognition of madness as *delirium* – that is, the taking of the unreal for the real; (4) an understanding of delirium (and hence madness) as a rationally structured *language;* (5) a consequent realization that madness is a state of reason, but of reason in a condition of blindness; (6) an analysis of this blindness as due not to a lack but an excess of light – that is, *dazzlement;* (7) a relation of this understanding of madness to the *fundamental Classical cosmology* of day and night. On the basis of this archaeological analysis, Foucault concludes that the Classical Age experienced madness as the fundamental negation of the reason that defined its world of truth; because of this, it rigorously excluded madness from every level of its existence.

Given the foregoing understanding of the Classical consciousness of madness, Foucault proceeds to discussions of the particular forms of madness that were generally recognized by Classical medicine and of the major therapeutic practices employed to treat the mad. With regard to the forms of madness, he finds one variety – dementia – that comes close to a pure realization of the general Classical conception of madness as the negation of reason. The other main Classical species of madness – the pairs mania/melancholy and hysteria/hypochondria – have, he notes, much more positive content of their own. Medical accounts of them were, as we saw above, in tension with the Classical Age's fundamental experience of madness and, as a result, never succeeded in taking on a coherent, generally accepted form. This seems to be a primary reason why Foucault thinks he cannot discover the Classical consciousness of madness in the "surface" concepts and theories Classical medicine developed about it but must rather work at the deeper, archaeological level.

Classical therapies for madness were not, according to Foucault, closely tied to Classical medical theory; indeed, they were not for the most part supervised by doctors. But he thinks they too directly reveal little about the Classical experience of madness, since they are almost all holdovers from medieval and Renaissance therapeutic practices. This, of course, is what we would expect, given the Classical Age's exclusion of madness. Medical treatment is a positive interaction inconsistent with the attitude of exclusion.

Although Foucault holds that the history of Classical medical theories and therapeutic practices has little to add to our understanding of the Classical experience of madness, he does think it important for understanding the transition to the new conception of madness as mental illness that arose at the end of the eighteenth century. He regards the development of theories of hysteria and hypochondria as particularly significant in this regard. These – as their names indicate – were long thought to be seated in specific organic locations. Indeed, in the early Classical period, they were, according to Foucault, thought to be entirely physical and not even regarded as varieties of madness. Gradually, however, their purely organic characteristics were reinterpreted in psychological terms. Women, for example, were originally thought to be more susceptible to hysteria because their internal organs were less dense. But eventually this lesser density was reinterpreted as a softness and delicacy that is induced by "soft" (luxurious) living. Foucault thinks that through this and similar reinterpretations (e.g., of the concepts of sympathy and of nerves) the original understanding of hysteria as entirely physical was transformed into an understanding of it as psychological. This, he says, laid the groundwork for the modern construal of hysteria as a "mental illness."

Similarly, Foucault sees Classical therapeutic practices gradually moving in the direction of modern psychiatry. He puts particular emphasis on Classical medicine's development of the concept of a *cure:* a specific remedy for a particular disease, in contrast to the idea, which dominated earlier medicine, of a *panacea* that would be sovereign for all cases. Obtaining a cure required a precise adjustment of the patient's suffering and the doctor's knowledge to one another. (This recalls Canguilhem's insistence of the role of the organism itself in the definition of the pathological.) Such an adjustment required "a common language, a communication – at least imaginary – between doctor and patient" (FD, 371). This notion of a cure, which was especially prominent in the treatment of "nervous diseases," moved away from the Classical attitude of rigorous exclusion and toward modern psychiatric practice.

With regard to specific treatments of madness, Foucault puts special emphasis on the fact that Classical therapies make no distinction between the treatment of madness as a physical disorder and as a mental disorder. In keeping with the fundamental perception of madness, all treatments deal with madness as a phenomenon of mind–body unity. There is a distinction between treatments that focus on the passion at the root of madness and those that focus on the delirium in which it is ultimately expressed; and, to our eyes, the former often seem entirely physical and the latter entirely mental. According to Foucault, however, closer examination always reveals both physical and mental aspects intertwined. Thus, the frequent recourse "to exhortation, to persuasion, to reasoning," which strikes us as entirely psychological, in fact corresponds to the Classical view that "language, the formulations of truths or morality, are in direct contact with the body. . . . The adaptation or rejection of an ethical principle can directly modify the course of organic processes" (FD, 397; MC, 183). However, he maintains that in the course of the eighteenth century, there was a gradual move toward a psychological construal of all therapies. For example, even procedures such as cold showers and "centrifugation" (whirling patients around on seats attached to revolving mechanisms), which produce obvious bodily effects, were applied to the mad merely as punishments designed to alter their mental attitudes.

Mental illness and the asylum

We now turn to Part III of FD, Foucault's analysis of the new, modern view of madness as mental illness. This analysis is different in one crucial respect from his earlier treatment of the Classical experience of madness. The latter was a history of a past that is, for the most part, no longer with us, whereas the former is a study of what has become our own view of madness. This is particularly significant because Foucault believes that our common modern self-understanding of our conception of madness is radically mistaken. According to this self-understanding, the idea that madness is an illness affecting the mind is merely a recognition of the objective reality that it has always had. Earlier ideas that the mad were filled with a god, diabolically possessed, had chosen to embrace unreason, and so forth, were merely mistakes that have been replaced by our scientific discovery that madness is actually mental illness. Further, this objective, scientific understanding of madness provides, for the first time, the tools for effectively alleviating the sufferings of the mad. Previous ages' treatments of madness were often really forms of cruelty, representing either innocent ignorance or deliberate maltreatment. But, on the basis of a correct understanding of the nature of madness, modern psychology and psychiatry offer the mad liberation from the cruelties of the past and the prospect of a scientifically based cure of their illness. Foucault's study of the origins of the modern view of madness aims to undermine this self-understanding. Without denying all objectivity to the modern view, he emphasizes its essential connections to contingent features of modern society. He also claims that the picture of modern psychology and psychiatry as disinterested searches for a truth that frees the mad from abuse and manipulation is a myth. In fact, our modern knowledge and treatment of the mad are devoted to a particularly thorough and insidious manipulation of them.

In the light of this "subversive" intent of Foucault's study of the modern experience of madness, his idea of an archaeological approach becomes particularly important. For, if he is correct about the faulty self-understanding of our psychology and psychiatry, a correct grasp of the significance of these disciplines will not be forthcoming from a straightforward study of the concepts and theories they put forward. Such a study would remain at the surface and fail to uncover an underlying structure that reveals, beneath their scientific pretensions, the true nature of modern psychology and psychiatry. Foucault's project therefore requires an archaeological approach.

He develops this approach to the modern experience of madness in terms of the two general types of consciousness – evaluative and cognitive – he used in treating the Classical experience. According to the modern self-understanding, the cognitive consciousness of madness in modern psychology and psychiatry is value-free, treating madness simply as an object of disinterested scientific inquiry. As for the corresponding evaluative attitude, it is said to be that of a compassionate scientist, eager to use his knowledge to improve the lot of his less fortunate fellows. According to Foucault, however, the modern evaluative consciousness of madness is much less striaghtforward and innocent and, moreover, is inextricably tied to the cognitive methods and content of scientific psychology and psychiatry.

Let us begin with the first dimension of evaluative consciousness, the critical consciousness that expresses a moral judgment of madness. Foucault sees the first major sign of something new here in the "Great Fear" of contagion from the houses of confinement that swept over Europe in the mideighteenth century. "People were in dread of a mysterious disease that spread, it was said, from the houses of confinement and would soon threaten the cities. They spoke of prison fevers; . . . it was said that the air, tainted by disease, would corrupt the residential quarters" (FD, 429; MC, 202). Although this fear was "formulated in medical terms," it was, Foucault maintains, "animated, basically, by a moral myth." This moral myth involved a new understanding of madness as a moral fault. In the Classical Age, madness was, on Foucault's account, condemned from a moral viewpoint because it was a choice of unreason – that is, a turning away from the world of human realities to a world of delusions. The madman was, by his own choice, outside the human world, an animal. In this view, madness was in essence external to the human history and society that it rejected; it was not a human fault, but a fault that gave up humanity. Foucault regards the Great Fear as important because it represented a break with this moral attitude toward madness. As an object of fear, the mad were once again implicitly regarded as part of the human world, not as those who had stripped off their humanity by a choice of unreason.

Foucault holds that this humanization of madness had two crucial dimensions. First madness was no longer located in a fantastic, "secret" world beyond human experience. It was, rather, a form of human experience, "lodged in the hearts, in the desires, the imagination of men" (FD, 436; MC, 209). It was a moral failing that, unlike the animality of Classical madness, was subject to correction. The mad thus needed to be reformed, and since the beginning of reform is agreement that one is in the wrong, the madman must be made to feel *guilt* over his condition. Second, since it was now part of the human world, the external factors that trigger madness were not sought in grand, enduring cosmic forces (e.g., lunar influences). Rather, they were sought in specific contingent features of local environments. As an example, Foucault cites melancholia, which was regarded as a distinctively English complaint, due to the freedom and wealth of English society. He also notes an emphasis on religious excesses and the artificialities of modern society (from stylized manners to novel reading) as sources of madness.

Foucault closely links this new critical consciousness of madness to a new practical consciousness, a new way of dealing with the mad. This had, in his view, a twofold origin. First, from within the Classical system of confinement, there arose protests that it was wrong to force the sane to live with the mad. Increasingly through the eighteenth century, the feeling grew that nonmad social offenders (e.g., criminals) should not have to endure the violence and other excesses of the mad. Consequently, he says, there developed a consensus that, within the system of confinement, the mad should be isolated from the rest of the confined population. Thus, just when the perception of madness as a form of unreason was abandoned, so was the method of confining madness with other forms of unreason.

Second, external social and economic changes were leading to the breakup of the old system of confinement. Here Foucault thinks the fundamental development was a new conception of the social and economic role of the poor. Previously, poverty had been regarded as a moral fault, the product of slothful idleness, and as we have seen, such idleness was the social mark of unreason. Now, however, poverty came to be viewed as frequently the result of economic forces beyond a person's control and, more importantly, as a necessary condition of the overall wealth of a society. "Because they labor and consume little, those who are in need permit a nation to enrich itself . . .; in short, a people would be poor which had no paupers" (FD, 492–93; MC, 229–30). This new appreciation of the poor was closely tied to the realization that population was a powerful positive economic resource. Foucault points out that, given the new view of the poor, confinement appeared to be a major economic mistake. It withdrew a significant body of cheap labor from the market and, even worse, required its support by public charity. (Presumably, the idea of using those confined as a controlled source of cheap labor had not worked out in practice.) Accordingly, there developed strong pressures for an end to confinement.

However, Foucault notes that a crucial distinction had to be made between the confined poor who were capable of work and those who were not. It was obvious that the former should simply be released from confinement – constrained by nothing but the iron laws of economics. The latter had no economic value and required (for ethical, not economic, reasons) care and support from society. This group, which included the physically ill and the mad (along with criminals, who posed a danger to society) constituted a subclass that still required confinement. Since it was agreed that the mad could not be confined with either the physically ill or criminals, it followed that a separate system of confinement would have to be developed for them. Further, although the general view at the end of the eighteenth century was that care for the needy should be handled by the private charity of neighbors and especially the family, the dangers the mad (like criminals) posed to public order required that their care be handled by the wider community.

But the great and difficult question was, on Foucault's account, precisely what method of confinement should be employed for the mad. The new evaluative consciousness of madness as a human moral failing requiring correction made the old Classical method of mere exclusion inappropriate. The two models available – from the other remaining subgroups requiring confinement – were the hospital and the (newly developing) prison. Eventually, the hospital model won out, primarily because of the case made by writers such as Tenon and Cabanis that the very fact of confinement would constrain the imagination and so have a positive therapeutic effect on the mad (FD, 526). Given this, the project of confinement itself led to a therapeutic approach to madness and hence to a form of confinement modeled on the hospital. Foucault emphasizes that this development followed from changes in the institution of confinement and not from any intervention (e.g., on compassionate grounds) by the medical profession. Indeed, as we shall see, he maintains that doctors precisely as experts on medical matters played little role in early treatment of the mad.

According to Foucault, then, the modern evaluative (critical and practical) consciousness of the mad led to the primary institutional locus of modern madness, the asylum. His next step is to analyze this institution with a view to discovering the true nature of the modern cognitive consciousness of madness. For his claim is that it is the structure of asylum life more than a disinterested scientific pursuit of truth that underlies modern psychology and psychiatry.

On the surface, of course, it appears that the asylum is precisely the locus of the objective scientific study and treatment of madness. It provides a space in which medical experts can carefully observe the mad, assess the nature of their condition, and prescribe an effective regimen of treatment. Foucault agrees that, in the asylum, the mad become objects of the "medical gaze" and of medical treatment, but he finds that the former is rooted in a moral judgment of the mad as violators of bourgeois society's values and that the latter consists of techiniques for compelling the mad back beneath the yoke of these values.

Foucault makes his case through a scrutiny of the work of the two great founders of the asylum movement, Samuel Tuke in England and Philippe Pinel in France, primary figures in the mythical origins of scientific, humanitarian psychology and psychiatry. Tuke freed the mad from the dank cells of Classical captivity and took them to live at the idyllic country "Retreat" he founded in York. The principle behind Tuke's Retreat was the idea, noted above, that madness derived from the artificialities of modern social life. At the Retreat, Tuke's madmen were to be restored by living in a simple, natural setting that would purge them of their diseases of civilization. According to Foucault, however, the Retreat was not strictly a return to a Rousseauian state of nature but to a primitive social group, structured along the social lines of the Biblical family: "a great fraternal community of patients and guardians, under the authority of the administrative directors" (FD, 570). Within this community, he says, the mad were required to submit themselves to the two constraints of *work* and *observation*. Through work they returned to the order of the divine commandments and submitted themselves to the laws of morality and of reality. Their success in doing so was monitored by the close observation of their caretakers, a scrutiny that "pursued in the madman the least perceptible signs of his madness" (FD, 584; MC, 249). A primary locus of this observation were the Retreat's famous "tea-parties," where patients met socially with directors and staff and the mad guests would "dress in their best clothes, and vie with each other in politeness and propriety" (cited, FD, 584; MC, 249).

Whatever Tuke's intentions, the effect of this sort of life was, on Foucault's view, not a return of the mad to a life of natural calm. Rather, it placed "the insane individual within a moral element where he [was] in debate with himself and his surroundings . . . a milieu where, far from being protected, he [was] kept in a perpetual anxiety, ceaselessly threatened by Law and Transgression" (FD, 580; MC, 245). As Foucault sees it, the mad were treated objectively – that is, as objects of scrutiny – in Tuke's Retreat, but the primary effect of this objectification was not scientific knowledge in those observing but fear and guilt in those observed. Of course the previous Classical system of confinement had had its terrors and had judged the mad guilty of moral fault. But in Tuke's regime fear and guilt were internalized: "He substituted for the free terror of madness the stifling anguish of responsibility; fear no longer reigned on the other side of the prison gates, it now raged under the seals of conscience. . . ." Similarly, "the asylum no longer punished the madman's guilt. . .; but it did more, it organized that guilt . . . [so that] the madman became an object of punishment always vulnerable to himself and to the Other. . . ."

(FD 582–83; MC, 247). So, although Tuke's asylum was in some ways more humane than the brutal physical constraints of houses of confinement, it was in other ways even more manipulative and dominating. Never before had the madman been controlled by the manipulation of his own feelings of responsibility and guilt. Never before had he been recruited as his own keeper.

Foucault offers a similar analysis of Pinel's celebrated "liberation" of the mad at Bicêtre. At first sight, it might seem that Pinel's asylum was based on essentially different principles from Tuke's, since the latter was modeled on the religious community of Quakers (to which Tuke belonged and for whom the Retreat was mainly intended), whereas Pinel opposed religion and particularly emphasized its role in the production of madness. However, Foucault thinks this difference is superficial since Pinel is opposed to only "the iconographic [imaginaire] forms, not the moral content of religion" (FD, 591; MC, 256). For him, "the asylum is a religious domain without religion, a domain of pure morality, of ethical uniformity. . . . The values of family and work, all the acknowledged virtues, . . . reign in [his] asylum" (FD, 592; MC, 257). The specifics of Pinel's treatment of the mad did differ from Tuke's. Instead of having the mad retreat from the world into an idealized "natural" community, Pinel tried to bring them back from the "lower depths" of society (where, in his view, their madness originated) and integrate them into the system of bourgeois society. For example, one of his patients – an English captain who was the first madman he freed – became Pinel's personal servant. But Foucault holds that Pinel shared Tuke's ultimate goal of subjecting the mad to bourgeois morality and, even more important, employed the same sort of internalizing techniques to attain it. One such technique was that of silence, the rigorous prohibition from uttering a single word to certain madmen until, humiliated by continual snubs, they abandoned the self-intoxication of their madness and accepted the norms of society. Another, "recognition by mirror," aimed at getting the madman to see (e.g., in other madmen) the absurdity of his pretensions. Finally, and perhaps most important, Pinel, like Tuke, subjected his charges to "perpetual judgment." "Everything was organized so that the madman would recognize himself in a world of judgment that enveloped him on all sides; he must know that he is watched, judged, and condemned" (FD, 601; MC, 267).

We have finally to discuss what Foucault regards as the most important feature of all in the structure of the asylum life that developed at the end of the eighteenth century. This is "the apotheosis of the medical personage" (FD, 604; MC, 269), the dominating role played by doctors in both the admission of patients to the asylum and their treatment once there. To us this no doubt seems entirely natural; since the mad are mentally ill, they require medical treatment. However, according to Foucault, the doctor did not rule the asylum in virtue of his scientific medical knowledge but in virtue of his moral authority. "A man of great probity, of utter virtue and scruple, who had long experience in the asylum would do as well" (FD, 604; MC, 270). The first doctor put in charge at Tuke's Retreat soon realized that his medical knowledge was of little use in improving the condition of the patients. There were cures, but "the medical means were so imperfectly connected with the progress of recovery, that he could not avoid suspecting them, to be rather concomitants than causes" (cited, FD, 606; MC, 271). Tuke insists that the doctor did have great influence on his patients. But Foucault maintains that this was clearly in virtue of his moral and social authority within the institution, not his scientific knowledge of madness. Similarly, "the medical personage, according to Pinel, had to act not as the result of an objective diagnosis, but by relying upon that prestige which envelops the secrets of the Family, of Authority, of Punishment, and of Love; it is by bringing such powers into play, by wearing the mask of Father and of Judge, that the physician . . . became the almost magic perpetrator of the cure." (FD, 607–608; MC, 273).

Foucault points out that, for Tuke and Pinel, there was nothing puzzling about this influence of the physician, since they accepted the efficacy of moral power. But with the development of medical practice in the nineteenth century in accord with a positivist ideal of purely objective, value-free knowledge, physicians were no longer able to invoke moral considerations to explain their power over the mad. They (and society in general) thought of themselves as working solely on the basis of medical knowledge. At the same time, the view of madness as a purely psychological disorder (the eighteenth-century beginnings of which we noted above) was coming to dominate. The natural result was the belief that doctors in asylums were curing the mad in virtue of their scientific knowledge of mental illness. With this was born the modern concept of scientific psychology and psychiatry. But in fact this concept was just a disguise for the doctors' moral domination of the mad in the name of bourgeois society and its values. Foucault sums the matter up this way: "[The] objectivity . . . of nineteenth-century psychiatry from Pinel to Freud . . . was from the start a reification of a magical nature . . ., beginning from a clear and transparent moral practice, gradually forgotten as positivism imposed its myth of scientific objectivity. . . . What we call psychiatric practice is a certain moral tactic contemporary with the end of the eighteenth century, preserved in the rites of asylum life, and overlaid by the myths of positivism" (FD, 610; MC, 276).

We see then that, according to Foucault, the modern cognitive consciousness of madness (our recognition of it as mental illness and our psychological and psychiatric knowledge about it) are in fact grounded in and subordinated to the modern evaluative consciousness of madness. At the archaeological level beneath the concepts and theories of psychological science, we find a structure defined by the project of moral domination. This, he says, is true even (and especially) of Freud's psychoanalysis. Admittedly, psychoanalysis does treat patients outside the setting of the asylum and even enters a dialogue in which the mad are, for the first time in centuries, allowed to speak in their own name. But on Foucault's account, Freud preserves and even augments the asylum's primary instrument of moral domination, the authority of the doctor. (The famous "transference" that is the key to psychoanalytic cures would seem to be the main locus of this authority and its dominating morality.) As a result, psychoanalysis allows the mad to speak, but it does not really hear what they say. Like the rest of modern psychological knowledge and psychiatric practice, it implements "that gigantic moral imprisonment which we are in the habit of calling, doubtless by antiphrasis, the liberation of the insane" (FD, 612; MC, 278).

The voice of madness

Throughout FD, Foucault's primary emphasis is on the ways that a society constitutes its experience of madness and thereby develops a language to speak to and about madness. But an important countertheme of the book, which comes to center stage in the concluding chapter, concerns the possibility of madness itself speaking to a society. Here Foucault turns from madness as an object about which truths are formulated to madness as a subject expressing truths of its own. As we have seen, during the early Renaissance, the tragic experience of madness was regarded as a source of terrifying truths about the world. And even the critical experience of madness that eventually dominated involved madness confronting reason with basic truths about its limitations and temptations. But, with the Classical Age, the rigorous exclusion of the mad left no room for communication between reason and madness. The latter was merely unreason – that is, reason in delirium – and there was no language worth listening to other than that of reason. But Foucault suggests that, toward the end of the eighteenth century, this began to change. He cites Diderot's remarkable dialogue, *Rameau's nephew*, as a first indication of a renewed possibility of real interchange between reason and madness. The "He" of the dialogue (the nephew of the great musician, Jean Philippe Rameau) presents himself as "ignorant, mad, impertinent, and lazy," whereas the "I" (ostensibly Diderot himself) is the embodiment of all the solid common sense and reasonableness of the Enlightenment. But in the course of the discussion, the nephew is disconcertingly perceptive and challenges his interlocutor (and the reader) to reassess his understanding of and commitment to the fundamental moral values of "normal" social life. On Foucault's interpretation, Diderot's brilliant dialogue marks "the reappearance of madness in the domain of language, a language in which it can speak in the first person and state, in the midst of all its empty talk and in the insane grammar of its paradoxes, something that has an essential connection to the truth" (FD, 618).

The concluding chapter of FD, "The anthropological circle," considers, on the basis of Foucault's analysis of the modern experience of madness, just what this "something" might be. As the anticipatory role of *Rameau's nephew* suggests, one place that madness finds a voice in the nineteenth century is in literary texts. Employing the same division of literary types that he used in the Introduction to *Traum und Existenz*, Foucault says that this voice arises neither in the epic (which is presumably always an expression of a society's accepted values and truths, not a challenge to them) nor, as for the early Renaissance, in tragedy, but in the alternating obscurity and illumination of the lyric. In poets such as Hölderlin and Nerval "madness finds once again its language"

(FD, 619), a language that does not (like the Renaissance's tragic experience) reveal "the invisible figures of the world" but rather "the secret truths of man" (FD, 620). These truths are a challenge to the sharp categorical divisions on which rational thought depends, telling us that "in man, the interior is also the exterior, that the extreme of subjectivity is identical to the immediate fascination of the object, that every end is a stubborn return [to a beginning]" (FD, 620).

But Foucault thinks that these same sorts of truths are conveyed in the nonlyrical context of discursive thought, particularly psychological theory. Here, however, we do not find the romantic poets' welcoming of the wisdom of madness. Rather, reason "protects itself by insisting . . . that the madman is only a thing, [specifically] a medical thing" (FD, 621). But, on Foucault's view, the results of scientific psychology themselves belie this claim. The consequence is that modern knowledge of madness is pervaded by a set of antinomies. Thus, on the one hand, madness appears as a return to a simpler, primitive stage of human existence. But, on the other hand, it is the ultimate outcome of overcivilization. Also, "in [madness] the organic triumphs, [it is] the sole truth of man that can be objectified and perceived scientifically." But, at the same time, madness is distinguished from bodily illnesses by the fact that "it makes surge up an interior world of evil instincts, of perversity, of suffering, and of violence. . . ." (FD, 622). Another conflict arises from the appearance of mad acts as simultaneously the product of determining reasons (desires, passions) and as done for no reason at all. A final (and perhaps fundamental) antinomy: Modern psychology thinks of itself as discovering, through its study of madness, fundamental truths about human nature, truths that are the basis of its cures. "But the human truth that madness reveals is the direct contradiction of the moral and social truth of man [in bourgeois society]." In fact, psychiatric treatment begins by "repressing this inadmissible truth" of madness and goes on to subject the madman to the truths of society (FD, 623).

Foucault suggest that it is because of these antinomies that modern psychology and psychiatry are characterized by a continual conflict of competing theoretical interpretations. Even the modern period, therefore, has been unable to develop a coherent theoretical account of madness. But now the obstacle to coherence is not, as in the Classical Age, the contradiction of offering a positive science of an essentially negative reality. It is rather the contradiction between that which madness itself reveals about human reality and the conception of human nature required by the social values that psychology and psychiatry serve.

The antinomies are expressed in continual conflicts between rival psychological interpretations and psychiatric approaches. Foucault remarks that, as with Classical medical views of madness, there may lie beneath these contending views of madness a coherent structure. Specifically, he suggests that in place of the "binary structure of Classical unreason (truth and error, world and phantasm, being and nonbeing, Day and Night)" there may be a modern "anthropological three-term structure [of] man, his madness, and his truth" (FD, 624). Presumably, a detailed archaeological analysis, parallel to that sketched for the Classical experience of madness, would reveal this structure; Foucault suggests that he plans to provide such an analysis in a "later study" that would draw up a "meticulous inventory" of the nineteenth century's "experience of madness in its totality; that is in the whole [composed] of its scientifically explicit forms and of its silent aspects" (FD, 624). (No such study ever appeared, although *Les mots et les choses* provided an archaeology of some related areas of nineteenth-century thought.) For the moment, Foucault contents himself with a brief discussion of some distinctive features of the nineteenth century's "surface" account of the types of madness. Here he focuses on aberrations – general paralysis, "moral insanity," and monomania – that had no Classical counterparts and that illustrate the conflicts of modern psychology and psychiatry.

But what, finally, is the place and importance for us of madness's first-person utterances? To answer this question, Foucault returns to the relation between madness and art. It soon becomes clear that for Foucault at this period, art offers our main hope of breaking out of the lies and self-deceptions of bourgeois values. His analyses of would-be sciences of man are consistently deflations of what they claim, but his analyses of artistic works are always appreciations of what they offer. Here, at the very end of his study of madness, Foucault first shows, through discussions of Goya's paintings of the mad and of De Sade's novels, how art can in different ways transmit the cries of madness. Moreover, he claims that, in the wake of Goya and De Sade, "unreason has belonged to whatever is decisive, for the modern world, in any work of art: that is, whatever any work of art contains that is both murderous and constraining" (FD, 640; MC, 285). Thus, there is a symbiotic relation between art and madness – the former expressing the latter, the latter giving the former its power. But this does not mean that the artist through whose work the voice of madness speaks is himself mad. Indeed, "Madness is precisely the absence of the work of art" and "where there is a work of art there is no madness" (FD, 641–42, 643; MC, 287, 288–89). Nietzsche's last demented postcards, for example, are "the very annihilation of the work of art" (FD, 642; MC, 287). But the artist's experience of the absence of his work in his madness can be the source of new artistic creation. In Artaud, for example, the work of art is nothing other than "all those words hurled against a fundamental absence of language" (FD, 642; MC, 287). Even when madness terminates rather than merely interrupts the artist's work, this dissolution of the work may, as in the case of Nietzsche, "be that by which [it] opens out onto the modern world," making the work immediate to us by the very shock of madness.

So for Foucault madness speaks through art, but only in the sense that art is a reaction to the madness that destroys it. We see madness in art only through the violence it does to art. The effect of this spectacle is that we recognize our culpability for the artist's laceration by madness. "The world is made aware of its guilt. . . . Henceforth, and through the mediation of madness, it is the world that becomes culpable (for the first time in the Western world) in relation to the work of art. . ." (FD, 643; MC, 288). Culpable for what? For refusing to recognize madness in its own terms, refusing to accept its voice as a legitimate one. It is this refusal that makes it impossible for there to be a mad work of art and so forces the artist into a destructive relation with the madness that is the root of his creativity. To be free of our guilt, to make reparation, we need to carry out "the task of restoring reason *from* that unreason and *to* that unreason" (FD, 643; MC, 288) – that is, of making a world in which reason (e.g., the coherent discourse of art) is not in violent confrontation with madness but exists with it in a harmonious complementarity. So, contrary to the project of modern psychology, through which the modern world aims at measuring and judging madness, "the world must justify itself before madness" (FD, 643; MC, 289).

The history of madness: methods and results

In the publications of 1954, seven years before FD appeared, Foucault had sought an understanding of the nature of the mental illness studied by psychology and treated by psychiatry. The two primary tools he employed were Heideggerian existential analysis of the lived world of the mad and a Marxist account of the real social factors (contradictions) that caused the formation of this world. Roughly, the existential analysis provided the deepest and richest level of the description of mental illness and the Marxist account provided the explanation of its occurrence. By the time he wrote FD, Foucault had become disenchanted with the Marxist explanation, though he still thought the ultimate account of mental illness must be found in its real historical (social and cultural) context. Now, however, he hoped to reach this account by some form of historical existential analysis that would explicate the nature of the "experience" of madness. This switch to "madness" from "mental illness" reflects another major change in Foucault's thought from 1954 to 1961. He has become distrustful of modern "scientific" psychology and its concept of mental illness.[10] As a result, he is no longer willing to take "mental illness" as a given, objective fact that needs explanation. Rather, he sees different historical periods as having distinctive experiences of madness, each of which – including that of modern psychology and psychiatry – needs to be understood in terms of its own historical context. The primary goals of FD are to analyze the experiences of madness of the Classical Age and of the modern period that followed it and thereby understand the true significance of the psychology and psychiatry of mental illness.

To carry out this task, Foucault employs a somewhat confusing variety of historical methods. Occasionally, he takes the standard historical approach of explaining events via political, social, and economic causes. He says, for example, that the Great Confinement was the French government's response to the crisis

---

10. Foucault's antipathy to contemporary psychology and psychiatry is very apparent in his 1957 essay, "La recherche scientifique et la psychologie" in *Des chercheurs français s'interrogent*, edited by J-E. Morère (PUF, 1957), 171–201. Foucault's critical attitude has some affinities with Canguilhem's views in his 1958 essay, "Qu'est-ce que la psychologie?" reprinted in E, 365–81. Cf. particularly pp. 376–81.

produced by the Spanish economic collapse and cites social and economic causes of the end of the Classical system of confinement. But this approach is not adequate for his primary purpose in FD. It accounts for events on the basis of the actions of groups and individuals, which actions are themselves explained by the agents' beliefs and intentions. Foucault, however, is interested in the "consciousness" (evaluative and cognitive) that underlies such beliefs and intentions. Consequently, the standard causal approach of historians, while useful as a starting point, cannot of itself answer the questions he is posing.

Foucault also sometimes refers to the effect of external events, such as the Great Confinement, on the way people think and perceive. He even says, as we saw, that the institutions and practices of confinement "constituted" the Classical experience of madness (FD, 102). But it is clear that he is not content with a reduction of thought to external material causes and that any relations of causality between practices of confinement and the Classical experience of madness are reciprocal.

Given Foucault's refusal of a materialist reduction of thought, we might expect that he would pursue the usual approach of the history of ideas, offering an internal account of the views developed by individual thinkers and showing how their work influenced and was modified by those following them. But, although Foucault does mention the ideas of a large and diverse set of thinkers, his discussion is by no means built around summaries and analyses of individual views. Indeed, FD does not provide a thorough exposition of what any single thinker, no matter how important, thought about madness.

It might seem that this lack of emphasis on particular accounts of madness reflects Foucault's interest in writing (à la Canguilhem) a history of the concept of madness rather than a history of theories of madness. Certainly, there is a sense in which Foucault is trying to disengage, for example, the concept of madness that somehow underlies the theoretical disagreements of Classical thinkers as well as the Classical treatment of the mad. However, in this case (in contrast to e.g., Canguilhem's history of the reflex) there is no commonly accepted concept of madness present in the medical and scientific literature of the Classical Age. At the level of scientific concepts and theories formulated in their terms, there is simply an irreducible pluralism. Accordingly, the sense in which Foucault is seeking a "concept" of Classical madness is different from the sense in which Canguilhem found the concept of the reflex in Willis and subsequent thinkers.

To some extent, a similar point can be made about the nineteenth century. As we have seen, the "antinomies" of modern psychology prevented consensus on a comprehensive theoretical viewpoint. However, it could nonetheless be argued that modern psychology has at least formulated a widely accepted concept of madness as mental illness that expresses a common consciousness of madness and is discoverable by the methods of Canguilhem's history of science. But even if this is so, an understanding of the modern consciousness of madness in these terms would be misleading, since it would ignore what Foucault regards as the essential dimensions of evaluative consciousness (madness as transgression of social values, and so on) that underlie a theory and practice that presents itself as merely objectively scientific.

In sum, although Canguilhem's history of concepts comes closer to Foucault's intention in FD than other available historical methods, any straightforward application of it is inadequate to his deeper purposes. This is because, first, operating only on the level of the cognitive content of scientific concepts and theories, it cannot discover a common cognitive consciousness located beneath irreducible conceptual and theoretical disagreement. Nor can it reveal any evaluative consciousness that may be the real source of what are purported to be merely objective concepts and theories. However, as we shall see, the new methods that Foucault eventually develops in his historical work can be plausibly viewed as extensions and transformations of Canguilhem's history of concepts.

Foucault's treatment of madness requires, then, another approach to the history of thought, an approach that may be called "archaeological" in virtue of its need to discover structures beneath the surfaces open to ordinary historical scrutiny. However, it never becomes entirely clear in FD precisely what this new archaeological method might be. It evidently must involve techniques for dealing with both texts and practices, since these are the data from which Foucault begins. Further, these techniques must be capable of operating on a level that is other and more fundamental than those of ordinary hermeneutics, which seeks the meanings of individual utterances and actions. Somehow, archaeology must be able to see structures that are common to all the texts and practices (in a given domain) of an age and that lie deeper than the level of "meaning" in any standard sense. Here, however, it is difficult for Foucault to give a clear sense to his new approach because of his insistence on presenting it as explicating a consciousness or experience. If this is taken seriously, we must ask who or what is the experiencing consciousness in question. But Foucault does not seem sympathetic to any of the range (from Hegel to Jung) of available answers.[11] Consequently, the archaeology of FD remains a technique of reading historical texts and practices for which Foucault is able to offer no satisfactory reflective account. In subsequent historical works he moves away from the existential viewpoint on which his talk of "consciousness" and "experience" is based. Admittedly, BC makes frequent references to medical "experiences" and even OT occasionally speaks of various aspects of Classical and modern "experience." But in these books experience is no longer, as in existential phenomenology, an ultimate category. It is subordinated to the linguistic structures underlying experience that are the true concern of Foucault's analysis. Moreover, in AK he presents archaeological analysis as dealing with a level of discursive structure in which the experiencing subject plays no role.

In addition to the methodological unclarities of FD, there are serious problems regarding its historical accuracy. There is no doubt that it remains an important pioneering work, one of the very first to question the standard Whiggish view of modern psychiatry as nothing more than a move to more humane treatment of the mad based on a correct understanding of the nature of their affliction. Over the twenty-five years since FD was published, there has appeared an impressive series of studies of the understanding and treatment of madness from the Renaissance on. On the one hand, this work has substantially confirmed Foucault's general claims that fundamentally different conceptions of madness have characterized different historical periods and that the historical move toward modern psychiatry has by no means been one of unequivocal progress. On the other hand, many of his more specific claims have been seriously questioned. Some important criticisms derive from the fact that, although

11. In AK, Foucault says that FD "accorded far too great a place, and a very enigmatic one too, to what I called an 'experience,' thus showing to what extent one was still close to admitting an anonymous and general subject of history" (AK, 16). (Sheridan's translation has "experiment" for the French *expérience*, but the context requires "experience.")

Foucault claims to provide a general account of Western attitudes toward madness since the Renaissance, the greatest bulk of
his evidence is restricted to French thought and practice. Thus,
Klaus Doerner and, more recently, Roy Porter have argued that
the Great Confinement that occurred in France had no significant parallel in Germany or England.[12] Similarly, David Rothman's history of nineteenth-century American psychiatry shows
it to have been far less concerned than Tuke and Pinel with the
medical treatment of madness.[13]

However, even in its own restricted domain of evidence, Foucault's account has been attacked as incomplete and inaccurate.
H. C. Eric Midelfort, for example, maintains that "many of his
arguments fly in the face of empirical evidence."[14] He criticizes, in
particular, Foucault's neglect or misreading of the medieval roots
of modern approaches to madness. Specifically, he says, Foucault
fails to see the extent to which confinement is not a radical innovation of the Classical Age but continues medieval monastic practices; moreover, he ignores major disanalogies between medieval
attitudes toward leprosy and later attitudes toward the mad.
Midelfort further objects to Foucault's sharp contrast between the
Renaissance acceptance and the Classical exclusion of madness.
This, he says, ignores the Renaissance's strong association of madness with sin and its frequent harsh treatment (even confinement)
of madmen. He also points out that the famous Renaissance ships
of fools, which Foucault takes as a major indication of the
"liminal" place of the mad in Renaissance society, almost surely
never existed. He maintains, moreover, that Foucault overempha-
sizes the Classical exclusion of the mad by downplaying what was
in fact a significant role of medical treatment.

In some cases, these sorts of criticisms can be met by pointing

12. Klaus Doerner, *Madmen and the bourgeoisie: a social history of madness and insanity*, translated by J. Neugroschel and Jean Steinberg (Oxford: Blackwell,
1981, German original, 1969). Roy Porter, *Mind forg'd manacles: a history of
madness in England from the restoration to the regency* (London: Athlone, 1987).
13. David Rothman, *The discovery of the asylum* (Boston: Little, Brown, 1971).
14. H. C. Eric Midelfort, "Madness and civilization in early modern Europe: a
reappraisal of Michel Foucault", in B. C. Malament, ed., *After the Reformation:
essays in honor of J. H. Hexter* (Philadelphia: University of Pennsylvania Press,
1980), 259. Cf. also Lawrence Stone's comments in "Madness," *New York
Review of Books*, Dec. 16, 1982, 36ff, and his ensuing exchange with Foucault,
New York Review of Books, Mar. 31, 1983, 42–44. Historical criticisms of FD
are also developed in *Evolution psychiatrique* 36 (1971), an issue entirely devoted to the book. Cf. particularly the essays by H. Ey and G. Daumézon.

out that Foucault is not concerned with formulating excep-
tionless empirical generalizations from the historical data but
with giving an overall characterization of a society's fundamental
attitudes toward madness. Such attitudes may well not be manifest in all texts and practices, and their existence can even be
compatible with a variety of contrary tendencies. Thus, when
Foucault presents the seventeenth and eighteenth centuries as
"the age of confinement," he should not be taken as maintaining
that there were no instances of confinement prior to that period.
His point is rather that in the Classical Age confinement takes on
a new and particularly central role in the treatment of the mad.
Such a thesis is not an empirical generalization that can be refuted by a few contrary instances. It is a general principle for
interpreting a large body of diverse and often conflicting data
and can be decisively refuted only by showing that there is a
more satisfactory overall interpretation of the data.

This is an important – and I think decisive – response to the
claim of some critics that Foucault's account is a blatant misrepresentation, easily dismissed by a few quick factual references. Nevertheless, it seems clear that, even as an overall interpretation,
Foucault's account is often seriously defective. Its fundamental
failure lies in the assumption that there is some simple unifying
conception of madness in each major historical period. Construals of Renaissance madness as the mocking inverse of reason,
of Classical madness as a free embrace of unreason, and of modern madness as a threat to bourgeois values masked as illness are
far too narrow to do justice to the complexity and diversity of
attitudes toward madness over the last three centuries. As usual,
simple unifying schemata do not sustain detailed scrutiny of the
historical record.

Foucault's history of madness was not written simply to provide an accurate overall picture of how people's views of and
treatment of the mad have changed through the years. It also
had the critical intent of discrediting the idea that our contemporary conception of mental illness is nothing more than the objective scientific truth about what madness really is. Accordingly,
beyond the question of the accuracy of Foucault's historical re-
constructions, we need to raise the issue of the success of his
critique of contemporary psychiatry and psychology.

In this regard, a major difficulty concerns the relevance of
Foucault's historical analyses to his critique of contemporary dis-

ciplines. For example, the purpose of his treatments of Renaissance and Classical madness is apparently to show that there have been alternatives to our modern conception of madness as mental illness. But what, we may well ask, is the point of doing this? Surely we can admit that past ages have thought differently about madness without having to regard this as a challenge to our conception of it. We do not, for example, find the historical fact that our ancestors thought very differently about the nature of matter or of the solar system a challenge to our current views of these topics. Beyond demonstrating the existence of alternative conceptions of madness, it would be necessary to show – as Foucault does not – that these conceptions are, at least in some respects, as well-grounded as our own.

Moreover, it is highly relevant that Foucault's discussion scarcely goes beyond the first beginnings of modern psychiatry with Pinel and Tuke. He simply does not offer the sort of detailed analysis of current psychological theory and psychiatric practice that would be necessary for a serious critical evaluation of them. Even if he has shown that some of the initial developments of the idea of madness as mental illness were not superior to the conceptions that they replaced, drawing conclusions from this about the status of contemporary work would be an egregious example of the genetic fallacy. Similarly, even if the views and practices of Pinel and Tuke involved an inappropriate dimension of moral judgment, it does not follow that this defect has carried over into contemporary psychology and psychiatry.

It seems clear, then, that, even if there were nothing to fault in Foucault's historical accounts of Classical and early modern views of madness, these accounts would not of themselves sustain a critique of contemporary psychology and psychiatry. The claim, often made by Foucault's followers, that FD undermines the authority of these disciplines is simply not sustainable.

This is not to say, however, that Foucault's history has nothing to contribute toward a critical assessment of psychology and psychiatry. One reason that established systems of thought and practice often maintain their authority in spite of basic flaws is that, precisely because they are so entrenched, it is difficult to think of any serious alternatives to their conceptions and procedures. Another reason is that they have, over years of dominance, developed subtle ways of masking their flaws. Historical analyses such as Foucault's can be used to overcome both these sorts of defense mechanisms. By unearthing alternative ways of thinking and acting, they end the de facto monopoly of the dominant systems. This is particularly so since the alternatives such historical analysis uncovers are not mere logical possibilities but have themselves been entrenched in the reality of our past. Thus, the fact that madness has been regarded as reason's mocking partner or as a fundamental rejection of humanity shows that there are serious alternatives to regarding madness as simply mental illness. Even if, precisely because they are in our past, there is no possibility of simply returning to these conceptions as such, they may still suggest numerous ways of modifying specific aspects of the entrenched viewpoint. A similar point holds regarding the techniques established systems have of masking their flaws. Historical analysis can suggest the sorts of flaws that might well be present (since they were there at the beginning) and even the kinds of techniques that have been developed to hide them. Simply knowing, for example, that early modern views of madness contained elements of moral judgment covered by a veneer of scientific authority makes it plausible to look for something similar in current elaborations of these views.

My suggestion, then, is that, on the one hand, Foucault's history in FD is simply not adequate to carry out its project of undermining the authority of contemporary psychology and psychiatry. On the other hand, it can be plausibly regarded as an important heuristic preliminary to such a critique. It is not, as Foucault and his supporters seem to think, decisive; but it is highly suggestive.

This view of FD as heuristic also reduces its burden of historical accuracy. If all we expect from it is the suggestion of possible directions for a critique of contemporary disciplines, then its failure to provide an adequate general account of Western views of madness over the last three hundred years is not fatal. Even if certain conceptions and attitudes were much less prevalent or important than Foucault suggests, they still correspond to real possibilities that provide plausible direction to our suspicions about the claims of current views about "mental illness." The relation of Foucault's history to the critique of psychology and psychiatry is like that of the medical history a patient gives his physician (in contrast to a highly reliable blood test) to the physician's diagnosis of his current illness. Both serve to generate plausible suspicions even though they may have serious limitations as accurate historical accounts.

My construal of FD as of primarily heuristic value is a significant backing away from the goals Foucault surely had in mind when he wrote it. On the other hand, it fits well with Foucault's later idea – for example, in "What Is Enlightenment?" – that historical critiques of reason have essentially local or regional import. Thus, the history of madness may well point toward specific criticisms of particular aspects of psychological theory and psychiatric practice; but there is no reason to think its critical suggestions will lead to their total undermining. Foucault himself made a very similar point in one of his last interviews. Speaking of the intimate tie between psychiatry and the mechanisms of modern power, he said: "This fact in no way impairs the scientific validity or the therapeutic efficacy of psychiatry."[15]

Indeed, I think we can go even further and maintain that there is nothing in FD's historical analysis inconsistent with the claim that the modern view of madness as mental illness is, in some major ways, both a cognitive and moral advance on earlier views. Even if, for example, modern psychological theories are by no means essentially correct and will require major rectifications in the future, it may still be true that they embody important objective truths about the nature of madness that were not available to the thought of previous epochs. They may, for example, correctly tie certain forms of madness to chemical imbalances or to unconscious Oedipal conflicts. Similarly, for all the ways modern psychiatric practice may be tied to forms of domination, it may still be true that many of its specific features are morally preferable to earlier procedures or even that it represents an overall moral advance over them. Foucault's history suggests many ways of deflating the pretensions of current views of madness to a privileged status. But it provides no basis for denying all credibility to modern views or for concluding that earlier views are superior to them.

This point requires particular emphasis because the rhetorical force of Foucault's prose often goes far beyond the evidentiary force of his arguments in condemning modern psychiatry. To speak of it as a "gigantic moral imprisonment" and to say that it can be called a liberation only "by way of antiphrasis" go far beyond anything established or even plausibly suggested by Foucault's historical analyses. Here his view is particularly distorted by his prejudice against bourgeois morality and by his romantic desire to see madness as an infrarational source of fundamental truth. Foucault simply assumes that a moral system built around respect for property and family relations strikes at the root of the individual's autonomy and happiness. His overwhelming emotional aversion to such a morality leads him to reject it in toto, with no analysis of its precise values and deficiencies. This is one respect in which Foucault (like Sartre and many other contemporary French literary intellectuals) remains unnecessarily constrained by the limits of his cultural milieu. Similarly, his romanticization of madness as a source of deep truth blinds Foucault to the fact that, quite apart from any exclusion or exploitation by society, the mad are often cripplingly afflicted by the distortions and terrors of madness itself. Here he has forgotten the perceptive analyses of his earlier book, *Maladie mentale et personnalité*, where he presented madness as "both a retreat into the worst of subjectivities and a fall into the worst of objectivities" (MMP, 56) and as a morbid stifling of the imagination.

In sum, FD has some major limitations, including an ill-defined methodology, significant historical inaccuracies, and uncritical evaluative presuppositions. However, it remains an impressive achievement that introduced a new and extremely fruitful approach to the history of madness and provides a powerful basis for the critique of contemporary psychology and psychiatry.

With regard to Foucault's own subsequent work, FD has a crucial germinal role. Its methodological and critical themes are carried forward by everything else that Foucault wrote. The archaeological method becomes more explicit and coherent in BC and OT, although there is an increasing emphasis on using it for the analysis of discursive rather than of nondiscursive practices. It is not until DP that Foucault returns to a central concern with the latter. Through all these developments, however, Foucault remains faithful to the fundamental goal of the archaeological method as it first appears in FD: to analyze structures lying beneath those elucidated by standard techniques in the history of thought. Similarly, the precise critical thrust of

Foucault's subsequent work varies from book to book, depending on the topics treated and the direction of approach. BC and OT are, for example, much less challenging to the objective truth-content of the disciplines they examine. But, throughout, the basic project remains that of FD: to use history to question the self-understanding of current knowledge of human beings. Beyond this, the specific content of Foucault's later works is often closely tied to that of FD. For example, the central questions of BC and DP are posed by a crucial episode in Foucault's history of madness. This was the point at which the system of Classical confinement was rejected as economically unsound and most of those confined were released to the job market. As we saw, special arrangements had to be made for three groups that were not able to be part of the work force: the mad, the sick, and criminals. Because of protests against inflicting the mad on the sane, a separate system of confinement was devised for them. Part III of FD studies this, the asylum system. BC analyzes the hospital system developed to care for the sick, while DP treats the prison that dealt with criminals. Both works thus begin from a historical crux defined by FD. Similarly, OT can be regarded as a historical generalization of the historical project of FD. Instead of focusing on the specific topics of madness and psychology, it attempts a general archaeology of all the modern human sciences through an analysis of the transition from Classical to modern views of life, labor, and language.

Overall, then, FD must be recognized as the foundation of the entire body of Foucault's work. Although there are many significant revisions and innovations, it lays down the basic methods, problems, and values that inform everything else he wrote.

3

CLINICAL MEDICINE

There is no simple or direct connection between *The birth of the clinic* (BC) and FD. We might be tempted to read BC as a history of the concept of bodily illness, paralleling FD's history of mental illness. But this would ignore the far more restricted range of analysis in BC, which says nothing about Renaissance medicine and offers only a relatively brief treatment of the Classical view of disease as a contrast to what emerged in the nineteenth century. Nor is BC a mere appendix to FD. Its historical locus is, as we have seen, defined by the crucial point in the history of madness at which the general system of confinement broke down and separate arrangements had to be made for the mad, criminals, and the sick. But, despite this connection, BC approaches its topic without reliance on the results of FD, which is never even cited. This no doubt reflects Foucault's Bachelardian tendency to eschew facile syntheses and treat each "region of rationality" in its own terms.

BC is generally regarded as Foucault's furthest move in the direction of structural analysis. The first printing of the book frequently referred to its approach as "structural," although Foucault deleted such references in later printings to avoid what he came to regard as a highly misleading characterization of his work. There is surely something broadly structuralist about certain aspects of BC's analysis, particularly the focus in the latter part of the book on language as a phenomenon, independent of speakers' intentions, to be analyzed as an autonomous system of rule-governed elements. (Much of OT and even parts of FD – e.g., the account of Classical madness as essentially linguistic – are similarly structuralist.) But, as we will see in Chapter 6, the fundamentally historical nature of his studies separates them from a pure structuralism. Moreover, I will argue that the methodology of BC is much closer to that of Canguilhem's history of concepts. Writing a book for a series edited by Canguilhem, Foucault's primary accomplishment is to write a history of the formation of the modern concept of disease.

Classical medicine

Foucault presents the modern understanding of disease as the result of a sharp break with the Classical conception. The latter is characterized in terms of what he calls three modes of "spatialization": a "primary spatialization" that situates disease in a conceptual configuration defining its fundamental nature, a "secondary spatialization" that relates disease to the individual bodies in which it is realized, and a "tertiary spatialization" that places disease in a social context. From our modern standpoint, the most striking feature of the Classical view is that it makes a sharp distinction between the primary and the secondary spatializations of disease. We think it entirely obvious that disease is to be conceived as something localized in an individual body; a disease simply is something that is wrong with a sick organism. But Foucault claims that "the exact superposition of the 'body' of the disease and the body of the sick man is no more than a historical, temporary datum" (3). Classical medicine, in particular, conceived of diseases as abstract essences (defined by sets of general qualities) that did not depend on the particular bodies in which they might be exemplified. Indeed, to understand a disease, doctors had to "abstract the patient" suffering from it to avoid being confused by idiosyncrasies that might obscure its true nature. "In relation to that which he is suffering from, the patient is only an external fact; the medical reading must take him into account only to place him in parentheses" (8).

The nonbodily space in terms of which Classical diseases are understood has two dimensions (which Foucault labels, respectively, vertical and horizontal). First, a disease is understood in terms of an ideal temporal sequence – not always realized in specific cases – in which the qualities of the disease unfold. Second, a disease is understood through analogies (similarities and dissimilarities in qualities) between it and other diseases. In both dimensions, disease is regarded noncausally. Any causal relationships that may obtain among the temporal succession of a disease's qualities are not essential to a grasp of its nature. Similarly, diseases are regarded as more or less closely related to one another solely in virtue of their degree of qualitative resemblance; considerations of genesis and causal relationships are not relevant.

As we shall see in Chapter 4, this view of disease is just one instance of a general Classical conception of knowledge in terms of tabular classification. All objects of knowledge are classified into species on the basis of their qualities, with members of the same species exhibiting an identical set of key overt qualities. Further, the system of identities and differences that defines the classificatory system is not seen as merely a convenient system of mapping; the system provides the "intelligible ordering" that represents their objectively true natures (7).

With regard to secondary spatialization (the ingression of the disease into the local space of the sick body), we have already seen that, on Foucault's account of Classical medicine, this has no essential connection with the nature of the disease. When someone is sick, the disease may, at a given moment, be localized in a particular organ. But this localization tells us nothing about the disease's nature, and in fact diseases circulate freely from one organic site to another with no essential alteration. Similarly, Foucault notes, the presence of a Classical disease is manifested by a temporal series of symptoms, but this developmental process need bear no relation to the pathological essence. Rather, the presence of a disease in a particular body is merely a matter of the appearance of the qualities that define the disease in the space of the body. Diagnosis requires only that the doctor carefully determine which qualities are present; where or when they occur is of no central importance. However, since the individual qualities of particular patients (e.g., their temperament, age, way of life) can obscure the "essential nucleus" of the disease, the doctor must take careful account of them, not as aspects of the disease but as factors that need to be abstracted to effect an accurate diagnosis.

Tertiary spatialization includes all the social techniques and structures whereby a society deals with disease. The term *tertiary* should not mislead us into thinking it is not of crucial significance in Foucault's account. In fact it corresponds to something of the highest importance: "a system of options that reveals the way in which a group, in order to protect itself, practises exclusions, establishes the forms of assistance, and reacts to poverty and the fear of death" (16). Moreover, as we shall see, Foucault regards tertiary spatialization as the point of origin for the overthrow of the Classical system of medicine.

According to Foucault, Classical tertiary spatialization has two fundamental characteristics. First is the idea that the true, simple essence of a disease is most fully realized in more primitive social structures. The sicknesses of more highly "civilized" societies take complex and diversified forms that obscure the real nature of diseases. Second is the parallel idea that "like civilization, the hospital is an artificial locus in which the transplanted disease runs the risk of losing its essential identity" (20). As a result, Classical medicine felt that disease should be cared for in the "natural" locale of the home, a view that fit well with the liberal economics of the eighteenth century. However, Foucault notes that this did not mean that the practice of medicine was to be free of state supervision. On the contrary, competent medical practice was regarded as so important for society as a whole that there had to be careful central control over the licensing of doctors. Accordingly, for the Classical Age, "the medicine of individual perception, of family assistance, of home care can be based only on a collectively controlled structure" (120).

Foucault points out that the new clinical medicine that arose at the end of the eighteenth and the beginning of the nineteenth centuries was not without Classical antecedents. There was, alongside the dominant medicine of species, a Classical medicine of epidemics. This had a distinctly marginal status because it was "opposed at every point to a medicine of classes [species]" (26). This opposition derived from the fact that the analysis of epidemics was not a matter of recognizing the qualities that defined the place of a disease in an abstract pathological classificatory scheme. It required rather the uncovering of particular processes, variable from instance to instance, whereby diseases spread among the members of an animal or human group. Thus, Foucault concludes that the medicine of epidemics required the analysis of temporal series with a view to determinations of causality, in sharp contrast to the medicine of species' concern with the placement of diseases in an abstract schema of classifications defined by atemporal qualities.

The practice of the medicine of epidemics required a distinctive form of tertiary spatialization. As much as the medicine of species, it needed its own "definition of a political status for medicine and the constitution, at state level, of a medical consciousness whose constant task would be to provide information, supervision, and constraint" (26). In France, in particular, a growing concern with the control of epidemics led to a social restructuring of medicine that began the undermining of the Classical medicine of classes and started the process of transformation that led to modern clinical medicine.

Foucault describes the main stages of this process. The initial restructuring of medicine to deal with epidemics led to a new form of "medical consciousness" that was just emerging at the beginning of the French Revolution. This medical consciousness converged in certain key respects with the political consciousness of the Revolution, a convergence that resulted, in the early Revolutionary period (before 1793), in a variety of proposals for radical reform of medical institutions and practices. However, Foucault argues that no radical reform could be effective until there was a correspondingly radical transformation of medical experience and discourse. This, he says, occurred only in the first part of the nineteenth century, in connection with the Consular government's reorganization of medical practice in 1803, which marked the birth of clinical medicine. Following this, there was the integration (by Bichat) of pathological anatomy into clinical medicine, which led to the displacement of clinical medicine by anatomo-clinical medicine. On Foucault's account, it is this discipline, finally constituted by Broussais's work on fevers, that has been the dominant form for the practice of medicine even into the twentieth century. We turn now to the details of Foucault's analysis of these developments.

A new medical consciousness

The pre-Revolutionary concern with epidemics led to the establishment of the Société Royale de Médicine as the central medical authority in France. This society was organized quite differently from the older *Faculté* of doctors associated with the University, whose authority it eventually replaced. Corresponding to this new organization (designed to monitor and control epidemics) was a new medical consciousness that was, first of all, characterized by its collective nature: "The Société . . . had become the official organ of a *collective consciousness* of pathological phenomena that operated at both the level of experience and the level of knowledge" (28). According to Foucault, this collective consciousness moved away from the Classical view of medical knowledge as an encyclopediac system that included all particulars in a preestablished structure. Instead, it presented medical knowledge as a body of "constantly revised information" in which the intersection of different informational lines marks causal (or other) connections between diseases that may have nothing in common from the standpoint of classical classificatory structures. In sum: "The locus in which knowledge is formed is no longer the pathological garden where God distributed the species, but a generalized medical consciousness, diffused in space and time, open and mobile, linked to each individual existence, as well as to the collective life of the nation, ever alert to the endless domain in which illness betrays, in its various aspects, its great, solid form" (31).

Foucault connects to the new medical consciousness and its conception of medical knowledge two complementary "myths" that he believes exercised a strong influence on Revolutionary thinking. The first was that of "a nationalized medical profession," replacing the clergy, with powers over bodies comparable to the latter's over souls. The second myth envisaged "a total disappearance of disease in an untroubled, dispassionate society returned to its original state of health," where there would be no need at all for doctors (32–33). Foucault thinks these myths were particularly important because they presented medicine as working for positive ideals and not just for the negative goal of curing illnesses. Corresponding to this was a switch from a medicine of health to a medicine of normality. That is, the doctor was no longer seen merely as someone who restores the body to a healthy (nondiseased) state but as the arbiter of standards that define positive norms of man's ideal physical state. "Instead of remaining . . . the dubious negation of the negative, [medicine] was given the splendid task of establishing in men's lives the positive role of health, virtue, and happiness" (34). Accordingly, whereas Classical medicine was primarily concerned with restoring "qualities of vigor, suppleness, and fluidity, which were lost in illness," the new medical consciousness looked forward to nineteenth-century medicine, which "formed its concepts and prescribed its interventions in relation to a standard of functioning and organic structure" (35). It was this transformation that led to the nineteenth-century conception of life as not primarily "the internal structure of the *organized being*, but [as] the *medical bipolarity of the normal and the pathological*" (35). (Here Foucault's discussion makes contact with Canguilhem's work, suggesting that the distinction of the normal and the pathological, which Canguilhem takes as a given for philosophical analysis, is a contingent – and fairly recent – product of specific historical transformations.) Foucault also notes that this medical distinction of the normal and the pathological was fundamental for the "sciences of man" that developed in the nineteenth century.

During the first years (1789–1792) of the Revolution, there was a strong impetus toward medical reform, deriving from a convergence of the demands of the new medical consciousness and of Revolutionary political ideology. The former required a "free field" of inquiry in which, unconstrained by ideal classificatory categories, doctors might pursue without restriction any information relevant to "the formation of an accurate, exhaustive, permanent corpus of knowledge about the health of the population" (38). This striving for freedom of inquiry fit in well with the Revolution's ideology of a free social space, "a space of free communication" (39) unfettered by the arbitrary privileges of the *ancien régime*. Specifically, medical and political considerations alike required the abolition of institutions such as the hospitals, doctors' guilds, and the University medical faculty, which were obstacles both to the pursuit of medical knowledge and the establishment of a free society.

But in spite of these mutually supportive demands for medical reforms and the many proposals they engendered, the Revolution failed to implement any new medical system. According to Foucault, this was because "the subject of medicine remained the same, and concepts were formed according to the same rules" (51). The new medical consciousness (and therefore the Revolutionary discussions based on it) had operated only at the level of theoretical formulations that could do no more than reorganize "already constituted elements of knowledge" and so did not effect any fundamental mutation. What was needed for radical change in medical thought and practice was "a new, coherent, unitary model for the formation of medical objects, perceptions, and concepts" (51). In effect, Foucault is claiming that there had as yet been no change in medicine at the archaeological level. The four elements of medical knowledge that he mentions – objects, perceptions, concepts, and theories – are precisely what he identifies in AK as the elements constituting the "discursives formations" that are the concern of archaeological analysis. Changes at the theoretical level that do not also involve fundamental ontological, epistemological, and conceptual transformations do not represent a change in discursive formation – that is, in the fundamental structures of thought and discourse for a domain.

But Foucault holds that the fundamental structures of the medical domain did change at the beginning of the nineteenth century with the development of what he calls "the clinic." The clinic is for him simultaneously a new institution, the clinical hospital, and a new form or style of medical thought and practice associated with it. On the latter level, the clinic, with its emphasis on careful and exact observation of patients as the foundation of medicine, was one of many instances in the history of medicine of a call for a return to direct experience. But, Foucault notes, such "returns" to experience are never as simple as they seem. They are not – contrary to their own standard self-interpretation – merely renewals of contact with an age-old accumulation of observational truths that persists through theoretical disagreements and transformations. Far from being mere returns to a constant basic experience, they have typically involved changes "in the very grid according to which this experience was given, was articulated into analysable elements, and found a discursive formulation. . . . The fundamental perceptual codes that were applied to patients' bodies, the field of objects to which observation addressed itself, the surfaces and depths traversed by the doctor's gaze, the whole system of orientation varied" (54). A primary task of BC is to chart the change of this sort that accompanied the "return to experience" heralded by clinical medicine.

The clinic as an institution

Foucault first, however, sketches his account of the institutional reforms associated with the epistemic change. The war conditions that existed from 1792 drew so many qualified doctors into military service that civilian medical practice became dominated by quacks and other incompetents. This led, especially after Robespierre's fall in 1794, to a strong movement for fundamental reforms in medical institutions. These were carried out between 1795 and 1803 and involved major changes in the organization of both the medical profession and the hospital system. With regard to the medical profession, Foucault maintains that the reforms ultimately adopted followed the essential lines of a report that Cabanis had submitted in 1798. This report was primarily concerned with the problem of restricting the practice of medicine to qualified physicians without reverting to detailed governmental regulation (which was repugnant to liberal principles) or to the pre-Revolutionary model of medicine as an autonomous corporation ruled by the self-interest of the doctors. Cabanis's solution was to give a central place to the concept of *medical competence*. The right to practice medicine would be a function merely of a person's knowledge, experience, and moral probity, not of his conforming to bureaucratic norms or gaining entrance to a socially privileged circle. Further, the source of medical competence was to be the sort of direct perceptual acquaintance with diseases that was provided by the clinical hospital. Foucault illustrates this by the new distinction between *doctors* and mere *officers of health*. This replaced the old distinction of physician and surgeon, in which the former was accorded a more eminent status in virtue of his theoretical knowledge as opposed to the latter's mere practical experience. The doctor also had a higher status because of his knowledge. But this was not speculative theoretical knowledge but concrete knowledge derived from close observation of patients in clinical hospitals.

These hospitals are, on Foucault's account, the second aspect of the reform of medical practice. There was still a strong attachment to the early Revolutionary idea that a well-regulated society should not need hospitals. Even if disease could not be eliminated, it should, according to liberal principles, be cared for in the home, not in state-controlled institutions. But it became apparent that the goal of eliminating hospitals was entirely unrealistic. There were too many poor and too much concern about the political consequences of distributing large amounts of money to poor families for the care of their sick. "A structure had to be found, for the preservation of both the hospitals and the privileges of medicine, that was compatible with the principles of liberalism and the need for social protection" (82). A solution was found in terms of the value of charity hospitals for medical research. On strictly liberal principles, it made good sense for the rich to support hospitals for the treatment of the poor provided that such hospitals were also used as a locus for study and training that would lead to advances in medical knowledge and improve the competence of doctors. "By paying for [the poor] to be treated, [the rich man] is . . . making possible a greater knowledge of the illnesses with which he himself may be affected" (84). Correspondingly, the poor "pay" for the treatment they receive by allowing themselves to be objects of medical study. "The clinic . . . is the *interest* paid by the poor on the capital that the rich have consented to invest in the hospital" (85). Thus, the clinic in the sense of a charity hospital that was a source of new medical knowledge and the training of new doctors became the focal point of the clinic in the sense of a system of medical practice founded on the direct observation of patients.

But what were the fundamental cognitive transformations that corresponded to this "birth of the clinic"? As we have already noted, Foucault maintains that the clinic's "return" to what is "directly observable" in fact involves seeing medical objects through a new interpretative grid. His next task is the analysis of the structure of this grid, of the new "codes of knowledge" that underlie the clinical gaze. There are, he maintains, two such codes: one expressing a new, linguistic structure of the signs of diseases, another expressing a new aleatory (probabilistic) structure of the domain of medical cases.

The linguistic structure of medical signs

Foucault sees the Classical account of disease as making a crucial distinction between signs and symptoms. The symptom has a privileged position because it "is the form in which the disease is presented: of all that is visible, it is the closest to the essential. . . . The symptoms allow the invariable form of the disease . . . to *show through*" (90). Signs, by contrast, merely announce what is happening, has happened, or will happen. They provide no knowledge of the disease but merely indicate how it is likely to develop over time. For nineteenth-century medicine, by contrast, there is no longer an absolute distinction between signs and symptoms; everything available to the observing gaze (both Classical sign and Classical symptom) is simply a signifier through which the signified (the disease) appears. Corresponding to this merging of sign and symptom is a reduction of disease from an ideal essence to a mere aggregate of phenomena. "There is no longer a pathological essence beyond the symptoms: everything in the disease is itself a phenomenon" (91). There is no room for a privileged class of symptoms because there is no disease beyond the observable signs.

However, the signs of a disease do not simply present themselves as such to the doctor's purely passive consciousness. In order for consciousness to recognize a phenomenon as a sign of a particular disease, it must compare it with phenomena associated with other organisms and with the normal functioning of the organism, notice the frequency with which it occurs in conjunction with other phenomena, and so forth. Calling any pathological phenomenon observed in an organism a "symptom," Foucault says that consciousness is the agency whereby a symptom is turned into a sign – that is, is recognized as an indicator of a disease (which is itself only the aggregate of all such indicators). In the ideal limit of complete knowledge, every symptom would be recognized as a sign of a disease so that "all pathological manifestations would speak a clear, ordered language" (95).

Corresponding to the view that the disease is simply the totality of its symptoms is the view that the nature of the disease can be exhaustively expressed in descriptive language. "In a clinical medicine *to be seen* and *to be spoken* immediately communicate in the manifest truth of the disease of which it is precisely the whole *being*. There is disease only in the element of the visible and therefore statable" (95). This contrasts with the Classical medicine of species, for which there is no direct correspondence between the nature of a disease and what we observe and for which consequently our empirical observation language is never fully adequate to express the essence of a disease.

Foucault notes that this new conception of signs and their role in medical knowledge is isomorphic to the philosophical account of signs developed at the same time by Condillac and others. For example, the process whereby consciousness turns phenomenal symptoms into signs of a disease is just an instance of what Condillac calls "analysis" – that is, "composing and decomposing our ideas in order to make different comparisons with them, and in order to discover by this means the relations that they have among themselves, and the new ideas that they may produce" (cited, 94). Also, the ability of descriptive language to capture totally the nature of disease fits perfectly with Condillac's view of the exact correspondence between empirical language and reality. "The doctor's reflective perception and the philosopher's discursive reflexion on perception come together in a figure of exact superposition, since *the world is for them the analogue of language*" (96).

The probabilistic structure of medical cases

According to Foucault, clinical medicine also deployed a fundamentally new understanding of the place of change and uncertainty in our knowledge of diseases. Of course, it has always been a truism that medical knowledge is uncertain, that the complexity and variety of the cases with which it deals makes its judgments particularly prone to error. But Foucault maintains that, with the advent of clinical medicine, the role of chance and uncertainty no longer merely expressed a defect in medical knowledge and began to take on a positive character. This was because the unpredictable variations among medical cases (the source of uncertainty) were gradually recognized as allowing for application of the mathematical apparatus of the probability theory developed by Laplace and others. "Medicine discovered that uncertainty may be treated, analytically, as the sum of a certain number of isolatable degrees of certainty that were capable of rigorous calculation. Thus, this confused, negative concept, whose meaning derived from a traditional opposition to mathematical knowledge, was to be capable of transforming itself into a positive concept and offered to the penetration of a technique proper to calculation" (97).

This new probabilistic understanding developed slowly from initial vagueness and incoherence. Foucault traces the development through four principal stages. The first involved a new perception of the "complexity of combination." On the Classical view, simplicity increased with generality. By contrast, there developed at the end of the eighteenth century the view that "simplicity is not to be found in the essential generality but at the primary level of the given, in the small number of endlessly repeated elements" (99). (Think, for example, of the status of Hume's "impressions.") As a result, the complexity of individual cases was no longer viewed as merely due to uncontrollable variations that occurred when one descended from the level of general truths about essences. Rather, the complexity was seen as something that could be analyzed into its constitutive elements and thereby exhaustively known.

The second stage involved a change in the use of analogy. For the medicine of species, analogy was merely a matter of similarity to an ideal pathological essence. Classical doctors invoked analogies between a patient's condition and such an essence to justify their diagnoses. But, since there was rarely a complete instantiation of the ideal essence, they were also led to explain away manifest symptoms that did not cohere with their diagnosis as accidental "complications" obscuring the essential truth of the disease. For clinical medicine, analogy was a matter of "an isomorphism of relations between elements" (100). This made diagnosis a matter of identifying the disease present in a given case with what had been observed in others. There was no longer any need to treat a disease as a "mixed reality" in which some elements were mere accidental accretions. It could rather be seen as "a *complex figure* in the coherence of a unity" (101).

This new, nonessentialist view of disease led, Foucault says, to the third stage: a new way of observing the range of different instances of a given disease. Such a range always reveals a number of variations and divergences among different cases of the same disease. Classical medicine merely ignored such deviations as of no significance. On the clinical view it was also true that in many instances the divergences among a large set of cases would prove to be of no ultimate importance. But if certain variant phenomena (e.g., conjunctions of apparently unrelated symptoms) continued through a large series of cases, then clinical medicine was prepared to recognize them as essential features of the disease. This new sensitivity to the "perception of frequencies" reflects the fact that medicine had taken "as its perceptual field not a garden of species but a domain of events" (102). Knowledge of this domain was not a matter of approximation of the eidetic insight of an ideal observer. Rather, it was something achieved only by "the totality of observers," for which the errors of individual observations are eliminated by statistical analysis.

Finally, as the fourth stage, clinical medicine formulated an ideal of developing a method for the calculation of probabilities, a method that would maximize the certitude of medical conclusions. Foucault points out, however, an unresolved ambiguity concerning just what such a method would achieve. Sometimes it seemed that medicine should be content with a *"pathology of phenomena"* – that is, with a knowledge of the laws of the appearance of phenomenal facts. But sometimes it seemed that more was required, that the manifold of phenomenal facts had to find its coherence in a "natural structure," knowledge of which would constitute a *pathology of cases* (103). So even though clinical medicine rejected the Platonism that took diseases as separately existing essences, it was not sure that it could go beyond an Aristotelian construal of diseases as natural kinds to a wholeheartedly positivist phenomenalism. However, this "fundamental contradiction" (105) remained unnoticed by clinical medicine.

As Foucault sees it, the above two codes of knowledge (the linguistic and the probabilistic) define clinical medicine as a science in the sense of a cognitive enterprise grounded in careful observation of specific cases and requiring the cooperation and consensus of an organized community of inquirers. He notes, however, that clinical medicine is not an experimental science. The latter involves putting questions to nature whereas the former is merely a matter of listening to what nature has to say. This, he says, does not mean that clinical medicine is antiexperimental. Its observations will naturally lead to experiment, but the questions posed will be expressed in the language of observation – that is, in the language spoken by nature to the clinical gaze.

Seeing and saying

The mixed visual and aural metaphors employed above are no merely rhetorical device or accident. Rather, they correspond to what we have already seen as a central feature of Foucault's account of clinical medicine: the essential connection between perception and language. "The purity of the gaze is bound up with a certain silence that enables [the doctor] to listen. . . . The clinical gaze has the paradoxical ability to *hear a language* as soon as it *perceives a spectacle*" (107, 108). This connection, already apparent in the notion of an "observation language" that emerged from Foucault's analysis of the linguistic nature of clinical signs, takes the central role in the next stage of his archaeology of clinical perception. This stage centers on the nature of and problems arising from the clinical connection of perception and language. Foucault formulates a first key issue this way: "If the clinical domain is open only to the tasks of language or to the demands of the gaze, it will have no limits and, therefore, no organization" (111). His point seems to be that the separate projects of observing facts about the body and of formulating statements in a clinical language will neither by themselves establish a coherent domain of medical knowledge. Left to themselves, looking and talking will just wander without end or structure from fact to fact, from statement to statement. An organized body of knowledge arises only when experience and language are connected with one another, when what we say is constrained by what we see and what we see is informed and guided by the categorical framework of our language.

Clinical medicine's project of connecting its experience and language began, Foucault says, with the simple demand that perception and speech alternate in medical investigations. Thus, Pinel proposed an ideal method of inquiry in which there is a "regular alteration of speech and gaze" whereby "the disease gradually declares its truth, a truth that it offers to the eye and the ear" (112). But a mere demand that speech and perception be alternately employed is not sufficient to specify a precise correlation whereby each limits and forms the other. According to Foucault, the needed correlation was successfully effected by the project of an ideally exhaustive description. A rigorously complete description requires both perception that omits nothing and language that precisely expresses all that is perceived. Linguistic precision requires that language be constrained by experience in the sense that it must "establish . . . a correlation between each sector of the visible and an expressible element that corresponds to it as accurately as possible" (113). Correspondingly, perceptual completeness can be meaningfully defined only on the basis of the categories implicit in "a constant, fixed vocabulary" (113). In this way, the drive for an exhaustive description of medical reality effects the needed mutually limiting relation between experience and language.

Foucault notes, however, that this crucial ideal of exhaustive description itself rested on a formidable postulate: "that all that is *visible* is *expressible* and that it is *wholly visible* because it is *wholly expressible*" (115). The assumption, in other words, is that the visible and the expressible are entirely convertible. In fact, however, the framework of clinical medicine was not able to support this complete convertibility. True, clinicians thought that there was an "unproblematic equilibrium . . . between the composition of the visible and the syntactic rules of the expressible" (117). It was assumed that what was perceived itself had a linguistic structure that could be unproblematically expressed. But the idea that the elements of perception have a linguistic structure makes sense only on certain conceptions of the nature of language. Foucault suggests that clinical medicine had no account of language capable of sustaining such a view. The assumption of the convertibility or mutual transparency of perception and language left "opaque the status of the language that must be its foundation, its justification, and its delicate instrument" (117). (He notes that a parallel difficulty arises for Condillac's philosophy.)

Foucault maintains that, in place of an appropriate account of the nature of language, clinical medicine offered a number of "myths" that served to cover up the lack. There was, for example, the myth of the "alphabetical structure of disease." This regarded "the singular impression . . . of a symptom" as an irreducible unit out of which a disease was formed, just as letters form words. Related to this was the acceptance of a nominalist view of disease, not only in the sense (which we have already encountered) that the disease has no substantial reality separate from its phenomenal signs but also in the sense (required for the clinic's basic postulate) that "the form of the composition of the being of the disease is of a linguistic type" (119).

He regards two other myths as much more important because they laid the foundation for the transition from clinical to anatomo-clinical medicine. First, there was the move to a chemical model of our knowledge of disease (in contrast to the Classical botanical model). The clinical analysis of diseases into their basic elements was regarded as similar to the chemist's "isolation of pure bodies and . . . depiction of their combinations" (120). Correspondingly, "the clinician's gaze becomes the functional equivalent of fire in chemical combustion; it is through it that the essential purity of phenomena can emerge: it is the separating agent of truths" (120). This is an important transformation of the role of the gaze, which now "no longer merely reads the visible" but also frees its "implicit structure." From now on, the gaze is not merely a reading of reality; "it has to discover its secrets" (120). A similar transformation is effected by a final myth, that of clinical observation as not mere sense perception but as a "fine sensibility," a facility of judgment developed from the doctor's erudition, training, and experience. Such observation is no longer so much a gaze as a *glance*. That is, it is not a matter of meticulously scanning every perceptual element in the field of a disease but of instantly penetrating, in virtue of a trained sensibility, to the essential meaning of what is observed. "The glance chooses a line that instantly distinguishes the essential; it therefore goes beyond what it sees; it is not misled by the immediate forms of the sensible . . .; it is essentially demystifying" (121).

These two myths were not, according to Foucault, just beguiling metaphors that covered over the problem of the convertibility of perception and language. They also suggested a view of medical knowledge that ascribed it a depth and penetration into its object that was not present in the original clinical view. They provided a basis for moving beyond the model of an "ear straining to catch a language" to the model of an "index finger palpating the depths" (122). This made room for clinical methods that did not merely look at the surface of the body but penetrated it to reveal the hidden seats of diseases. These methods, in turn, opened the way for the acceptance of pathological anatomy and its primary instrument, the autopsy, as sources of medical knowledge. The result, as we shall now see, was a fundamental modification in the structure of clinical medicine.

Anatomo-clinical medicine

Standard medical history has always connected the development of clinical medicine to the discovery of pathological anatomy. But it is also generally admitted that this anatomy developed only at the end of the historical process leading to the clinical standpoint. Why was such an essential factor so late in arising? The standard answer has been that the dominance of pathological anatomy was delayed because of the opposition of "religion, morality, and stubborn prejudice" (124) to the dissection of corpses. According to Foucault, however, this view is simply contrary to the historical facts. Doctors generally had no difficulties obtaining corpses and carrying out dissections during the eighteenth century. The standard view confuses what happened during the Renaissance, when there was deep religious and moral opposition to dissection, with the situation during the Enlightenment. In fact, the true reason why pathological anatomy was so late in developing was rooted in the nature of clinical medicine itself. Its concern with directly observable phenomena, carefully scrutinized for temporal patterns and probabilistic frequencies, "was, by its structures, foreign to the investigation of mute, intemporal bodies" that was carried out by dissection (126). Accordingly, before pathological anatomy could be a significant factor, there had to be a basic modification in the clinical viewpoint. This modification was, Foucault argues, effected by Marie-François-Xavier Bichat and his successors.

Bichat shares the viewpoint of clincial medicine in that his "eye is a clinician's eye, because he gives an absolute privilege to the *surface gaze*" (129). However, Foucault thinks his work significantly transforms the meaning of "surface gaze" by putting it into an anatomical context. The surfaces scrutinized by the doctor are those opened up by anatomical dissection, not merely those forming the external body. This change led to a basic shift toward a realistic view of the results of medical analysis. Through Bichat's work, pathological anatomy appears as "an objective, real, and at last unquestionable foundation for the description of diseases" (129). Medical analysis is no longer merely of words or of perceptual units convertible with words but of the real causes of disease. As a result, the contradiction, noted above, between the "pathology of phenomena" and the "pathology of cases" was eliminated in favor of the latter. Thus, there was a move away from the earlier clinical nominalism and toward something more like the realism of the older classificatory medicine. There was no question of a return to the separated essences, but the anatomical approach gave "the old nosological project . . . new vigour, insofar as it seemed to provide it with a solid basis: real analysis according to perceptible surfaces" (131–32).

However, the project of a medicine that would understand and classify diseases on the basis of anatomical truth faced, on Foucault's account, two major difficulties. First, there was the problem of connecting the "simultaneous set of spatial phenomena" revealed by anatomy to the "temporal series" of the external symptoms (134). How, for example, can one tell which anatomical lesions are essential causes of the disease and which only its effects? Similarly, there was no simple correlation between the intensity of anatomical causes and the strength of their effects; for example, a very small tumor might cause death, while major organic changes might have little effect on health. The second major difficulty centered on death. The death of an organism is a major disturbance that may well obscure the true nature of the killing disease. How do we know that what our postmortem dissection reveals is a cause of the disease and not just an effect of the process of dying? Bichat's anatomy provided answers to these questions but, in the process, effected major changes in the meaning of clinical medicine.

Foucault says that, in response to the first difficulty, Bichat and his successors employed a simple method of the comparison of facts. They compared, for example, healthy bodies with diseased ones, different patients who had died from the same disease, and the nature of organs observed in autopsies with what was known about their normal functioning. In this way, it was possible to discern the true place of anatomical lesions in the development of diseases. But this simple comparative method resulted in an important change in the conception of disease. "Disease is no longer a bundle of characters disseminated here and there over the surface of the body. . . . It is no longer a pathological species inserting itself into the body wherever possible; it is the body itself that has become ill" (136).

It might be objected that Foucault is wrong to present this as a major change, since it was just the outcome of a continuous series of successively closer and more fine-grained observations of the body. But he rejects the idea that "the access of the medical gaze into the sick body was . . . the continuation of a movement of approach that had been developing in a more or less regular fashion since the day when the first doctor cast his somewhat unskilled gaze from afar on the body of the first patient" (139). This view misreads history by projecting onto it "an old theory of knowledge whose effects and misdeeds have long been known" (139). Using a distinction that will become fundamental for him in AK, Foucault maintains that the move to pathological anatomy "was the result of a recasting at the level of epistemic knowledge [savoir] itself, and not at the level of accumulated, refined, deepened, adjusted knowledge [connaissances]. . . . It is not a matter of the same game, somewhat improved, but of a quite different game" (137).

In support of his position, Foucault points to the major difference involved in the move from a mere observation of symptomatic correlations to a specification of the anatomical *site* of a disease. The move meant that the essential condition of a disease was no longer any particular set or order of symptoms (which may in fact vary widely) but a specific anatomical lesion. Thus, "the *chronological series* of symptoms" was subordinated to "the *ramifications of the lesional space*" (139). Foucault does not go so far as to say that the earlier clinical view of disease was simply abandoned. But he does claim that it has been fundamentally modified by being introduced "into the specified volume of the body," with the result that "the notion of *seat* has finally replaced that of *class*" (140). That is to say, although medical diagnosis is still a matter of classifying the body's disease, this classification is no longer a primitive fact but rather derives from facts about the location of anatomical lesions.

With regard to the problem of death, Foucault notes that a first step toward a solution was built into the structure of the clinical hospital, which allowed autopsies to be performed immediately after death, so that there was minimal time for distorting effects to operate. But beyond this Bichat employed an important distinction between phenomena connected with a disease itself and phenomena that were part of a relatively autonomous process leading to death. On the basis of this distinction, death is no longer "that absolute, privileged point at which time stops and moves back"; it is rather a process, "multiple, dispersed in time" (142). As such, death can be understood in its own terms and "can no longer be confused with the disease or with its traces" (143). With its distorting effects thus controlled, death, in virtue of the dissections it allows, becomes the key to the knowledge of disease. The analytic knowledge that the myths of the clinic had vainly sought in mathematical, chemical, and linguistic models, it now found in death.

This new view of death represented a major change from the view, dominant since the Renaissance, that "the knowledge of life was based on the essence of the living" (145). After Bichat, "knowledge of life finds its origin in the destruction of life." (145). This required that medicine free itself from its long-standing fear of death as the abolition of medical skill and knowledge. But, more than this, Bichat's work "integrated . . . death into a technical and conceptual totality" of a new medical viewpoint. Because of the fundamental changes effected by the integration of anatomical pathology, Foucault is even willing to claim that "the great break in the history of Western medicine dates precisely from the moment clinical experience became the anatomo-clinical gaze" (146). This break involves, first of all, a new conception of disease, which is no longer "an event or nature imported from the outside" but rather a specific form of life itself. "The idea of a disease attacking life must be replaced by the much denser notion of *pathological life*" (153). Foucault thinks this new conception derives from the localization of disease as a disorder at a specific site within the body. Disease is a form of life in the precise sense that it is a particular direction the body's life takes. This direction is one of degeneration, leading ultimately to death. Hence, disease is a form of life to the extent that life itself has an intrinsic connection to death. Death is the ultimate end toward which life moves, and disease lies on the trajectory of that motion. "Now death is the very source of disease, a possibility intrinsic to life that makes disease possible" (156). Accordingly, death becomes the crucial third term that defines the relationship between life and disease. "In anatomical perception, death was the point of view from the height of which disease opened up onto truth; the life/disease/death trinity was articulated in a triangle whose summit culminated in death" (158).

Foucault argues that, corresponding to this new conception of disease, there is a major transformation of medical perception, signaled by a new construal of the notion of *sign*. The phenomenal signs doctors observe on the surface of the body lose their privileged status as direct indicators of disease. They are significant only to the extent that they refer to lesions within the body, which are now the only sure signs of disease. Given this new understanding of signs, medical perception takes on a very different character. It is no longer a two-dimensional reading of a series of symptoms but rather a three-dimensional mapping of a volume, the third dimension representing the connection of surface symptoms to events and structures within the body. Foucault sums up this new form of medical perception as a "structure . . . of *invisible visibility*" (165). Previously, the primary object of medical perception was the sensory data visible on the surface of the body. Now it sees through this "superficial" visibility to the "fundamental visibility" within the body that is unveiled by pathological anatomy.

Foucault also maintains that the new mode of perception involves a reconstrual of the notion of medical *case*. In clinical experience, the case was viewed as part of a series that revealed the essential nature of the disease, a series in which individual idiosyncrasies of particular cases would be eliminated as not statistically significant. But for anatomo-clinical experience, each case can be appreciated in its full individuality. "Only individual illnesses exist" (168). This is because the space of illness has now been entirely identified with the bodily space of the individual suffering from it. The entire reality and meaning of disease resides in its specific bodily sites. In this way, Foucault notes, contrary to the long-standing Aristotelian doctrine, a science of the individual is not only possible but necessary. Ironically, it was death, the destruction of the individual, that was the key unlocking this "forbidden, imminent secret: the knowledge of the individual" (170).

Carried to its logical conclusion, the anatomo-clinical view required the identification of the disease itself with the corresponding internal lesion. The lesion could not be just an effect (sometimes, perhaps, not even present) of the disease. This full identification, however, was not made by the early developers of pathological anatomy. Bichat himself, for example, allowed for some cases of diseases for which there was no corresponding organic lesion at all. Foucault holds that the full flowering of the anatomo-clinical view came only with Broussais's work on fevers. Broussais opposed the claim, defended, for example, by Pinel, that there were "essential fevers," which did not originate in organic lesions. Attacking Pinel's account, Broussais established the view that all fevers and indeed all diseases are locally situated. "From now on, the organic space of the localization is really independent of the space of the nosological configuration" (186).

On Foucault's account, Broussais's fulfillment and completion of Bichat's work effects the final transformations of medical perception. He sees, in particular, two main final changes. First, the order of priority between visibility and localization is reversed. For Bichat, diseases are localized because they are visible to anatomical scrutiny. After Broussais, localization in an organic site is the fundamental feature, from which visibility follows as a consequence. Second, Broussais makes "the local space of the disease . . . also, immediately, a causal space" (189). For Bichat, the local site of a disease is merely its point of spatial and temporal origin. For Broussais, what happens at this site (specifically, the irritation of tissues) is the cause of the disease, which indeed has no longer any reality other than that of the effect, perhaps eventually spread throughout the body, of a disorder (lesion) of an organ. "Disease is now no more than a certain complex movement of tissues in reaction to an irritating cause: it is in this that the whole essence of the pathological lies" (189).

With these final transformations, the Classical view of disease as something independent of the sick body is entirely eliminated. "The space of the disease is, without remainder or shift, the very space of the organism" (191). Foucault agrees that Broussais's work has been rightly criticized for some respects in which it was a return to antiquated medical concepts such as sympathy and practices such as bleeding. But he thinks that medical historians have overemphasized these reversions and failed to notice that even they are part of a structure that, as a whole, represents the essence of modern medicine. In spite of all the limitations and regressions of his work, Broussais "had fixed for his period the final element of *the way to see*. . . . The historical and concrete a priori of the modern medical gaze was finally constituted" (192).

The birth of the clinic: methods and results

In his concluding remarks, Foucault presents BC as an exercise in a method of writing intellectual history: "This book is, among others, an attempt to apply a method to the confused, understructured, and ill-structured domain of the history of ideas" (195). His understanding of the purpose and nature of this method was earlier expressed in the book's preface. There he begins with the skeptical thought that our age is, no doubt, one of criticism, but not, as for Kant, criticism (critique) that can start from the fact of knowledge. Rather, our critique can start only from the "fact that language exists," with no assumptions about its truth or validity. We cannot expect to find large truths about our nature and destiny in the wisdom of what has been said or to evaluate this wisdom on the basis of our own uncovering of such truths. We can only try to understand "the innumerable words spoken by men" through which "a meaning has taken shape that hangs over us." There is no hope of breaking through this web of language to a world of fundamental truths. "We are doomed historically to history, to the patient construction of discourses about discourses, and to the task of hearing what has already been said" (xvi).

But Foucault also maintains that our discourse about discourses need not take the form it almost always has in the modern world: that of *commentary*. Commentary is an effort to "uncover the deeper meaning of speech." It is based on the assumption that there is, in what has been said, something not explicitly expressed that is nonetheless implicitly present as the fundamental meaning intended by those who have spoken. In short, "commentary" is the technique employed by modern efforts at the hermeneutic understanding of texts.

As we have seen, even in FD, Foucault saw the need to move beyond this sort of hermeneutic analysis of meaning. But, although FD employed a nonhermeneutic (archaeological) method of analysis, it did not articulate a reflective understanding of that method. The preface to BC shows that Foucault has at least begun to develop such an understanding. He suggests that, as an alternative to commentary, it may be "possible to make a structural[1] analysis of discourses that would evade the fate of commentary by supposing no remainder, nothing in excess of what has been said, but only the fact of its historical appearance" (xvii). Such an approach, he says, would not construe the meaning of a statement in terms of a speaker's intention; rather, meaning would be a function of the statement's role in a system of statements, determined by "the difference that articulates [the statement] upon the other real or possible statements." Here Foucault adumbrates the view of the archaeological level of analysis that AK works out in detail.

He proposes this sort of analysis as an alternative to the methods of standard history of thought. These methods he characterizes as either "aesthetic" or "psychological." The former works from analogies between the views of different thinkers, which are charted either diachronically as "geneses, filiations, kinships, influences" or synchronically as "the spirit of a period, its *Weltanschauung*, its fundamental categories, the organization of its sociocultural world" (xvii). In either case, the history operates entirely on the level of the intentional content of what has been said. The psychological approach operates at the same level but tries to reverse the apparent meanings of texts through, for example, a

1. Later printings of BC omit the adjective "structural" in this passage.

"psychoanalysis" of thought that would show how a certain thinker or age was not as rational or irrational as a surface reading indicates.[2] Neither of these methods allows us to overcome the limitations of thinking of meaning in terms of the speaker's conscious or unconscious intentions.

In BC, then, Foucault explicitly sets out to employ the sort of archaeological approach he had, because of the exigencies of his discussion, implicitly developed in FD. His approach initially parallels FD in its focus on both discursive and nondiscursive factors. The development of modern medicine is portrayed as a complex of new ways of thinking and perceiving and new institutional forms. As in FD, no clear priority is given to either; the reforms of the early Revolutionary period and the first moves toward a new conception of illness seem to be mutually constitutive. However, as Foucault's analysis progresses, it comes to deal almost exclusively with the concepts (both substantive and methodological) of medical discourse. There is a thorough analysis of the clinical and the anatomo-clinical concepts of illness and of the new conceptions of medical observation associated with them, but very little discussion of how these are related to the institutional structure of the clinical hospital.

In this analysis of illness Foucault's method is essentially that of Canguilhem's history of concepts. As we saw, Foucault was not able to use this method in FD for two reasons. First, Classical and (to some extent) modern views of madness lacked the canonical set of concepts and theories needed to guide a normative history of science. But this was not so for the modern view of disease that is the primary concern of BC. Here there is a single, generally accepted concept of disease as an internal disorder of the patient's body that does in fact guide Foucault's historical account. Thus, just as Canguilhem identifies Willis as the originator of the concept of the reflex, Foucault identifies Bichat as the originator of the modern concept of disease. And, just as Canguilhem follows later important modifications of the concept of the reflex by Astruc, Unzer, and others, Foucault traces later developments of the concept of disease by Broussais.

The second factor that moved the history of madness beyond

<hr>

2. Foucault may mean to include Bachelard among those employing the "psychological" approach, although Bachelard does not typically use his psychoanalysis of knowledge as a way of undermining the apparent significance of scientific texts.

the resources of the history of scientific concepts was the need to take account of an evaluative consciousness of madness that underlay the allegedly value-neutral conceptions of modern psychology and psychiatry. To the extent that Foucault connects medical discourse to institutional practices (and hence to the values implicit in them), his discussion does, like that of FD, go beyond any straightforward applications of Canguilhem's method. But, as we have seen, this aspect receives progressively less emphasis in BC, and the final detailed analyses of both the clinical and the anatomo-clinical concepts of illness are almost entirely a matter of the history of concepts.

Besides its methodological connections to Canguilhem's historical work, BC also has important affinities with his philosophical analysis of the normal and the pathological (in NP). In fact, BC can be plausibly viewed as providing a historical background to Canguilhem's philosophical discussion. However, Foucault does not discuss Canguilhem's main theses (e.g., concerning the qualitative differences between the normal and the pathological); and, overall, his historical account is consistent with but strictly neutral with respect to Canguilhem's philosophical views of norms and the normal.

Despite the decreasing emphasis in BC on the tie of clinical medicine to the new bourgeois institutions and values of the French Revolution, Foucault's discussion does provide some basis for a critique of the moral values hidden beneath the alleged pure objectivity and value-neutrality of modern medicine. Moreover, we get a sense of how he himself would carry out such a critique from his acid comments in the Preface (xiv–xv) on the purported humanity and compassion of modern medical treatment and from the irony of his discussion of the "contract" between rich and poor that set up the clinical hospital. However, the thrust of BC is much more toward a purely epistemological critique of clinical medicine. Specifically, it undermines medicine's positivist conception of its method as merely the direct observation of what is immediately apparent. Foucault shows that what presents itself as nothing more than fidelity to what is simply given to any naive gaze is actually a mode of perception based on a complexly structured interpretative grid. His analysis is a splendid instance of laying bare the a priori presuppositions involved in reports of allegedly uninterpreted data. As such, it has the same general significance as the critiques of the theory/observation distinction developed at about the same time by English-speaking philosophers of science such as Hanson, Kuhn, and Feyerabend. (However, like Canguilhem, Foucault sees concepts rather than theories as the primary interpretative elements.)

It is important to note that neither aspect of his critique of modern medicine leads Foucault to deny that it is based on an objective body of scientific knowledge. Like Bachelard, who emphasized the controlling role of reason in the experiments of physics and chemistry without denying the objectivity of these disciplines, Foucault does not present the interpretative grid of modern medicine as undercutting its scientific status. Nor does he think that the value-ladenness and ideological content of medicine exclude its objectivity.[3] In AK (181), as we shall see, he explicitly notes that it would be a mistake to deny that pathological anatomy is a science because of the connections of clinical medicine to institutional norms. And he goes on to maintain that, in general, ideological significance is compatible with scientific objectivity. Consequently, as was the case with psychology and psychiatry, the critique of medicine supported by BC does not lead to a global rejection of it.[4] Rather, it suggests specific ways of calling into question important aspects of its self-understanding. Once again, Foucault's critique of reason is limited and local, not an all-dissolving skepticism.

Among historians, BC has been the best received of all Foucault's books.[5] There have been (entirely justified) complaints about the often opaque style, but few serious objections to his main theses. This is no doubt due, first, to the fact that Foucault here operates on a much smaller scale than in FD (or OT) and so avoids the sorts of sweeping generalizations we find in his other books. Further, his critique of medicine, as we have seen, primarily takes the form of an epistemological analysis of its conceptual framework and does not seriously challenge its status as scientific

3. François Dagognet (like Foucault, a student of Canguilhem) criticized BC for taking too positive a view of clinical medicine and not developing the sort of critique that FD provided for psychiatry. Cf. "Archéologie ou histoire de la médecine," *Critique* 21 (1965), 436–47.
4. Similarly, the same points made in Chapter 2 about the difficulties of moving from the history of Classical and early modern madness to a criticism of contemporary psychiatry apply to the use of Foucault's history of the clinic for the critique of current medicine.
5. Cf., for example, reviews by Karl Figlio, *British Journal for the History of Science* 10 (1977), 164–67, F. N. L. Poynter, *History of Science* 3 (1964), 140–43, and Stanley J. Reiser, *Social Science and Medicine* 10 (1976), 124.

knowledge. Thus, there is much less to make conventional historians uneasy.

From the point of view of Foucault's own project, one major flaw in BC is its failure to follow through on the connections, discussed in the earlier part of the book, between clinical knowledge and the nondiscursive structures (e.g., institutions) associated with it. Further, even to the extent that these connections are discussed, Foucault fails to give a clear account of just how discursive and nondiscursive factors are related. He notes, for example, that the French Revolution's efforts at medical reform effected no fundamental change because they were not correlated with any fundamental (i.e., archaeological) changes in thought. Real reform, he seems to say, was contingent on the prior development of a new form of knowledge (clinical medicine). But then he seems to present clinical medicine as itself an outcome of the institutional reforms (based on Cabanis's proposals) that produced the clinical hospital. This leaves us wondering how these reforms, any more than those undertaken earlier, could have effected a fundamental transformation without a prior change in the system of medical knowledge. Unfortunately, it is at just this point that Foucault turns to a purely internal analysis of clinical discourse and abandons the queston of its nondiscursive connections.

Foucault's next book, OT, explicitly limits itself to the internal analysis of discourse, and apart from some tentative methodological suggestions in AK, Foucault does not return to the interrelations of the discursive and the nondiscursive until DP. All this reflects the great difficulty he had, while developing his archaeological method, in coming to grips with the central issue of the place of knowledge in the realm of historical causes and effects.

Another limitation of BC from Foucault's own point of view is precisely its restriction to a history of concepts. This no doubt put him on firmer ground historically, but it kept him from developing the connections of medical discourse with other systems of discourse – the sort of connections that are essential to an archaeological analysis. This may be what Foucault has in mind when, in AK, he criticizes BC for tending to "bypass . . . the level proper to archaeology" (AK, 16). In OT, however, as we shall now see, the archaeological method returns in full force.

4

THE ORDER OF THINGS: I. FROM RESEMBLANCE TO REPRESENTATION

The ultimate concern of *The order of things* (OT) is the cognitive status of the modern "human sciences" or "sciences of man." Foucault maintains that, to understand this status, we need to understand the place of these sciences in the overall epistemological field of modern knowledge. This in turn requires a grasp of what knowledge means in modern culture, what forms it takes, and where, among these forms, the human sciences are situated. OT's effort to achieve this understanding is based on several fundamental propositions. The first is that what knowledge means has varied from one historical period to another; specifically, in recent Western culture, the Renaissance (roughly, the sixteenth century), the Classical Age (from the mid-seventeenth century to the end of the eighteenth century), and the Modern Age (from the beginning of the nineteenth century to at least the middle of the twentieth) have all had very different conceptions of knowledge. Second, a given epoch's conception of knowledge is ultimately grounded in its "experience of order" – that is, the fundamental way in which it sees things connected to one another. For example, in the Renaissance, things were ordered through resemblance, whereas in the Classical Age order was a matter of relations of strict identity and difference. Third, since knowledge is always a matter of somehow formulating truths about things, its nature in a given period will depend on the period's construal of the nature of the signs used to formulate truths. Fourth, since the signs most important for formulating knowledge claims are linguistic ones, the nature of knowledge depends on an epoch's conception of language.

Accordingly, in order to understand the cognitive status of the human sciences, we need to understand the modern conceptions of order, signs, and language. Put roughly, such a set of conceptions, along with the conception of knowledge they entail, constitutes what Foucault calls the *episteme* of a period. Moreover, since an episteme is not an invariant cultural absolute, we need to understand it against the background of previous epistemes, specifically, in the case of our modern period, those of the Renaissance and the Classical Age. From this, we can appreciate the overall structure of OT. It begins with a relatively brief description of the Renaissance episteme and the knowledge based on it, moves to a much more detailed analysis of the Classical episteme and knowledge, elucidates the nature of the modern episteme and its knowledge through a comparison with that of the Classical Age, and, finally, uses this understanding of modern knowledge to determine the status of the human sciences.

The Renaissance episteme

As already noted, the Renaissance, on Foucault's account, saw things as ordered through their resemblances to one another. The nature of resemblance (or similarity) can be appreciated by reflecting on what Foucault presents as its four principal forms: convenience, emulation, analogy, and sympathy. The first connotation of convenience (*convenientia*) is spatial proximity rather than similarity. But the Renaissance idea is that at "the hinge between two things a resemblance appears" (18). In fact, spatial proximity involves resemblance in two ways. Things are together because of an antecedent similarity between them, and they become more similar as a result of their proximity. The soul and the body provide a good example. "The soul had to be made dense, heavy, and terrestrial for God to place it in the very heart of matter. But through this propinquity, the soul receives the movements of the body and assimilates itself to that body" (18). Through relations of convenience, everything in the world is linked together in a chain, each link bound to those adjacent by resemblances associated with convenience. The second principal form of resemblance is emulation (*aemulatio*). Unlike convenience, it is not tied to spatial proximity. Rather, through it things resemble one another even from great distances, like reflections in mirrors. There are, for example, relations of emulation between the human face and the sky, between man's intellect and God's, between the features of the human face (eyes, nose, mouth) and various heavenly bodies. Like convenience, emulation unites the world into a whole. But here it is not a matter of adjacent links in a chain "but rather a series of concentric circles reflecting and rivaling one another" (21).

Whereas convenience and emulation involve resemblances between properties, Foucault presents analogy as a matter of resemblance between relations. Because of this, it effects much more subtle and less obvious connections between things. Like convenience and emulation, analogy unites the entire world, but it is distinctive in that it makes man the center of this unity. This is because, for Renaissance thought, "all analogies can find one of their necessary terms in him. . . . He is the great fulcrum of proportions – the center upon which reflections are concentrated and from which they are once again reflected" (22, 23).

Finally, there is sympathy, resemblance operating as a principle of spatial movement and qualitative change. It is, for example, by sympathy that heavy objects are attracted to the earth and light things to the weightless ether. Moreover, things that move through space in virtue of sympathy also change their qualities, becoming more like the realm into which they move. For example, when fire rises into the air, it undergoes a series of changes that eventually change it into air. This illustrates the dangerous tendency of sympathy to assimilate things to one another. "Left to itself, sympathy would eventually reduce the entire world to a homogeneous mass, to the featureless form of the Same" (24). This is prevented, however, by the compensating force of antipathy (illustrated by natural enmities between animals and by herbal medicines that produce offsetting effects), which isolates things and works against their assimilation. Through the counterbalancing play of sympathy and antipathy, things "can resemble others and be drawn to them . . . without being swallowed up or losing their singularity" (24–25). Foucault notes that the Renaissance saw "the movement and dispersion created by . . . the sympathy-antipathy pair" as giving rise to and explaining the other three forms of resemblance (25).

The above discussion should give us a sense of how, on Foucault's account, Renaissance thought ordered the world in terms of relations of resemblance. The next question concerns the nature of the signs through which knowledge of the world's resemblances can be formulated. Foucault argues that a key feature of the Renaissance episteme is that the signs whereby the resemblances of the world are known are themselves resemblances. A resemblance functioning as a sign of another resemblance is called a *signature*. As an example, Foucault mentions the case of aconite, a plant that was used to treat diseases of the eye because of a "sympathy" between it and the eye. The sign (signature) by which we are able to recognize this relation of sympathy is the analogy between the eyes and the seeds of the plant: "They are tiny dark globes seated in white skinlike coverings whose appearance is much like that of eyelids covering an eye" (27). Thus, the sign of one kind of resemblance (a sympathy) is another kind of resemblance (an analogy). This is typical of Renaissance knowledge. The sign of a sympathy may be an analogy, the sign of an analogy an emulation, of an emulation, a convenience, of a convenience a sympathy once again. In this (and similar) ways, Renaissance thought pursued knowledge of its world through an unending spiral of linked resemblances, each a sign of another. The system of the world and the system of knowledge of the world had, accordingly, the same essential structure, that of a complex of interconnected resemblances. Knowledge of signs in their own right (which Foucault calls semiology) and knowledge of what signs tell us about the world (hermeneutics) were collapsed onto one another. The collapse, however, did not, in his view, mean that knowledge and nature entirely coincided. This would have required that each resemblance in the world be its own sign (signature) and that, in consequence, all truth be immediately apparent. Instead, truth had to be sought through the endless pursuit of the chain of signs.

At this point, Foucault is able to draw some important consequences regarding the nature of knowledge for the Renaissance. (Others will follow from the specific nature of linguistic signs.) First, Renaissance knowledge is "plethoric yet absolutely poverty-stricken" (30). It is plethoric in the sense that the system of resemblances is endless, any one leading to an infinite chain of others. But for this very reason it is also poverty-stricken: "The whole world must be explored if even the slightest of analogies [for example] is to be justified and finally take on the appearance of certainty" (30). Sure knowledge requires an infinite accumulation of successively dependent confirmations. To be certain, for instance, that a given relationship of sympathy exists, we may have to know that a given analogy holds; to be sure of the analogy, we may have to be sure of an emulation, and so on. To some extent, this difficulty is overcome by the famous Renaissance doctrine of the mirroring of the macrocosm by the microcosm. This guarantees that knowledge of a subsystem of the world can be an adequate guide to knowledge of the whole and so limits the extent of our pursuit of similarities. Foucault notes that for his analysis, in contrast to the ordinary view, the microcosm–macrocosm relation is not part of the fundamental structure of Renaissance knowledge but merely a "surface effect" functioning to solve a problem.

Another important consequence concerns a feature of Renaissance knowledge that is particularly puzzling for us: its acceptance of magic and of erudition (citations of ancient authorities) on a par with what we can recognize as scientific rationality. Even in as late a figure as Newton, we find enduring achievements in mechanics and optics disconcertingly side by side with the serious pursuit of alchemy and bizarre Scriptural exegesis. To us, such combinations seem unstable, reflecting an unfortunate confusion that was eventually overcome by recognizing the priority of rational, scientific methods. But, on Foucault's account, the acceptance of science, magic, and erudition on equal epistemic terms follows from the basic structure of the Renaissance episteme. As an example, he cites the magical practice of divination (foretelling the future from present signs), which is merely an instance of the interpretation of signatures (i.e., inference from a sign to a resemblance it signifies) that is knowledge for the Renaissance. Moreover, since the signs interpreted are themselves resemblances and, as such, part of the world, it is surely to be expected that operations carried out on or with them will have effects in that world. So there is nothing bizarre in, say, Paracelsus's claim that snakes are repelled by certain Greek words. According to Foucault, then, the "Natural Magics" that historians of thought have encountered at the end of the sixteenth century are not "a vestigial phenomenon in the European consciousness"; they arise "because the fundamental configuration of knowledge consisted of the reciprocal cross-reference of signs and similitudes. The form of magic was inherent in this way of knowledge" (33).

Similarly, it made perfect sense for Foucault's Renaissance to seek knowledge of the world through the interpretation of the texts of ancient authors. For these texts (of Scripture and of Greek and Roman antiquity) were just further sets of signs put into the world by God as indicators of truth about resemblances. "There is no difference between the visible marks that God has stamped upon the surface of the earth, so that we may know its inner secrets, and the legible words that the Scriptures, or the sages of Antiquity, have set down in the books preserved for us by tradition" (33). Thus, both magic and erudition have a natural place in the Renaissance conception of knowledge.

To complete his account of Renaissance knowledge, Foucault turns to the status of language. As a particular system of signs, language in the Renaissance was, of course, a part of the world itself, one segment of the complexly intertwined system of resemblances. As a result, language was studied (e.g., by Ramus) in the same way as any other natural object. Further, since language was assimilated to the enduring marks (signatures) found on physical objects, priority was given to its written form. Foucault suggests that this privileged position of written over spoken language is closely related to such well-known Renaissance developments as the invention of movable type, the interest in ancient manuscripts, and the priority assigned the text of Scripture over Church tradition. (He says, however, that it is not possible to determine which are causes and which effects of the priority of writing.)

The primacy of writing in the Renaissance view of language accounts for two other distinctive features of knowledge in this period. The first – again, very difficult for us to understand – is the failure to distinguish between "what is seen and what is read," between directly observed facts and claims made by possibly unreliable sources. For example, in the work of Ulisse Aldrovandi on "serpents and dragons," there is "an inextricable mixture of exact description, reported quotations, fables without commentary" (39). For Buffon, writing from the standpoint of the later Classical episteme, this made Aldrovandi's works a "hotch-potch" containing only a small portion of real natural history. But for Aldrovandi the distinction between the observed and the merely reported, which meant so much to Buffon, was of little significance. For him, natural signs, directly observed, are just as much writing (*legenda*) as are words themselves. Accordingly, there is no particular reason to emphasize the differences between, say, the fact that an animal has a certain color skin and the fact that it figures in certain myths. Foucault's point is not, it seems to me, that Renaissance naturalists believed the myths they recounted; there is no reason to think they were more credulous than people a century and a half later or that they were doing anything more than recording the fact that certain stories had been told. The difference between the Renaissance and the Classical Age – between Aldrovandi and Buffon – is not about whether the myths are true but about whether information about myths has an essentially different status from information about direct observations of an animal. Renaissance naturalists were certainly capable of understanding the distinction in question; but, because of their subsumption of both observations and myths to the category of written signs, they had no reason to give it any special weight.

The second consequence Foucault draws from the privileged place of writing in the Renaissance is the central epistemic role of *commentary*. Given the assimilation, via the primacy of writing, of language to natural "signatures," knowledge becomes nothing other than "relating one form of language to another form of language" (40). Accordingly, knowledge is inevitably expressed in the "secondary discourse of commentary," languages interpreting language. Since commentary is itself language, it too can be commented on; hence there is no limit to it, no end, as Montaigne said, to books about books. However, the Renaissance's projects of commentary are ultimately controlled by the "sovereignty of an original Text" that "offers its ultimate revelation as the promised reward of commentary" (41). This, of course, is the fundamental truth of the world as expressed by God in His creation. It is the ultimate reality that provides the standard for the truth of Renaissance linguistic expressions.

In summary, then, Foucault presents the Renaissance episteme as ordering the world in terms of relations of resemblances and as likewise construing signs as constituted by their resemblance to what they signify. Language (with writing given primacy) then becomes itself a part of the world, a subsystem of resemblances.

The resulting conception of knowledge is one that places magic, erudition, and science on a par, that makes no essential distinction between direct observations and reported stories, that takes the form of commentary, and that is the essentially incomplete pursuit of an unending chain of similarities.

Classical order

Around the middle of the seventeenth century, there occurred what Foucault regards as a radical break with the Renaissance episteme, and Western thought took on a fundamentally different character during the Classical Age. This new structure of thought (new episteme) was based on a new conception of how things in the world are ordered. The principle of ordering ceases to be resemblance and becomes relations of identity and difference. Foucault finds the Classical viewpoint first fully apparent in Descartes's *Rules for the direction of the mind*, which explicitly presents resemblances as occasions of error rather than objects of knowledge. A similar critique can be found in Bacon's discussion of the idols of the mind, but Foucault thinks that Bacon, unlike Descartes, does not offer a method for avoiding the deceptions of resemblance and for building a positive body of knowledge. He expresses the uneasiness of the Renaissance with itself rather than the new Classical viewpoint.

Foucault allows that for Descartes – and the Classical Age in general – resemblances between things must still be the starting point of inquiries leading to knowledge. But resemblances are no longer regarded as expressing the true order of reality, an order that is rather to be found in the structure of the elements into which things and their resemblances can be analyzed. These elements are related not by vague and ambiguous resemblances but by strict identities and differences (presence or absence of particular properties). On the basis of these identities and differences, elements can be arranged in series (e.g., from the simplest to the most complex) in terms of precise criteria.

The properties that characterize things and enable them to be related to one another via a precise system of identities and differences may be quantitative and hence expressible in terms of a common unit of measurement. To the extent that this is so, the world (nature) will form a mathematical system and our knowledge of it will be a kind of algebra. However, Foucault maintains that the Classical order of things was not an essentially mathematical one. Even nonmathematical, purely qualitative properties could be the basis of relations of strict identity and difference. (A good example, which we will discuss more fully, is the ordering of living things in the classifications of natural history.) Consequently, Foucault opposes the standard view that finds the essence of Classical thought in reductionist projects of mechanism and mathematization (56). The Classical episteme does see the world as a set of elements ordered by precise identities and differences rather than vague resemblances. But these identities and differences need not be – and in many important cases were not – quantitative. The general science of order (*mathesis*) to which Classical thought aspired was not identical with a mathematical understanding of nature; the analysis by which it moved from resemblances to properly ordered elements was not reducible to algebra.

The Classical conception of the order of things, even apart from its new conceptions of signs and language, which we will discuss below, has major effects on the conception of knowledge. Foucault's fundamental point, of course, is that knowledge is no longer a matter of recognizing resemblances but of extracting from resemblances precise comparisons of the identities and differences of things' properties. From this he thinks there follow two major sets of modifications in what is meant by knowledge. First, there are changes in the process whereby knowledge is attained. The primary instrument of knowledge becomes the analysis of resemblances, not their mere recognition. No resemblance will be accepted as of any cognitive significance until it is "subjected to proof by comparison [of identities and differences]" (55). Consequently, the mind's essential activity in knowing is no longer the connecting of things but their discrimination. Its primary role is no longer to draw things together on the basis of their resemblances but to separate them on the basis of their differences. Second, there are changes in the character of the knowledge the mind attains. Because it dealt with an unending chain of resemblances, Renaissance knowledge was necessarily incomplete and merely probable. By contrast, the elements revealed by Classical analysis could be completely enumerated and exhaustively understood. Accordingly, Classical knowledge could, at least in principle, attain complete certitude. Further modifications in the conception of knowledge are tied to new

Classical conceptions of signs and language, to which we now turn.

Classical signs and language

Foucault finds three fundamental contrasts between the Classical conception of signs and that of the Renaissance. The first concerns the relation of signs to the human minds that deal with them. For the Renaissance, a sign was a part of the world given to man, like any other resemblance. It was there for us to discover, but there whether or not we did in fact discover it. For the Classical Age, by contrast, a sign as such exists only for a knowing mind: "There can no longer be an unknown sign, a mute mark" (59). This means, then, that signs are no longer antecedently present objects given to our knowledge but rather intrinsic parts of knowledge itself. The locus of signs has moved from the world to the mind. As a result, degrees of certainty (from minimal probability to absolute certainty) are now intrinsic characteristics of signs, not merely states of the minds that employ them.

A second contrast with the Renaissance is that signs (no longer construed as resemblances) do not serve to draw things together but to separate and disperse them. This is because the sign is now essentially connected with analysis. This connection is, in fact, twofold. The sign is both the result of analysis (since for an element of our experience to become a sign it must be differentiated from the impression in which it is confusedly given) and the instrument of analysis (which is carried out by applying signs to further impressions).

Thirdly, whereas the Renaissance gave priority to natural signs, for Classical thought conventional signs have pride of place. This follows from the placing of signs in the mind. Natural signs are awkward and inconvenient because they typically do not fit easily and effectively into the mind's workings. Conventional signs – arbitrary in that we construct them but not arbitrary in that our construction is constrained by the functions we need them to perform – are much easier to deal with. The ideal system of arbitrary signs would achieve two complementary goals. On the one hand, it would provide a framework for identifying the simplest elements out of which any system being analyzed is composed; on the other hand, it would provide a means of combining these elements to produce every possible configuration of the system. For us, there seems to be a tension between these two functions of a sign system. Why, we may ask, should we expect the signs that accurately pick out the actual elements from which a real system is built to be also effective logical instruments for constructing all possible combinations of these elements? Doesn't it often happen that calculational efficiency requires a fictional construal of the system being dealt with (as when we find geocentric astronomy a more efficient instrument for calculating motions on the surface of the earth)? But, as Foucault presents it, the Classical episteme leaves no place for such questions, since it sees reality itself as ordered in terms of the very same system of relations (identities and differences) that order signs. Because of this, a sign system built from primitives that adequately correspond to the basic elements of the world would have exactly the same logical structure as the world.

This last point brings us to the fundamental question of the relation of Classical signs to what they signify. According to Foucault, for the Renaissance this relation was, as we have seen, resemblance. Just as things in the world resembled one another, so signs resembled what they signified. Indeed, as resemblances, signs were simply part of the world they signified. For Classical thought, by contrast, he holds that signs are ontologically separated from the world and instead exist in an ideal mental order. But Foucault also argues that, precisely because they are ontologically separated, Classical signs as such are directly related to what they signify, without any intermediary such as a resemblance to the signified. Whether or not a sign happens to resemble what it signifies, it directly *represents* it in the way that an idea represents its object. In fact, Classical signs are ideas (or similar mental representations such as perceptions, images, or sensations). (Foucault, following Classical writers, will also speak of material things such as maps and pictures as signs, but presumably this is only in virtue of their relations to the complexes of ideas that they instantiate.) However, a sign is not merely an idea or other mental representation. An idea is a sign only on the condition that "it manifests . . . the relation that links it to what it signifies" (64). In other words, the sign "must represent; but that representation, in turn, must also be represented within it" (64).

Foucault recognizes, accordingly, two essential features of a Classical sign in relation to what it signifies. First, it signifies its object by representing it and, indeed, "has no content, no function, and no determination other than what it represents" (64). In contrast to a Renaissance sign, which signified in virtue of the similarity of its intrinsic content to the content of what it signified, the Classical sign directly ("transparently") represents the content of the object it signifies. Second, "this content is indicated only in a representation that posits itself as such . . ." (64). This is what Foucault means by speaking of the Classical sign as a "duplicated representation" (65). It is "doubled over on itself" in the sense that it refers to its own representative function. Foucault suggests that both these features are particularly apparent in maps or pictures (or the ideas they express), which the Port Royal Grammar gives as primary examples of signs. A map or a picture is exhausted in its representation of its object; every property that it has (precisely as a map or a picture) corresponds to some aspect of what it represents. And maps and pictures, by their very natures, present themselves as signs of something else; a map is necessarily a map of some region, a picture a portrayal of some person or thing.

According to Foucault, the distinctive nature of Classical signs entirely excludes certain questions about signification that other periods find natural and even necessary. He says, for example, that "in the sixteenth century, one asked oneself how it was possible to know that a sign did in fact designate what it signified" (42). The Classical Age abandons this question and instead begins "to ask how a sign could be linked to what it signified" (43), a question that still occupies modern thought. On the other hand, Classical thought excludes fundamental modern questions about what signification is, since it "precludes even the possibility of a theory of signification" (65).

These claims are initially puzzling, but understanding them clarifies important features of Foucault's account of the Classical conception of signs. I propose the following interpretation of his cryptic comments. The reason the Classical Age no longer asks how we can know that a sign designates what its signifies is that this question presupposes that there is something in addition to the sign and the signified in virtue of which the former signifies the latter. For the Renaissance, a sign signified in virtue of its resemblance to what it signified. Since we might have doubts about the existence of this resemblance (e.g., about whether there really is an analogy between aconite seeds and human eyes), it is appropriate to ask how we know that a sign does in fact signify what it seems to. But for the Classical Age, there is no intermediary such as resemblance between sign and signified. The sign directly represents what it signifies and, moreover, presents itself precisely as so representing. For this reason, there is no basis for doubting whether it in fact signifies what it seems to; the "transparency" of the sign guarantees it. On the other hand, precisely because there is no term intermediate between sign and signified, it is appropriate to ask how the two can be linked. The answer requires an analysis of representation, showing how its nature permits the direct connection of two terms with no role for a *tertium quid* such as resemblance.

But if Classical thought appeals to the nature of representation to understand the link between sign and signified, how can it exclude the possibility of a theory of signification? In Classical terms, after all, signification – the function performed by a sign – is precisely representation. How can there be an analysis of the nature of representation but no theory of representation (signification)? The answer turns on the meaning Foucault gives here to *theory*. I suggest that he understands it to involve not an analysis of the nature of representation but rather an account of how representation originates – that is, of how consciousness comes to have a capacity to form representations. This latter question is pointless from a Classical viewpoint, for which all consciousness (thought) is necessarily representative. The question presupposes that "signification [representation] . . . is a determinate form in our consciousness" (65) that needs to be accounted for by some specifying cause (e.g., some "specific activity of consciousness," 66). Classical thought denies this, since it holds the consciousness *as such* provides representations of things. It is only at the end of the eighteenth century, with Kant and the beginning of the modern episteme, that consciousness is no longer regarded as intrinsically representational and questions are raised as to how the mind is able to form thoughts that represent objects.

It needs to be emphasized that such questions are not the same as those that concern the actual existence of the objects conceived by thought. The latter were obviously raised – and in very radical forms – by Classical philosophers from Descartes on. But even in asking these questions, Classical thinkers took for granted that the mind's thoughts had a coherent representational content, even if the objects of representation were themselves merely other thoughts. Thus, when Descartes asked if there really is an external world corresponding to our thoughts of one, he presupposed that those thoughts at least represented the sense impressions that we ordinarily regard as of material things. With Kant, however, the representational character of thought is no longer taken for granted. A representation of sense impressions by thought requires a synthesis of them by the mind, and the possibility of such a synthesis does not follow merely from the nature of consciousness as such. Only a consciousness that is appropriately structured (by, for example, the forms of sensibility and the categories of the understanding) will be able to achieve the synthesis and thus represent objects. Even a successful Cartesian argument for the existence of the external objects that we find ourselves thinking of will not explain what it is that enables us to think of such things at all. And if Foucault is right, Classical thought is not even able to seek such an explanation because it cannot conceive of thought as other than representative.

To sum up my interpretation of Foucault's often obscure account of Classical representation: For the Classical Age, representation is the necessary form of all thought, so that thought can never "step back" from it and understand it in terms of anything else. There is, in other words, no possibility of treating representation itself as one of the elements of an ordered system and thereby understanding it in terms of its relationships of identity and difference to the other elements. But this is simply to say that representation itself cannot be represented. It is the point from which any Classical thought originates and which, accordingly, cannot be just another object of that thought. This, of course, is not to say that Classical thought was unaware of its own representational character or even that it could not develop analyses ("theories") of representation in the sense of descriptions of the elements and types of representation. But what was not possible was for Classical thought to represent the very act of representation – that is, to regard this act, which constitutes all thought, as just one element among others in an ordered series (e.g., a table of the faculties of the mind).

Foucault illustrates this Classical nonrepresentability of representation through his ingenious and tortuous analysis of Velazquez's *Las Meninas* in Chapter 1 of OT. He begins with a detailed discussion of the painting's spatial structure, showing how at every level this structure is built around a single point outside the painting. This is the point that is, most obviously, occupied by us who are looking at the painting. But it is also the point at which the artist must have stood in painting it, and the point where, by the spatial logic of the painting, we must place the models (the King and Queen of Spain) that the painter portrayed on the canvas is painting. Each of the three figures "located" at this focal point of the painting corresponds to one element in the process of representation: the King and Queen to the object represented, the painter to the subject representing, the spectator to the subject viewing the representation. Further, all three of these elements are themselves represented in the painting as, respectively, the image reflected in the mirror on the back wall, the self-portrait of the artist, and the man standing at the back doorway. However none of the three are portrayed as performing their role in representation. The painter and the spectator appear, but not in front of the picture, where they must be when actually painting or viewing. The models appear only in mirror image and not as objects of the painter's gaze. The painter's and the spectator's roles could be portrayed only by putting them as reflections in the mirror, but then they would not be directly represented in the picture. The models are represented as they look to the painter, but they are present only as reflections and not in the position they must occupy to be objects of the painter's gaze. Accordingly, Velazquez's painting can be regarded as a Classical effort to represent representation. As such, it does successfully portray all the separate elements that are involved in representation. But it fails – not through any inadequacy of Velazquez's art but because of the logic of the situation – to represent any of these elements in its precise role in the process of representation. Foucault's suggestion is that this corresponds to an essential feature of the Classical Age: There was in principle no way of "thematizing" (explicitly representing) the act of representation itself.

Corresponding to the new Classical view of signs in general, there is, Foucault maintains, a new view of those particular signs that make up languages. As signs, words now belong to a separate ontological realm. Language is no longer intertwined with the world, a reality of the same nature as the things it signifies. It ceases to resemble and instead represents, which means that "discourse was still to have the task of speaking that which is, but it was no longer to be anything more than what it said" (43). The representations of language express a content that they themselves do not possess. An important epistemological consequence is that erudition ceases to be a form of knowledge. This is because words can no longer be regarded as natural signs forming a part of the world, included in it as marks of the truth. "It is the task of words to translate the truth if they can; but they no longer have the right to be considered a mark of it. Language has withdrawn from the midst of beings themselves and has entered a period of transparency and neutrality" (56). This new status of languages also explains why, in the Classical Age, natural history, for example, ceases to include what has been said about an animal (myths, and so on) as knowledge about it.

Foucault sees the transition from the Renaissance to the Classical view of language expressed in Cervantes's *Don Quixote*. Part 1 of the novel exhibits the folly of seeking resemblances in a world where they have no place. Don Quixote, in good Renaissance fashion, believes the books he has read will blend in with reality, that writing is still "the prose of the world." But this is no longer so: "Resemblances and signs have dissolved their former alliance; similitudes have become deceptive and verge upon the visionary or madness . . .; words wander off on their own without content . . ." (47–48). But while Part 1 exhibits the failure of the Renaissance conception of language, Part 2 reveals a new power of language. For, as Don Quixote meets people who have read Part 1 and recognize him as the hero of the book, he comes to achieve his own proper reality as a literary character. "Don Quixote has achieved his reality – a reality he owes to language alone, and which resides entirely inside the words" (48). This corresponds to the switch from language as part of the world, woven into the system of resemblances, to language as an autonomous system of representation.

Foucault presents this new status of language as entailing an important change in the status of language about language. During the Renaissance, as we have seen, this took the form of *commentary*, a continual probing of the depths of language's intrinsic meaning content. But for the Classical Age, the meaning of language is entirely exhausted in its representative function, with the result that the only questions about it concern how it performs this function. Such questions belong to what Foucault calls the domain of *criticism* rather than commentary. Criticism covers such issues as the critique of available vocabularies as bases of science and philosophy, the analysis of the relative values of various linguistic devices (e.g., syntactical forms, rhetorical figures) for carrying out the function of representation, and the relation of special languages (e.g., that of Scripture) to their representational content. Whereas commentary "sacralizes" language by treating it as a fount of wisdom, criticism "judges . . . and profanes" it by treating language as a mere means of expressing truths independent of it (81).

Classical knowledge

Now that we have surveyed Foucault's account of the Classical conceptions of order, signs, and language, we are in a position to sketch his view of the general structure of knowledge during the Classical Age. The overall project of knowledge is that of achieving a "general science of order" – that is, a linguistic representation of things that places them in series according to the identities and differences existing among their properties. The appropriate expression of such a representation is a *table* (like the tables of genera and species developed by natural history) that lays out all the categories of being and places each thing in its proper place. Foucault distinguishes two important divisions or poles of the general science of order. The first is *mathesis,* the part of the science of order that deals with "the ordering of simple natures" and employs an algebraic method of analysis. Mathesis handles those aspects of reality that are susceptible to a quantitative, mathematical treatment. (Here Foucault is using *mathesis* in a narrower sense than he does when he employs it as the name of the general science of order.) The second division is *taxinomia,* which deals with "the ordering of complex natures" – that is, of things as they occur in the natural order of our experience (72). Taxinomia provides a qualitative ordering of things and is the method used by the "empirical" (i.e., nonmathematical) sciences of the Classical Age that we will discuss in some detail below.

But the mathesis and taxinomia that comprise the general science of order do not, on Foucault's view, exhaust the domain of Classical knowledge. For the methods they employ presuppose that there has already been a preliminary ordering of the impressions from which our efforts to attain knowledge must always begin. Here we need to recall that, even though the Classical episteme deprives resemblance of a central role in knowledge and signification, it does not entirely elminate it. Resemblance still remains as "an indispensable border of knowledge" (67). Specifically, the flux of impressions from which we inevitably begin could not be ordered at all if some impressions did not resemble others. Knowledge begins with our recognition of resemblances among impressions and the consequent connection (ordering) of them in the imagination. Thus, at the very root of our knowledge are the corresponding factors of resemblance and imagination (i.e., the mind's power to recognize resemblances and connect impressions in terms of them).

Knowledge of the process whereby imagination transforms the flux of impressions into a preliminarily ordered series is the domain of what Foucault calls *genetic analysis* (or *genesis*). He presents this area of inquiry as a major concern of philosophers from Locke to the Ideologues. It united two complementary areas of analysis. One, the *analysis of nature*, "gives an account of the resemblances between things . . . before their reduction to order" (69). The other, the *analytic of imagination*, shows how the imagination is able to order the flux of similar impressions and thus provide a basis for the further orderings of taxinomia and mathesis. Genetic analysis thus provides the philosophical foundation and justification for these two enterprises and with them comprises the entire body of Classical knowledge.

With this account of the general structure of knowledge, Foucault completes his delineation of the Classical episteme. His next step is to undertake detailed studies of three particular domains of Classical knowledge: general grammar, natural history, and the analysis of wealth. All three of these are, he reminds us, subdomains of taxinomia; that is, they undertake qualitative orderings of the complex representations belonging to specific regions of our experience of the world. In this sense they are empirical rather than mathematical disciplines. One of Foucault's reasons for focusing on them as examples is no doubt that they exhibit the structure of the Classical episteme in a particularly clear way. But even more important is the fact that these three areas of knowledge are extremely valuable for the comparative understanding of the philology, biology, and economics that emerge in the context of the modern episteme and that, as we shall see, exercise an essential role in the formation of the human sciences. We turn, then, to Foucault's analysis of the Classical disciplines treating language, living things, and wealth.

General grammar

For the Classical Age, language is identified with discourse – that is, "representation [thought] itself represented by verbal signs" (81). But what is the special feature of linguistic representation that "distinguishes language from all other signs and enables it to play a decisive role in representation?" According to Foucault, it is the fact that language "analyses representations according to a necessarily successive order" (82). This order is foreign to that of thought in itself, for though "thoughts succeed one another in time, . . . each one forms a unity" in which there are no discernible temporal divisions. But in language the different elements of a thought must be expressed successively. "To my gaze, 'the brightness is within the rose'; in my discourse, I cannot avoid its coming either before or after it" (82). It is precisely this feature of language that is the focus of "that new epistemological domain that the Classical Age called 'general grammar,' " which Foucault defines as "the study of verbal order in its relation to the simultaneity that it is its task to represent" (83, emphasis omitted). General grammar was of particular importance for Classical philosophy because the discourse it studied ("natural language") is our first ("spontaneous and unthought-out") analysis of thought. "It constituted, as it were, a philosophy inherent in the mind . . . and one that any philosophy had to work through if it was to rediscover . . . the necessary and evident order of representation" (83–84).

Foucault emphasizes that general grammar is not an effort to discover grammatical structures common to all languages. There is, in fact, a different general grammar for each human language. The "generality" of these grammars consists in the fact that they explicate the fundamental system of representation that underlies *all* the grammatical rules of a given language. A general grammar aims at establishing "the *taxonomy* of each language," the "system of identities and differences" that defines its particular mode of representation and provides "the basis, in each of them, for the possibility of discourse" (91). Specifically, any general grammar can be understood in terms of the four key features of a language's representative function: attribution, articulation, designation, and derivation. These features are not always the explicit focus of the theories of particular general grammarians. Foucault's discussion of general grammar consists

not in a survey of such theories but in an analysis of the structure
of any general grammar as it is determined by the above four
features.

According to Foucault, a necessary condition for any linguistic
representation of thought is the connection of two mental representations – that is, the *attribution* of one to the other. This is
achieved in a proposition by the verb's affirmation of the coexistence (in thought) of the two representations. This affirmation is
the essential function of the verb, and accordingly the basic force
of every verb is that of *to be* (though of course a given verb may
also exercise further functions of adjectival attribution, expression of tenses, and so on). The being asserted by verbs in this
function is not that of extramental reality but merely that of
connection or coexistence in thought. This is the fundamental
meaning of attribution.

Foucault points out that, of itself, the verb's connection of two
representations says nothing about the specific content of those
representations. This content is provided by words (in the first
instance, nouns) that name what is contained in a given representation. The process whereby different words express different
representational contents is *articulation*. In theory, of course, every noun could be a proper noun, giving a unique name to the
complex unity of content present in each different representation. But language that is of any human value needs nouns that
designate representations in a more general way. This leads to
two sorts of articulation. The first is "horizontal articulation,"
which groups "together individuals that have certain identities in
common and separates those that are different," thus yielding
various common nouns. The second is "vertical articulation,"
whereby we distinguish "entities that subsist by themselves from
those . . . [e.g., qualities] that one can never meet in an independent state," thus obtaining adjectives, adverbs, and so on, in
addition to nouns (97).

Through theories of attribution and articulation, a general
grammar provides an account of the structure of a language considered as an autonomous system. But of course the point of a
system of representation is to represent something outside itself.
Specifically, the names of a language do not just delineate a complex system of contents; they denote objects existing outside language. A general grammar's treatment of designation and derivation covers this essential aspect of language as denotation.

According to Foucault's analysis of general grammar, the linguistic function of *designation* originates in the initial association of the cries and other sounds that people naturally emit in certain situations to objects involved in those situations. Thus, a person will naturally give a cry of pain when hit by a falling tree branch. Such cries are "the effect and consequence of our animality" and are not in themselves the signs of anything. But they are biological universals in that they "depend solely on the conformation of our organs" and so will be the same in all humans. As a result, someone can associate another's cry "with the same representations that have . . . accompanied his own cries" (105). When this occurs, the cry begins to function as a linguistic sign (and similar processes occur in more complex ways). In this way, language originates from a "language of action," developing out of natural human responses to events in the world. But it becomes language properly speaking only to the extent that it detaches itself from the world, through the universalizing process that makes a cry not merely a cry (i.e., merely a biological response). The origin of language from the language of action explains both its essential arbitrariness and the nonetheless close connection of words to what they name. Language is arbitrary because "cries and other natural reactions will, in general, have no identity of content . . . with what they designate" but merely "relations of simultaneity and succession" (106). On the other hand, the basic linguistic signs are linked to what they designate in virtue of facts about our biological condition (e.g., our propensity to cry out when in pain). Therefore, there is a strong causal tie (at the fundamental level) between words and their objects.

On the basis of the above analysis of the language of action, general grammar develops a theory of roots. Roots are "rudimentary words," found in many if not all languages, that have been "imposed upon language by nature in the form of involuntary cries spontaneously employed by the language of action" (107). But, beyond this origin, roots have been specifically selected by people as part of their languages because of perceived resemblances to what they designate. For example, a particular root may be chosen because of an onomatopoetic resemblance to a sound it designates, or a root involving an *r* may be regarded as resembling the "harshness" of the color red. By means of this process of selection on the basis of resemblance, each language comes to have a set of basic roots from which the rest of its words are derived. These roots are the basis of the language's tie to a reality outside itself and hence to its power of designation. Our languages have, of course, greatly developed from their primitive roots. Not only have the forms of words changed, but so have their meanings. This process whereby the meanings of a language have developed, with increasing subtlety and complexity, from the meanings of its initial roots, is what Foucault calls *derivation*. To each stage of derivation, there corresponds a new level of the language's articulation. General grammars emphasize the role of writing in the process of derivation. They put particular stress on the fact that alphabetical forms of writing (as opposed to "figurative" forms such as hieroglyphics) encourage the development and transmission of new meanings and thus support linguistic (and, correspondingly, intellectual, social, and political) innovations. Figurative systems are so difficult to learn that the energy of a society is spent in simply preserving what it has received. Moreover, their more concrete, pictorial character encourages imaginative credulity (rather than the scientific analysis supported by alphabetical systems) and thus impedes human progress.

But though the form of writing is crucial in the development of a language from its roots, it is not, according to Foucault, the ultimate force behind this development. This force is rather the "rhetorical dimension" of language, whereby a word takes on a new meaning because of some similarity (or other relation) in form or content to another word. Rhetoric is tied to what Foucault calls the "spatiality" as opposed to the temporality of language. By this he means that rhetorical transformations of meaning are implicit in a language as a static system. Even though they may in fact occur over a period of time, their basis lies not in any temporal laws of causal development but in the atemporal structure of the language. For example, the move, via metonymy, whereby "roof" comes to mean "house" is based on the relation between the meanings of these words and is not an instance of some law governing the development of language over time. Consequently, although derivation obviously does take place over time, it is not at root a temporal phenomenon. The laws it follows are determined by the atemporal structure of the "tropological space" of language.

Foucault notes that the four basic functions of language we have been discussing can be arranged as the vertices of a quadrilateral (beginning with attribution and proceeding clockwise through articulation, designation, and derivation). He uses this "quadrilateral of language" (115) to summarize the relationships in general grammar among the four functions. The general principle is that functions located at adjacent points both "reinforce" and "confront" one another. Thus, articulation reinforces the proposition's attributive function by providing it with specific content, but, on the other hand, articulation differentiates things whereas attribution connects them. Designation reinforces articulation by revealing the point at which nouns developed by the latter attach to the world; but its pointing to the particular contrasts with the generality achieved by articulation. Derivation shows how words develop continuously from their origin in designation, but it destroys the one-to-one representation characteristic of designation. Finally, completing the circuit, derivation provides the generality that is required for the attribution effected by a proposition; but it has a "spatial" structure in contrast to the temporal sequence of terms in the uttering or writing of a proposition. There are also important relations between functions at opposite ends of the diagonals of the quadrilateral. Articulation and derivation are related by the fact that a language's "articulative capacities are determined by the distance it has moved along the line of derivation"; and attribution and designation by the fact that "words always name something represented" (116).

At the center of the quadrilateral, where the two diagonals intersect, is the element around which "the entire Classical theory of language is organized": the name (116). Every one of the four functions is essentially tied to naming. A proposition can connect (via attribution) representations only if they have been named; articulation is a process of generalizing proper names; designation relates a name to an object, and derivation changes the meaning of names. It is even the case that the use of language to express truths is, for the Classical Age, intimately tied to naming. Of course, only propositional judgments, not names, are strictly true or false. But naming things properly is the key to formulating true propositions. "If all names were exact, if the analysis upon which they are based had been perfectly thought out . . ., there would be no difficulty in pronouncing true judgments. . ." (116). This is because it is through the proper naming of things that language enables us to move from the vague confusion of

resemblances to the identities and differences that define their
true reality.

Natural history

Unlike general grammar, seventeenth and eighteenth century
work in natural history has received considerable attention from
historians of science. Foucault is therefore, from the outset, concerned to distinguish his (archaeological) approach to this work
from the standard ones. He begins with a sketch of views that, he
says, correspond to those of "an average cross section" of historians of the life sciences in the Classical Age. Such historians begin
with the idea that, during the seventeenth century, there arose a
new "curiosity" that led to unprecedented developments in the
scope and accuracy of the life sciences. Given this, their concern
is, first, to ascertain the causes of this new curiosity and, second,
to trace the course of its manifestations. The causes are said to
include both factors within science – such as the new emphasis
placed on observation and the recent prestige of the physical
sciences, which made them a model of rationality – and ex-
trascientific influences, such as interests in agriculture, exotic
plants and animals, and in "the ethical valorization of nature"
(126). The manifestations of the new curiosity are described
primarily in terms of a set of conflicts between scientific concepts
and theories. There are, for example, conflicts between mechanism and vitalism, between experimentalists and systematists,
and between fixism and transformism. Further, underlying all
these conflicts, there is thought to be a basic tension between
factors (mechanism and theology) that work to keep Classical
natural history as close as possible to its Cartesian origins and
factors (vitalism and irreligion) that were pushing it toward its
nineteenth-century future.

Foucault is highly critical of this picture. For one thing, he
thinks it is incapable of explaining why some of the conflicts it so
emphasizes arose. It must, for example, accept the disagreements between fixists and transformists and between experimentalists and systematists as brute facts. Similarly, it is unable to see
the connections between such diverse phenomena as taxonomy
and the use of the microscope. Secondly, the standard account
fails to do justice to the sharp gaps that exist between different
modes of thought about living things; it treats as parts of a single

historical fabric such mutually alien frameworks as Aristotelianism, Newtonianism, Cartesianism, and Darwinism. Most importantly, it applies to the Classical Age anachronistic categories such as that of *life*, which, as Foucault will try to show, had no fundamental place before the nineteenth century.

Foucault's archaeological approach is very different from the standard one. For one thing, it puts in brackets all questions about the causes of new forms of scientific thought. This is not because Foucault thinks such questions are pointless or unanswerable but because he thinks we need descriptions of the phenomena in question at a much deeper level before we can profitably seek their causes. (Cf., OT, "Foreword to the English Edition," xii–xiii.) Further, archaeology purports to supply this deeper description and thereby repair the defects noted above in the standard account of the "manifestations" of Classical natural history. In particular, Foucault thinks that his archaeological approach will reveal the structure of Classical natural history that sharply distinguishes it from both previous knowledge of living things and from nineteenth-century biology, and that it will show how, in relation to this structure, the conflicts so central to the standard account appear as mere surface disagreements.

On Foucault's account, natural history arose from the Classical episteme's separation of signs from the world and the resulting emphasis on the distinction between what was known of a thing by direct observation and what had merely been said about it. As we have already noted, for the Renaissance, signs (including legends and fables) were part of the world on a par with, for example, the organic structures of plants and animals. As a result, Renaissance descriptions of living things included accounts of both on equal terms. But with the Classical separation of signs from the world, "the words that had been interwoven into the very being of the beast have been unravelled and removed" (129). The idea of a natural "history" takes on a meaning closer to the original Greek sense of a "seeing." Whereas for the Renaissance, the historian (of nature or of anything else) "was defined not so much by what he saw as by what he retold," for the Classical Age, history (particularly natural history) means "a meticulous examination of things themselves for the first time, and then of transcribing what has been gathered in smooth, neutralized, and faithful words" (130–31).

According to Foucault, then, Classical natural history is the enterprise of representing things in language as exactly as possible. Its task is to reduce the distance between words and things "so as to bring language as close as possible to the observing gaze, and the things observed as close as possible to words" (132). Therefore, "natural history is nothing more than the nomination of the visible" (131). This is the source of the sense that Classical natural historians have of merely pointing out what has been there to see from the beginning but escaped people because of inattention. But in fact their descriptions were possible not because they had overcome distractions from the obvious but because "a new field of visibility" had been "constituted" (132). This field, moreover, omitted a great number of the "obvious" facts about plants and animals, even in the already restricted domain of the directly observable. For, Foucault points out, not only hearsay but also taste, smell, and most of touch (except for some fairly obvious distinctions) were excluded from the descriptions of natural history. Sight becomes the almost exclusive organ of observation, and even here not everything (e.g., colors) is admitted. Therefore, he concludes, instead of being a simple return to what is obviously there, Classical natural history is a strongly constrained and limited system of description. For it, "to observe . . . is to be content with seeing . . . a few things systematically. With seeing what, in the rather confused wealth of representation, can be analyzed, recognized by all, and thus given a name that everyone will be able to understand" (134).

The object of this special sort of description is what natural history calls the *structure* of a plant or animal. According to Foucault, structure encompasses just four aspects of the elements that make up a natural thing: their form, their number, their mutual spatial arrangement, and their relative magnitudes. It thus provides a grid that, "by limiting and filtering the visible . . . enables it to be transcribed into language" (135). Viewed as structures in this sense, natural objects appear as visible patterns of "surfaces and lines" and not as organic unities of "functions or invisible tissues." "Natural history traverses an area of visible, simultaneous, concomitant variables, without any internal relationship of subordination or organization" (137). This, he says, explains why botany rather than anatomy had epistemological priority among disciplines dealing with living things. In the nineteenth century, anatomy would return to the kind of prominence it had had in the Renaissance. But for the Classical Age, "the fundamental arrangement of the visible and the expressible no longer passed through the thickness of the body" (137). It was not, as historians often claim, that a shift in interest to botany during the Classical Age led to an emphasis on techniques for describing visible surface structures. Rather, it was a shift to the epistemological primacy of such structures that made plants rather than animals the living things more accessible to our knowledge.

Structure alone, however, is not adequate as a basis for Classical knowledge of a living thing. This is because structural description presents each plant and animal as merely an individual reality and does nothing to place it in relation to other plants and animals. Therefore, out of the descriptions of individual structures, natural historians had to extract the essential nature of each thing described – that is, the features that would enable us to assign the thing its exact place in an ordered table of natural beings. These features constitute what was called the *character* of a plant or animal.

Historians of science recognize, in the Classical Age, two competing ways of determining characters. One, called the system, began with the arbitrary specification of a small set of descriptive elements (an initial character). For example, Linnaeus selected those parts (elements) of the plant that were relevant to fructification. Each individual plant was analyzed in terms of these elements and characterized as the same as or different from others on the basis of the sameness or difference of the elements. The second way of specifying character was known as the *method*. This (as practiced, e.g., by Adanos) did not begin with arbitrarily selected elements but with an arbitrarily chosen species of plant or animal. The chosen species was described in exhaustive detail, taking account of all its elements. The next species encountered was likewise exhaustively described, except that any features already included in the description of the first were not mentioned. Similarly, each subsequent species was described with the omission of features already encountered in preceding species. On the basis of this series of description, there would eventually emerge a "general table of relations" (142), as various species were seen to share the same characters.

Foucault acknowledges that there are some obvious and important differences between these two ways of determining the characters of natural objects. For example, whereas the method is unique, there are as many systems as there are ways of selecting the set of elements that specify the initial character. On the other hand, once the arbitrary initial character is chosen, the system's characterizations are fixed, whereas knowledge of new species may require modifications in the method's division of the natural world. But Foucault emphasizes that "despite these differences, both system and method rest upon the same epistemological base." They are merely alternative means to the same ultimate goal: "a knowledge of empirical individuals . . . [in terms of] the continuous, ordered, and universal tabulation of all possible differences" (144). Method and system, for all their superficial differences, "are simply two ways of defining identities by means of the general grid of differences" (145).

Foucault notes that a fundamental problem for the project of natural history was raised by the possibility that there might not be sufficient continuity from one individual to another to allow us to group them according to shared characters. He says that, to eliminate this possibility, natural history had to lay down a postulate of the *continuity of nature*. It is obvious that this continuity is not immediately revealed in our experience of nature, which is full of gaps and confusions in comparison with the ideal tables of natural history. However, according to Foucault, these gaps and confusions have, in the Classical view, nothing to do with the nature of animal genera and species themselves. They are due to extrinsic conditions of the earth, such as climate and geological change, that have, for example, destroyed some species and forced others with nothing essential in common to live in the same area. As a result, natural history had to distinguish between two different groupings of living things. On the one hand, there was the ideal "spatial" grouping, expressed in the great tables of taxonomic orders, that represented the true continuity of nature. On the other hand, there was the experienced grouping of living things that had resulted from the temporal series of events in the history of the Earth. The task of natural history was to reconstruct the ideal order of the former from the fragments presented by the latter.

According to Foucault, this shows "how superficial it is to oppose . . . [in Classical natural history] a 'fixism' that is content to classify the beings of nature in a permanent tabulation, and a sort of 'evolutionism' that is supposed to believe in an immemorial history of nature. . . ." (150). Natural history does involve both the idea of a fixed and continuous network of species and the idea of a temporal dispersion that has blurred that network. But these are not alternative conceptions of nature. The first alone expresses the fundamental Classical understanding of living things; the latter is merely the explanation of why our experience does not immediately reveal the true fixed divisions of natural species.

But what, then, are we to make of the discussions of the transformations of living things offered by thinkers such as Bonnet, Maupertuis, and Diderot? Are these not, as is commonly held, the precursors of the evolutionary ideas of Lamarck and Darwin? In this regard, Foucault puts forward the following very strong thesis: "There is not and cannot be even the suspicion of an evolutionism or a transformism in Classical thought" (150). The fundamental reason is that a genuinely evolutionary view of nature conceives "time . . . as a principle of development for living beings in their internal organization," whereas for Classical thought time is always extrinsic to the essential reality of a living thing and has no role in determining its nature. Because of this, the ideas of the so-called precursors of evolution are in fact "incompatible with what we understand today by evolutionary thought" (151).

To establish this point, Foucault discusses the two different Classical approaches to the development of species over time. One (proposed by Bonnet) regards the entire fixed taxonomy of living things as "affected by a temporal index" whereby the whole system moves forward in a way that preserves the fixed relations between species. Each species simply moves up to occupy the place on the scale of perfection previously occupied by its predecessor in the table of natural beings. (For example, man moves to a new order of perfection, and his old place is taken by the lower primates, so that "there will be Newtons among the monkeys.") This is obviously a performationist view that in no way regards species as emerging from one another in time. The taxonomical table of species is given from the beginning, and time serves merely as an arena for "the infinite chain of being [expressed in the table] to continue its progress in the direction of infinite amelioration" (152).

The second approach (developed, for example, by Maupertuis) does not involve the temporal displacement of the entire system of species but rather has particular species appearing one after another. Here Foucault agrees that there seems to be a similarity to evolutionary thought because the appearance of new species is causally tied to "changes in the condition of life" such as air, climate, and water. But he insists that this similarity is merely apparent. The changes in conditions of life may cause the emergence of a particular species at a given time, but they have no role in determining the nature of the species. This nature is given ahead of time by the ideal taxonomic table. Accordingly, the conditions of life do not play the role of *environment* in an evolutionary theory; they do not transform a species by changing the functions of its organs. In sum, "for this form of thought . . . the sequence of time can never be anything but the line along which all the possible values of the preestablished variables succeed one another" (153). So neither Classical approach to the development of species is genuinely evolutionary, for in neither does time precede and produce the continuum of species. "It is . . . impossible for *natural history* to conceive of *the history of nature.*" (157).

Foucault maintains that it is not just in the absence of evolutionary ideas that Classical natural history differs from the biology that emerges at the beginning of the nineteenth century. The two enterprises are radically different and should not be regarded as parts of the same intellectual project. This, he says, is due to the essentially different status of the concept of *life* for natural history and biology. Although natural history dealt primarily with living things, it was not in principle limited to them. Its general project was to develop a language that could classify taxonomically all natural beings, not just those that happened to possess the attribute of being alive. Accordingly, when natural history speaks of "life," it means only "one character – in the taxonomic sense of that word – in the universal distribution of beings" (160). Moreover, the range of the objects of natural history that possess this character will vary depending on how life is defined. On Maupertuis's loose definition in terms of motility and relations of affinity, everything dealt with by natural history is alive; on Linneaus's stricter definition, the range of life is much more restricted. But no matter how wide or narrow its range, life remains just one possible character of the objects known by natural history. "Life does not constitute an obvious threshold beyond which entirely new forms of knowledge are required" (161). By contrast, Foucault says, biology is a *science of life,* a mode of knowledge peculiarly appropriate to the category of living things. There could be no biological knowledge of non-living things. But life is only a contingent character of some objects of natural history; it is not a fundamental category that specifies the objects of natural history (or any other Classical science) as such. This is what Foucault means by his perhaps overdramatic claim that, before the nineteenth century, "biology did not exist" and that this was because "life itself did not exist. All that existed were living beings" (127–28; cf. also 160).

Analysis of wealth

We come finally to Foucault's treatment of a third empirical domain of Classical knowledge: the analysis of wealth. Once again, he cautions against construing this domain anachronistically, as either a continuation of Renaissance thought on wealth or as an anticipation of nineteenth-century economics. And, as before, he sets out to show that the domain constitutes a distinct body of knowledge.

Foucault recognizes one important similarity between the Classical approach to wealth and that of the Renaissance: both begin with the problem of how to understand money (the medium of economic exchange) and its relation to the prices of the goods exchanged. For the Renaissance, he holds, the fundamental fact about money was that it had value in its own right. In virtue of the precious metal from which it was made, it had an intrinsic worth. Because of this, money was able to function in exchanges as a sign (mark) of the value of other things. Although the Classical analysis of wealth begins from the same problem, it reverses the solution. Instead of basing money's function as a sign of wealth on its intrinsic value, it bases the value of money on its function as a sign. As a medium of exchange, money has value only because it represents the value of other things. Here there is an exact parallel with Foucault's account of the general views of the Renaissance and the Classical Age regarding signs, with the former treating a sign (money) as signifying in virtue of its resemblance to what it signifies and the latter making the sign a pure representation with no content (value) of its own. Foucault says that this Classical construal of money was developed by the "complex of reflections and practices" called "mercantilism" (175). Although the mercantilist view of wealth parallels Classical developments in the treatment of language (and of nature), it took hold much more slowly because of its much closer tie to institutions and practices.

The practical significance of money as a representation of wealth is that it is able to serve as a *pledge* offered in exchange for commodities: "It has exactly the same value as that for which it has been given, since it can in turn be exchanged for that same quantity of mechandise or the equivalent" (181). The value of a given amount of money as a pledge is, of course, the price of the merchandise exchanged for it. Money's role as a pledge, expressing the price of commodities, raises the question of how it is able to fulfill this role. What is the economic basis for the pledge that is implicitly made when money is exchanged for goods? What supports the value of money as a pledge? Here standard history finds another of the fundamental controversies of which it is so fond. One group (Law and others), it is said, held to the view (which Foucault has presented as *the* Classical view) that money is a pure representation. Consequently, this group claimed that its value as a medium of exchange must be guaranteed by some intrinsically valuable goods other than money itself. But another group (Condillac, Destrutt, and others) held that the value of money was guaranteed by its intrinsic value as a marketable commodity. On that standard account, then, this issue led to a fundamental split between those who maintained the representative view of money and those who did not.

Foucault, however, argues that this is a misunderstanding. In fact, both sides of the controversy accepted the basic Classical doctrine that money's representative function is not based on its intrinsic value as a commodity. The crucial conceptual point, however, is that to accept this is not to deny that money may, quite apart from its representative function, in fact have a value as a commodity. All that the view of money as a pure representation requires is that it not represent wealth *in virtue of* any intrinsic value it has as a commodity. Indeed, both sides to the controversy in question agreed that money was an intrinsically valuable commodity. They differed merely over the question of whether this value of money or the value of some other commodity was the guarantee for money as a pledge when it was exchanged for merchandise. So, as in other cases, controversies that standard history presents as representing fundamental divisions in the thought of an age turn out, from Foucault's perspective, to be superficial disagreements among thinkers working within the same fundamental framework.

The same, he argues, is true of another "great controversy" among Classical analysts of wealth, that between the Physiocrats and the "utilitarians" (Condillac, Galiani, Graslin). This disagreement arose from reflections on the things that are bought and sold in the process of economic exchange. Obviously, they are bought and sold because they have *value* for people. But how is it that things come to have value and what determines the precise values they have? We can summarize Foucault's account of the Physiocrats' view as follows: They held that all values originate from an excess of commodities. A commodity has economic value precisely to the extent that I have more of it than I need and so am able to sell it to someone who has less of it than he needs. Moreover, the Physiocrats located the source of the surplus of commodities in the fecundity of the land. It is only in agricultural production that there is a net gain once all production costs have been deducted. Only when God (or Nature) is acting as our uncompensated coproducer do we reap more than we sow. (In manufacturing, any apparent increase in value is balanced by expenses of production and entrepreneurial profit.) Accordingly, the Physiocrats see all value as ultimately due to the fecundity of the land, which generates a surplus of commodities that have value as possible objects of exchange. Furthermore, the process of exchange itself does not increase the value of commodities. True, a higher price may be obtained by, for example, selling the commodity in another market, but any such profit will be offset by added expenses such as transportation. On the Physiocrats' view, then, all value ultimately originates in land, which produces a surplus of commodities. This surplus takes on value by entering into the process of exchange, which process cannot itself create more value but can only employ what has come to it from the land.

By contrast, Foucault says, the "utilitarians" held a psychological theory of the origin of value that exactly reverses the Physiocrats' account. They begin from human needs, which are, of course, due to a lack, not a surplus, of commodities. Commodities have an initial value precisely because they would be useful for satisfying our needs. Moreover, contrary to the Physiocrats, the process of exchange serves to augment this value, when it turns out that others are willing to give me commodities that I value more than what I give them in exchange. Thus, the diamonds that may be of rather small value to me in themselves become of great value to me because of the price others will pay for them.

It is, then, quite true that the Physiocrats and the utilitarians propose sharply opposed theories of the origin of value. The former locate the source of value in the surpluses produced by the land and see exchange as merely a means of distributing this value, not of increasing it. The latter locate the source of value in human need (hence in the insufficiency of the land's production) and see exchange as a means for increasing this initial value. But, according to Foucault, the disagreement is merely a matter of reading the same "theoretical elements" (199) in opposite ways. Both sides think about the origins of economic value in terms of the same fundamental ideas. Both see land as the sole source of wealth, but the Physiocrats assert its superabundance and the utilitarians its insufficiency. Both admit an essential connection between value and exchange. But, although the Physiocrats assert that commodities have value only as possible objects of exchange, they deny that exchange can increase this value. The utilitarians, on the other hand, see commodities as valuable (because of their usefulness) apart from any possibility of exchange, but they think exchange increases their value. Thus, "what plays a positive role in one theory becomes negative in the other" (199). The two views are just inverse construals of the same basic elements. The disagreements between them are real and important. But they occur within the same basic context of thought about wealth.

Foucault concludes by commenting on the possibility, pursued by many historians, of explaining the disagreements between the Physiocrats and utilitarians in terms of the opposing social and economic interests of the two groups. "Perhaps it would have been simpler to say that the Physiocrats represented the landowners and the 'utilitarians' the merchants and entrepreneurs" (200). Foucault does not dispute the possibility or even the value of this sort of explanation. But he notes that "though membership of a social group can always explain why such and such a person chose one system of thought rather than another, the condition enabling that system to be thought never resides in the existence of the group" (200). Archaeological analysis of Classical thought about wealth is concerned precisely with this condition of possibility. It is not interested in the sources of individuals' opinions, which Foucault says is the concern of "doxology."

The common structure of the Classical domains

Throughout his discussion of the three Classical empirical domains, Foucault emphasizes not only their radical distinction from corresponding sixteenth- and nineteenth-century systems of thought but also the deep structural similarities they exhibit among themselves. Because of these similarities, he argues, each is, in its own domain, an expression of essentially the same conceptions of order, signs, language, and knowledge – that is, an expression of the Classical episteme. Given the central role of the conception of language in any episteme, we should expect that general grammar would, as it does, exhibit the structure of the Classical episteme in a particulary clear manner. Attribution and articulation define a language as a system of Classical representation. The former connects representations through the affirmation of the verb; the latter defines a system of identities and differences which express the specific content of the representations connected. Then designation and derivation relate the system of representation to the objects it represents, the former effecting fundamental connections between things and primitive roots, the latter transforming the meaning of the roots in the direction of increasing complexity and subtlety.

Foucault argues that natural history and analysis of wealth exhibit the same essential structure as does general grammar. Natural history's descriptions of structures connect the elements composing a plant or animal just as attribution does the terms of propositions. Moreover, structural description not only provides (as attribution does) the general form of representation; it also, like articulation, specifies the particular content of the representation. Further, the specification of character complements the description of structure just as designation and derivation complement attribution and articulation. The character designates the particular species to which a described structure belongs. But this designation is not like the simple "pointing" of a primitive root; it also functions like derivation, placing the species in a developed system, which complexly relates it to other species. Similarly, in the analysis of wealth, value functions in a way that parallels both attribution and articulation. It both connects items of equivalent value and defines a system that specifies each thing's particular value. And, finally, the function of money parallels that of designation and derivation. It initially represents (designates) commodities as having certain values and also represents the development (changes) of this value through repeated exchanges.

Foucault points out that the pairs, attribution/articulation and designation/derivation, are paralleled by just a single function in natural history and analysis of wealth. The reason, he says, is that the languages treated by general grammar have developed spontaneously whereas those treated by the other two domains have been deliberately constructed by men. In natural languages, the initial acts of designation by primitive roots have been developed without unified purpose and in different ways by groups speaking different languages. As a result, there are different systems of articulation through which propositional attributions can be given content. Corresponding to this various and unguided development are the vagueness and inaccuracies of natural languages. By contrast, the language of natural history and that of the analysis of wealth have been consciously devised to express highly developed scientific and social conceptions. Therefore, initial designations of objects are made in terms of an already derived system of meanings, so that any propositional attribution connects terms already belonging to an articulated grammatical system. This, Foucault concludes, is why functions separated by general grammar are combined by natural history and the analysis of wealth.

The Classical episteme that pervades the three empirical domains we have just examined is dominated by representation, just as the preceding Renaissance episteme was dominated by resemblance. Like resemblance, representation is not only the way in which signs (including language) relate to what they signify; it also constitutes the way in which things in the world relate to one another. For it is precisely in virtue of relations of identity and difference (by which the Classical world is ordered) that things represent one another. This is why not only the four basic functions treated by general grammar but also their parallels in natural history and analysis of wealth are all means of representation. "Representation governs the mode of being of language, individuals, nature, and need itself. The analysis of representation . . . has a determining value for all the empirical domains" (209).

Accordingly, when representation lost its central place, there was a fundamental break with the Classical episteme. In Foucault's view, this occurred rather abruptly in about a fifty-year period spanning the end of the eighteenth century and the beginning of the nineteenth. Just as *Don Quixote* reflected the transition from the Renaissance to the Classical Age, the Marquis de Sade's pair of novels, *Justine* and *Juliette,* reflect the move from the Classical to the modern era (cf. 208–11). Chapter 5 will discuss Foucault's account of the modern episteme and, particularly, of the "human sciences" that it sustains.

Critical reactions

Of all Foucault's books, OT has been the most severely criticized by historians. Some see it as a free-floating prose fantasy rather than a serious work of historical scholarship. G. S. Rousseau, for example, begins his review by contrasting OT with FD, in which, he says Foucault "was tied to solid facts and still concerned with historical accuracy" and ends by commenting that he is "sorely disappointed at this necromantic performance."[1] Such negative assessments were partly the predictable reaction of sober academics to the book's portentous, self-important tone and to its dazzled reception by an intellectual public far more impressed than its comprehension of Foucault's fuliginous pronouncements could possibly warrant. But there were also often solid historical reasons for the reaction.

In order to assess the impact of these criticisms, it is important to distinguish several different historical levels on which OT operates. The first might be called the level of *specific history:* the interpretation of particular texts (e.g., Descartes's *Regulae,* the Port Royal Grammar) in their own terms. Second, there is the level of *constructive history,* which builds general interpretative frameworks connecting a range of texts. Foucault pursues constructive history at different levels of generality, ranging from the characterization of a set of texts as forming a unified empirical domain (natural history, analysis of wealth), through analysis of the common structure of several empirical domains, to claims about the overall character of the thought of an entire epoch

---

1. G. S. Rousseau, "Whose Enlightenment? Not man's: the case of Michel Foucault," *Eighteenth-Century Studies* 6 (1972–73), 239, n. 3; 256.

(Renaissance resemblance, Classical representation). Third is the level of *critical history:* the use of the results of specific and constructive history to question the self-understanding of various contemporary disciplines (philosophy, the human sciences). (We might also include a fourth level of *speculative history,* which projects future directions of Western thought.) Foucault's critical (and speculative) history derive mainly from his discussion of the modern episteme, which we will take up in the next chapter. But criticisms of his specific and constructive history have primarily focused on his treatments of the Renaissance and Classical Age and so are most appropriately considered at this point.

Foucault's specific historical analyses have attracted the least amount of critical fire. George Huppert has taken strong exception to his presentation of Ramus and Belon as instances of the Renaissance system of magical similitudes and signatures.[2] He argues that Foucault simply misreads what are in fact bodies of essentially scientific research. Similarly, John Greene has expressed strong reservations about Foucault's interpretations of Buffon and Lamarck.[3] But it seems that what most distresses historians are not Foucault's specific interpretations of texts and authors but the use he makes of them in his constructive history. The particular cases he discusses are not marshaled, in the careful way of the serious historian, to establish the truth of his sweeping claims. They function not as *evidence* but as *illustrations.* Foucault seldom makes any effort to show that his claims are supported by all the relevant texts of a given period, nor does he pay much attention to apparent counterexamples to his views. As a result, historians have rightly felt that they are being presented with oracular pronouncements rather than well-supported conclusions.

Beyond this, most historians who have discussed OT have found the more ambitious conjectures of its constructive history not only unsupported but also highly questionable. Two sorts of difficulties are particularly prominent. First, specialists in particular periods maintain that Foucault's characterizations of epistemes are gross oversimplifications that not only ignore important differences between individual figures but also contradict major aspects of the periods' thought. Thus, Huppert argues

2. G. Huppert, *"Divinatio et eruditio:* thoughts on Foucault," *History and Theory* 13 (1974), 200–203.
3. J. Greene, "Les mots et les choses," *Social Science Information* 6 (1967), 131–38.

that Foucault's account of the Renaissance gives untoward prominence to a marginal group of hermetic and magical writers,
whose work was disdained by the period's empirical scientists
(e.g., Copernicus, Vesalius), whom Foucault almost entirely ignores.[4] Foucault's unified episteme, in which science and magic
coexist as two ways of following the infinite chain of resemblances, ignores the sharp Renaissance division between magi-
cians and natural scientists. (Similarly, I would add, it is difficult
to see how rationalistic Scholastic philosophers such as Suarez fit
into Foucault's scheme.)

A second major area of difficulty concerns Foucault's claim that
each episteme expresses an entirely distinctive way of thought,
representing a sharp break with everything that comes before
and after. This, of course, contradicts the search for "precursors"
that constitutes so much of standard research in the history of
ideas, so it is not surprising that there has been a critical deluge of
examples of thinkers who pre- or postdate what Foucault presents
as the distinctive features of a given episteme. G. S. Rousseau, for
example, maintains that the view of language developed in the
Port Royal Grammar, which for Foucault is uniquely associated
with the Classical episteme, is already present in a work by the
Spanish grammarian, Sanctius, published in 1585. (Similarly, he
argues that the notion of organic structure, which, as we will see,
Foucault thinks is distinctive of the modern episteme, is in fact
present in numerous thinkers from Plato and Aristotle, through
Albert the Great, Leonardo da Vinci, and Leibniz.[5])

There are several ways of defending Foucault against the
above criticisms of his constructive history. We might, of course,
dispute the critics on the level of the specific examples and interpretations that they advance. We may, perhaps, be able to offer a
Foucaultian reading of Copernicus or Suarez that is more persua-
sive than his critics' or show that Sanctius's grammar bears only
superficial similarities to that of Port Royal. OT has the merit of
suggesting numerous areas where we might fruitfully reexamine
standard historical interpretations. However, its failure to support its claims with anything even approximating a comprehensive survey of the relevant evidence has left its defenders with an
immense body of apparent counterexamples to explain away.

4. Huppert, 196.
5. Rousseau, 246–47.

Foucault himself suggests another line of response in AK and his Foreword to the English translation of OT. In AK he refers, for example, to his comparison in OT of the Classical domains of general grammar, analysis of wealth, and natural history. The comparison, he says, revealed some striking similarities in these domains but was not part of an effort to describe "a mentality that was general in the 17th and 18th centuries" or to "reconstitute . . . the forms of rationality that operated in the whole of Classical science" (AK, 158). He agrees, moreover, that the unity he found in these particular domains could not be extended to include other aspects of the history of Classical thought. Taking account of, for example, cosmology, physiology, and Biblical exegesis would have resulted in a very different analysis. This, he says, in fact illustrates an essential feature of his archaeological method, which is an instrument of local studies and "is not intended to reduce the diversity of discourse" (AK, 150).

As Foucault is aware, readers of OT may well be surprised at this characterization of its results. He says: "In *The order of things*, the absence of methodological sign-posting may have given the impression that my analyses were being conducted in terms of cultural totality" (AK, 161). (The same point is made more fully in the Foreword to the English edition of OT, where Foucault insists that he offered a "strictly 'regional' study" [x].) In fact, the problem is surely not just that he failed to make explicit the implicit restrictions on his discussion. His own direct statements clearly claim generality for his analysis. He consistently uses terms such as *Classical thought, modern thought* and *Western thought* in a global sense. For example, after explaining Descartes's rejection of resemblance in favor of identity and difference, he says: "All this was of the greatest importance to Western thought. . . . As a result, the entire *episteme* of Western culture found its fundamental arrangements modified" (OT, 54). There is, moreover, Foucault's frequently cited explicit statement: "In any given culture and at any given moment, there is always only one *episteme* that defines the conditions of possibility of all knowledge. . ." (OT, 168). In fact, this same sort of view is present in the definition of an episteme that Foucault offers in AK itself. It is, he says, "the totality of relations that can be discovered, for a given period, between the sciences" (AK, 191). There is surely much more than an "absence of methodological sign-posting" that leads Foucault's readers to think that he is making global claims about the thought of an entire period.

A more honest response would be to admit frankly that, on one level, OT does offer a highly interesting and stimulating comprehensive constructive history of Western thought since the Renaissance. No doubt this history is highly conjectural and based more on Foucault's intuitions than on solid evidence, and no doubt much of it will not withstand close scrutiny. However, this does not mean that it is worthless. The value of sweeping historical constructions such as Foucault's is precisely as sources of fruitful suggestions rather than as ultimately accurate generalizations. As J. H. Hexter has pointed out, the striking and spectacular claims of constructive history are almost always refuted by detailed studies of specific issues.[6] But such refutation is frequently followed by what Hexter calls a "reconstruction" in which the constructive claims return in a more circumscribed and qualified form. The value of Foucault's constructive history lies, then, not in its initial accuracy but in its ability to stimulate a fruitful process of criticism and reconstruction. It must be admitted, however, that, in contrast to Foucault's work on madness (and also his later work on the prison and sexuality), OT has not yet provided a major stimulus to further historical work.[7] It therefore remains to be seen whether it will be justified by its refutations.

We now turn to OT's treatment of the modern episteme and the place in it of the human sciences. This will be followed by a discussion of the book's methodology and an assessment of its critical history of the human sciences.

6. J. H. Hexter, *On Historians* (Cambridge, Mass.: Harvard University Press, 1979), 5–6.
7. One important exception is Ian Hacking, *The Emergence of Probability* (Cambridge: Cambridge University Press, 1975).

5

THE ORDER OF THINGS: II. THE RISE AND FALL OF MAN

The modern episteme

As is the case with any episteme, that of the modern age involves a fundamental reordering of reality, a new way of regarding things and their interrelations. The basic realities are no longer elements related to one another by identities and differences in their properties. Foucault presents them as rather "organic structures," connected to one another by analogies between their structures and hence between their functions. As a result, he says, the essential reality of things is not located in the continuous series that they form in an ideal conceptual space. It is found rather in their existence as discrete structures. Further, their similarities of structure are not due to "their adjacency in a classificatory table [but to] the fact that they are close to one another in a temporal succession" (218). A thing is what it is not because of its place in the ideal classification system but because of its place in real history. The order of concretely existing things is from now on determined not by ideal essences outside them but by the historical forces buried within them.

Corresponding to this new conception of order, there is, Foucault maintains, a new conception of the sign, one that displaces the central role the Classical Age gave to representation. He therefore speaks of modernity as closely tied to a "decline" or "failure" of representation. In this regard, however, it is crucial to keep in mind that Foucault does not mean that the modern episteme eliminates representation as a function of thought. Representation still has a crucial place in the modern conception of signs (as well as of language and of knowledge). His point is just that it is no more an unquestioned, self-justifying starting point; it is no longer simply accepted as a function identical to thought itself.

Rather, representation must be understood and grounded in terms of something other than itself. This is because "representation has lost the power to provide a foundation . . . for the links that can join its various elements together. No composition, no decomposition, no analysis into identities and differences can now justify the connections of representations one to another" (238–39). The power of representation to connect must instead be sought "outside representation, beyond its immediate visibility, in a sort of behind-the-scenes world even deeper and more dense than representation itself" (239).

Foucault sees Kant's project of critique as a primary focus of this new view of representation. Kant allows that some forms of knowledge – that is, empirical ones – are essentially representational. But he does not accept the Classical assumption that all thought (and hence all knowledge) is by its very nature representational. His critique "questions representation . . . on the basis of its rightful limits" and thereby "sanctions for the first time . . . the withdrawal of knowledge and thought outside the space of representation" (243). Thus, the entire system of representation, which, for the Classical Age, is the necessary form of thought and reality as such, appears, to Kant's critical eye, as just a particular form of thought and reality that needs to be grounded in something more fundamental. Philosophies based on the uncritical acceptance of representation are simply systems of dogmatic metaphysics. However, Foucault notes that, whether or not it was his intention, Kant's work also "opens up . . . the possibility of another metaphysics; one whose purpose will be to question, apart from representation, all that is the source and origin of representation." This, as we shall see, is the root of the various nineteenth-century "philosophies of Life, of the Will, and of the Word" that develop in the wake of Kant's critical philosophy (243).

The new views of order and of signs had, in Foucault's view, major consequences for the modern conception of knowledge. He thinks that the single most important development was a fragmentation of the field of knowing. For the Classical Age, knowledge formed a homogeneous whole, with each domain (from mathematics to philosophy to empirical sciences) just a particular form of the general science of order. To know, in any domain, was to construct ordered tables of identities and differences. "But, from the nineteenth century, the epistemological field . . . exploded in different directions" (346) and could no longer be understood as a linear series of inquiries employing the same basic method in different domains. Rather, there were three distinct dimensions to the space of knowledge. One was that of mathematical sciences (including pure mathematics and mathematical physics), which construct deductive systems "linking together . . . evident or verified propositions" (347). Another was that of what Foucault calls the "empirical sciences," such as biology, economics, and philology, which relate the "discontinuous but analogous" elements of the experienced world so as to reveal "causal relations and structural constants between them" (347). The third dimension was that of philosophical reflection, which seeks a unified understanding of the grounds of knowledge and of the order of reality.

Foucault sees these divisions in the field of knowledge as due to the decline of representation. The splitting off of philosophy as a methodologically distinct mode of inquiry is the direct result of the fact that representation is no longer the unquestionable form of thought and knowledge. Some areas of knowledge (specifically, those dealing with empirical realities) can, he agrees, continue to operate without themselves dealing with the question of the grounds of representation. (Though, even these he sees as developing fundamental concepts that cannot be reduced to representation). But there is a need for a new sort of reflective inquiry that probes the origins and basis of the mind's powers of representing objects. Foucault presents the split between the mathematical and the empirical sciences as a consequence of a new distinction between analytic and synthetic knowledge, which itself follows from the questioning of representation. For the Classical Age, there was no important distinction between analytic (a priori) and synthetic (a posteriori) knowledge. An analysis of representations in terms of identities and differences was at the same time a connection (synthesis) of them in the ordered tables that express their essential reality. But with the modern refusal to accept representation as the inevitable form of thought and reality, this unity of analysis and synthesis disappears. There is no longer any basis for assuming that the representative system of identities and differences yielded by, say, a logical or a mathematical analysis will express the sorts of connections that in fact constitute the concrete reality of things. For these connections will not in general be those of identities and differences but, as we have seen, those of structural and functional similarities. Accordingly, the analytic knowledge of the mathematical and logical sciences becomes sharply separated from the synthetic knowledge of empirical sciences.

Although the three dimensions correspond to irreducibly different kinds of knowledge, Foucault notes that it is possible to apply the methods of one dimension to the problems of another. Thus, we have mathematical formulations of empirical sciences such as biology and economics and projects for formalizing thought that combine mathematics and philosophy. He also refers to efforts to develop philosophies that employ empirical concepts such as life and production (labor) and to philosophical analyses of the foundations of empirical sciences.

Philosophy

Foucault notes that modern philosophical reflection takes three different forms, corresponding to three different approaches to the question of representation. Representation is essentially a relation between a subject and the objects it thinks and experiences. One approach to a philosophical account of representation begins from the side of the experiencing subject and seeks in it the conditions for the possibility of objects of representation. Here the idea is that the mind is a transcendental reality that constitutes the objects of representative knowledge. This, of course, is the approach taken by Kant in his transcendental philosophy of the subject. But Foucault notes that it is also possible to approach the question from the side of the object. Here the idea is to find in the object the conditions of the possibility of the subject's representational experience, thereby developing a transcendental philosophy of the object. Such philosophies particularly focus on life, labor, and language, which, as we will see, are introduced in the empirical sciences as nonrepresentational sources of representational systems. Thus, life, labor, and language define fields of what we might term "transcendental objectivity," opposite poles to Kant's field of transcendental subjectivity. The result is a series of philosophical systems (for example, Schopenhauer's) that may superficially appear to be reversions to precritical metaphysics. But Foucault argues that in fact they are simply another way of taking the transcendental turn introduced by Kant.

   Both of the above philosophical approaches assume that there is a need to connect the representations in terms of which our experience occurs to either a subject or an object that lies outside that experience but grounds its possibility. However, Foucault points out another option: simply to restrict ourselves to our experience, with no effort to provide it with any transcendental grounding. This amounts to accepting what Kant would call the "phenomenal" world as the only domain of which we have any knowledge. This, Foucault says, is positivism, the third form of modern philosophical reflection. Like transcendental philosophies of the object, positivism might seem to be a reversion to Classical modes of thought. Is it not, after all, the identification of reality with the world of representations? Should we not, therefore, regard it as a mere revival of the empiricist philosophies of the Classical Age? Although Foucault does not raise this question, he might respond by maintaining that it is not possible to separate positivism from the critical turn that it rejects. The point would be that, once this turn has been made, there are, in contrast to the Classical Age, alternatives to regarding thought as merely a system of representations. Positivism may maintain that in fact this is all our thought is, that there is nothing beyond the phenomenal realm. But it does so in a context that, in contrast to the Classical Age, at least allows the possibility of other construals of thought. Of course, the positivist can try to exclude these other construals (as, for example, meaningless). But how can he do this except by methods (for example, the appeal to a principle of verification) that themselves go beyond the resources of thought limited to the phenomenal realm? Thus, positivism seems to face the alternative of either making the merely dogmatic assertion that thought is to be identified with representation or else falling into incoherence by attempting to establish the assertion. In either case, it is sustained (although as an essentially unstable philosophy) by the modern, not the Classical, episteme. In this way, Foucault might justify joining positivism to "criticism" (transcendental philosophy of the subject) and "metaphysics" (transcendental philosophy of the object) to form the "triangle" of modern philosophical thought (245).

Modern empirical sciences

Foucault says very little about the mathematical dimension of modern knowledge but has a substantial discussion of the empirical sciences of biology, economics, and philology, paralleling his earlier treatments of natural history, analysis of wealth, and general grammar. (This is presumably because the empirical domains are far more relevant to an understanding of the modern human sciences and perhaps because the nature of the modern episteme is more sharply revealed in them.) Like his treatment of the Classical empirical domains, Foucault's discussions here are concerned, first, to show that modern biology, economics, and philology correspond to sharp breaks in the history of thought and are not merely (more successful) extensions of previous ways of thinking. He also attempts to show, as before, that certain controversies regarded as fundamental by historians are just alternative manifestations of the same archaeological structure of thought.

Economics

In Foucault's account of the Classical analysis of wealth, value is understood in terms of representation. This is because the economic value of a commodity is essentially related to the system of exchange. According to the Physiocrats, commodities have value only as possible objects of exchange; according to the utilitarians, their initial value is increased through exchange. But exchange is a system of representation; things enter into it only by being represented by money, which itself has value only insofar as it represents. The decisive break of modern economics with the Classical approach is due to its reconception of economic value as due to the productive power of labor rather than to any connection with representation. Foucault thinks that the initial step in the direction of the modern view was taken by Adam Smith, when he employed labor as an absolute measure of the value that a commodity has in the system of exchange. For Smith, this value was not measured by the money or the equivalent amount of goods that would represent the commodity in an exchange but by the amount of labor needed to produce it. Moreover, Smith did not (as had earlier thinkers who employed the concept) define labor in terms of the needs and desires that are represented by commodities in the system of exchange. He used it as an irreducible measure of value. To this extent, Foucault sees him moving beyond a purely representational view of wealth. On the other hand, Foucault holds that Smith never decisively broke with the Classical approach. Even though he viewed labor as the *measure* of a commodity's value, he still held that the commodity *had* value only because of its connection with the representational system of exchange.

On Foucault's view, the decisive break occurred only with Ricardo, who presented labor not only as the measure of value but also as the sole source of value. From this point on, things ceased to have economic value because they could be traded for money or other commodities that represent them in the system of exchange. They had value because (and to the extent that) people worked to produce them. "Value has ceased to be a sign, it has become a project" (254).

Foucault sees this new view of value based on labor as having three fundamental consequences for the new science of economics. First, it leads to a new conception of economic history as a linear causal series. For Classical analysis of wealth, economic "history" is merely a cyclical repetition of sequences of events – for example, increased demand causing higher prices, causing less demand, causing lower prices, causing, once again, increased demand. This is because value is always related to the system of exchange, in which any changes in value (for example, of money or of commodities) are always correlated with inverse changes in other values. Since the system always involves only a finite number of correlated values, changes can be only cyclical. For Ricardo, by contrast, the value of a commodity is determined by something outside the cyclical system of exchange: the quantity of labor needed to produce the commodity. Moreover, this quantity of labor itself depends on the available "forms of production" such as the tools used, the system of the division of labor, and the amount of capital invested in the production process. Further, the forms of production have themselves been produced by previous labor, which itself depended on previous forms of production, and so on. Therefore, current values are the result of a linear series of causes that extends back in time indefinitely. This means that economic developments, which depend essentially on changes in the values of commodities, are now viewed as occurring in the linear succession of historical time. "All value is determined, not according to the instruments that permit its analysis, but according to the conditions of production that have brought it into being. . . . The mode of being of economics is no longer linked to a simultaneous space of differences and identities, but to the time of successive productions" (255–56). Not that the system of exchange, defined in terms of representation, ceases to exist. But it now depends on labor to produce the valuable commodities that it circulates. "After Ricardo, the possibility of exchange is based upon labour; and henceforth the theory of production must always precede that of circulation" (254).

A second fundamental consequence of the role of labor in modern economics is a new conception of man as an economic agent. Since economic values are created by the historical forces of production, man as seeking and depending on these values is now regarded as dependent on these forces. The role of human beings in the analysis of wealth was exhausted by their capacity to form representations of things that they needed or desired. Modern economics deals with the factors that have caused men to form such representations – for example, with the barrenness of nature that forces us to work, with the bodily deficiencies and the external threats that limit our ability to produce. Consequently, it presents a view of man not available for a Classical analysis that required him only as a bearer of representations. This is man as a finite being struggling in an indifferent or even hostile world. "*Homo oeconomicus* is not the human being who represents his own needs to himself, and the objects capable of satisfying them; he is the human being who spends, wears out, and wastes his life in evading the imminence of death" (257). Modern economics is ultimately based not on an analysis of representations but on an "anthropology" of human finitude.

The third consequence involves the relation of the new linear time of economics to the finitude of men. The history of labor is a history of increasing human want as population increases and resources diminish. Consequently, as time goes by, human

THE ORDER OF THINGS II 189

"The more man makes himself at home in the heart of the
world, the further he advances in his possession of nature, the
more strongly also does he feel the pressure of his finitude, and
the closer he comes to his own death" (259). Accordingly, economic history is now seen as directed toward some sort of conclusion, in which men will encounter the ultimate consequences
of their material limitations. Here, however, there are two directions taken by modern economic thought. Ricardo himself takes
the pessimistic view that the end result of economic history will
be the stabilization of mankind in a permanent state of scarcity.
Marx, on the other hand, offers an optimistic vision according
to which, at the very point of utmost scarcity, when human
finitude has reached the extremity of its distress, there will arise
a new consciousness among men. This will be an awareness that
the abject condition to which they have come is not the inevitable fate of their finitude but just an "alienated" form of it that
can be overcome by a radical transformation of economic and
social arrangements.

According to Foucault, then, both Marx and Ricardo see economic life as the linear history of finite man's struggle to survive
through his labor. Moreover, both see this history as moving
toward a culminating point at which man will face the ultimate
consequences of his finitude. However, Ricardo sees this culminating point as a mere dead end that makes permanent the
scarcity against which man has so long struggled. Marx, on the
other hand, sees it as the end of scarcity and the beginning of a
new form of human existence. These two lines of thought are
just two different ways of developing the same basic picture of
economic reality; both are founded on the identical archaeological structure of modern economics. Therefore, no matter how
revolutionary Marx's ideas may be as challenges to the power of
the ruling class and to the economic theories that support this
power, they do not represent a radically new form of thought.
"At the deepest level of Western knowledge, Marxism introduced no real discontinuity" (261). It is, of course, opposed to
bourgeois economic views. But this opposition is merely a surface effect. The opposition and the controversies following from
it "may have stirred up a few waves and caused a few surface
ripples; but they are no more than storms in a children's pad-

dling pool" (262). At the level of archaeological analysis, Marxism is not a revolutionary event but one that fits exactly into the structure defined by the modern episteme.[1]

Biology

Like the analysis of wealth, Classical natural history was based on a system of representation: the taxonomic tables in which species were classified in terms of their identities and differences. The move to modern biology begins, according to Foucault, with the introduction (by e.g., Lamarck) of the notion of *organic structure*. However, Lamarck (as well as Jussieu and Vicq d'Azyr) employed organic structure merely as a means of establishing character, which was itself still understood as the representation of a species' place in the taxonomic tables. Foucault therefore maintains that Lamarck and the others were still (like Adam Smith in his analysis of wealth) essentially tied to the Classical episteme. He holds that the decisive break, constituting modern biology, was rather effected by Cuvier, who was the first to give organic structure a role prior to and independent of taxonomic classification. For Cuvier, the structure of an organ is to be understood in terms of the function that the organ performs. In drawing up a list of species, what is of importance is no longer identities and differences in plants' and animals' properties but only functional similarities in their organs. Thus, organs (e.g., gills and lungs) that have no elements at all in common may nonetheless be grouped together on the basis of their similar functions. Likewise, organisms themselves will be classified on the basis of their similarities as functional systems.

In this way, Foucault says, we arrive at the modern definition of a living thing as a functional system. Given this definition, the property of *life* is no longer just one category of natural classification. Rather, all classifications express subdivisions of life (de-

1. In an interview given after the publication of OT, Foucault notes that his claims about Marx's lack of originality may apply only to the domain of economics. "I do not believe that [Marx's] economic analyses go beyond the epistemological space set up by Ricardo. On the other hand, one might suppose that Marx introduced into the historical and political consciousness of men a radical break and that the Marxist theory of society indeed inaugurated an entirely new epistemological field." Raymond Bellour, "Deuxième entretien avec Michel Foucault," in R. Bellour, *Le livre des autres* (L'Herne, 1971), 192. The interview originally appeared in *Lettres françaises*, June 15, 1967.

fined in terms of functional system); to define a thing's species is to specify the precise sort of functional system that it is. As a result, life becomes the category that defines the objects of biological inquiry as such, and modern biology becomes, in contrast to Classical natural history, the *science of life*.

Foucault characterizes the life with which biology after Cuvier is concerned in terms of three key features. The first is the discontinuity of its forms. There is no possibility of ordering the variety of functional systems (living things) in a continuous series. Every living thing is a complex system of organs, each of which performs a function related to the survival of the organism as a whole. Some organisms are more complex than others in the sense that they have more organs exercising more functions. But more complexity in this sense is a basis for no more than loose groupings of organisms into broad categories. It is not, for example, possible to make an unambiguous determination of the number of organs and of the number of functions each performs. There may be more precise ways of ordering organs themselves (e.g., according to how well they perform their functions). But these will not provide an ordering of species, since one sort of organ will be superior in one species, another in another. As a result, the continuum of Classical order is replaced by a discontinuous proliferation of species of life.

The second key feature of life is its connection with environment. For natural history, distinctions of species were explained by preestablished differences expressed in the taxonomic tables. The differentiation of species was not produced by any external causal factors operating on real plants and animals. But for Cuvier and those who came after him, the separation of living things into different classes is due to the different ways that living things are linked to the surroundings on which they depend for their survival. External factors are no longer, as for natural history, mere occasions for the appearance of species whose natures and interrelations are already determined by their place in the system of representation. For modern biology, the nature of a species is causally dependent on the environment in which its members exist.

The third fundamental characteristic of life is its temporality. Precisely because living things are scattered into discontinuous groups that have been formed by the pressure of environmental forces, they are essentially tied to the time in which these forces and their effects exist. For the Classical Age, living things were, so to speak, in but not essentially of time. Individuals existed temporally, of course, but their natures, the genera and species to which they belonged, were not determined by the course of temporal events. In this sense, natural "history" was profoundly nonhistorical. With Cuvier, however, life is essentially tied to time; it is a thoroughly historical reality.

Foucault argues that it is this temporality and historicity of life that provides the basis for the introduction (by Darwin and Wallace) of the idea of evolution, which, as we have seen, he regards as totally foreign to Classical thought. It may seem that Foucault is obviously wrong to point to the work of Cuvier as the basis of evolutionary theory. He was, as is well known, a "fixist" who opposed Lamarck's ideas about the development of species. Doesn't this show that we should follow the standard histories of biology in regarding Cuvier's thought as a throwback to earlier times and Lamarck as the true precursor of Darwin? Foucault, however, argues that the standard view here is very mistaken. There are, he admits, some superficial resemblances between Lamarck's ideas and those of Darwin. But they differ fundamentally and in just the way that, according to Foucault, Classical ideas of development (advanced by Diderot and others) differed from genuinely evolutionary thought. Specifically, Lamarck conceives the development of living things as "an unbroken process of improvement" through which the stages of a preestablished "ontological continuity" were gradually unfolded (275). His views, accordingly, are, as we saw Foucault argue above in a different context, squarely within the Classical episteme of natural history. Cuvier rejected Lamarck's developmentalism, but this for Foucault was merely a consequence of his break with Classical thought about living beings. It is also true that he treated species as fixed and did not put forward any evolutionary view of them. But Foucault holds that his fixism is just one way of construing, from the modern viewpoint, the historicity of life. Just as Ricardo heralded a future permanent state of economic stability, so Cuvier saw himself as describing a present permanent state of biological stability. But in each case, the stability was determined by the very forces that make labor or life radically historical. Darwin, like Marx, introduced a different construal of this historicity. But his approach is made possible by the same general conception of life (as essentially temporal and historical) that was the basis of

Cuvier's work. In sum, Cuvier and Darwin both belong to the modern episteme, Lamarck to that of the Classical Age. Once again, Foucault concludes, standard historical accounts of "fundamental" disagreements (and arguments) are undermined by archaeological analysis.

Philology

Foucault says that the development of modern philology was similar to that of biology, although it proceeded more slowly because of the particularly central place of language in the Classical episteme. An initial move away from representation – but still (like the parallel work of Smith and Lamarck) within the Classical episteme – was involved in the work of William Jones and others on inflections. But for Foucault the decisive break that separates philology from general grammar comes only with Bopp. For Bopp words do, of course, have representative functions; we can and do use them to express what we mean. But these functions no longer define their basic reality as words. Rather, words are understood as first of all elements of a grammatical system defined by the rules governing their use. Their power to represent derives entirely from their roles in this system.

Foucault specifies modern philology's new conception of words in four of its main features. The first is its methods of distinguishing one language from another. For the Classical Age, this was done by reference to the different ways that languages analyzed the thoughts they represented. For modern philology, however, languages are distinguished on the basis of differences in the formal features of their grammars. Foucault points out, for example, that much attention is paid to the differences between languages (e.g., Chinese) that form complex expressions solely by juxtaposing autonomous grammatical elements and those (like Sanskrit) that form complex expressions by inflectional modification of roots. Moreover, philology does not merely use these formal characteristics to distinguish languages from one another. It also – and this is its second main feature – takes these characteristics as a primary object of its detailed study of a language. There were, for example, thorough studies of the phonetic nature of languages that treated them as more like systems of musical notes than systems of visible signs.

The third distinctive feature of philology is its new theory of the root. For general grammar, primitive roots were nouns, names representing objects in man's environment. On Bopp's analysis, the roots of a given language can be determined entirely by a study of its properties as a formal system, with no need to work back to a primitive language and its initial connections with objects. On the other hand, philology does recognize that language has its origins in human existence and specifically in human efforts to come to terms with the world. This recognition is apparent in Bopp's account of the roots of verbs. For general grammar, the root of all verbs was *to be*, which asserted a connection between representations. All other verbs were regarded as combinations of this assertion (attribution) and various adjectival modifications (e.g., "he runs" = "he *is* [in a state of] running"). According to Bopp, however, verbs have their own roots, independent of the copula and the representative functions of adjectives. Moreover, nouns are, for Bopp, derived from verbs, so that the fundamental connection of language as a whole to reality is effected by the roots of verbs.

Foucault maintains that this is of great significance because verbal roots do not represent objects; they rather express the actions and volitions of a subject. "Language is 'rooted' not in the things perceived but in the active subject." This suggests that we regard it as "a product of will and energy, rather than of the memory that duplicates representation" (290). In this way, language becomes that which "manifests and translates the fundamental will of those who speak it" – that is, "the fundamental will that keeps a whole people alive" (290). This leads to a view that ties the development of languages and hence of civilizations not to what elites have learned but to what peoples as a whole desire – not, in sum, to knowledge but to freedom. Thus, philology, which seems so distant from practical affairs, links "language and the free destiny of men in a profound kinship" and hence comes "to have profound political reverberations" (291).

The fourth feature of philology is its new method for defining "systems of kinship between languages" (291). Based on the theory of roots, which allowed their determination in purely formal terms, this method is similarly able to chart the relationships between languages without reference to their representative character. Furthermore, study of these relationships reveals laws of linguistic change that enable philologists to draw conclusions about temporal relations between languages. For general grammar the succession of languages in time – like the temporal series of species – is merely a matter of the sequential appearance of forms already determined apart from time and its laws. But now the mutations of language follow laws of temporal succession that are part of philology's account of their inner structure. Thus, like living beings, languages become essentially historical realities. Indeed, Foucault maintains that, since the historicity of languages derives from laws of development that are essential to it, its history necessarily involves evolutionary change. By contrast, as we have seen, living things do not evolve because of principles built into their very nature as living but because of contingent relations between them and their environments. This is why there is no philological parallel to Cuvier's fixism.

Language and modern thought

With the decline of representation and the consequent fragmentation of knowledge, language, Foucault says, lost the central place it had held in the Classical episteme. The structure of language is no longer that of knowledge as such (i.e., an ordering of representations); nor is all scientific knowing just a refinement of the knowledge implicit in ordinary language. Language is now itself just "one object of knowledge among others" (296). (This is why, in contrast to our discussion of the Classical episteme, we could sketch the main features of modern knowledge without reference to language.) However, Foucault notes that this "demotion" of language does not mean that it has no special significance for modern thought. Even though its structure is no more the structure of knowledge, it still remains the medium through which any knowledge must be expressed. (This implies, Foucault says, that language cannot be entirely reduced to an object, since it always reappears in the subject's effort to express what he knows.) However, precisely because of its historical nature, our use of language burdens us with meanings and presuppositions that confuse and distort what we are trying to say. We express our "thoughts in words of which [we] are not the masters" (297).

Foucault discusses two complementary projects modern thought undertook to gain some control over language. The first was an effort of purification via formalization, designed to purge alien, distorting linguistic elements. This included both the positivists' constructions of ideal formalized languages and what Foucault sees as an even more radical effort (by Boole and others) to develop a symbolic logic that would express thought independently of any language. The second project was that of the critical interpretation of language. Here the idea was not to purify or replace historical language but rather to understand the meanings that were implicit in it. The aim of such interpretation (as practiced, e.g., by Marx, Nietzsche, and Freud) is not, as in the Renaissance, to discover the fundamental truth buried in language. It is rather to reveal the myths through which we are "governed and paralyzed" by our language.

On Foucault's view, then, formalization and interpretation – the two great and apparently opposed modern approaches to language – are both rooted in the new status of language as a historical reality and object of our knowledge. Moreover, the practice of either is implicitly connected to the other. Interpretation seeks to understand language as a historical reality; but, as we learn from philology, this reality is, in its essence, a formal structure. Correspondingly, the project of formalization must begin with some implicit understanding of the meaning of the linguistic forms with which it deals. Accordingly, Foucault maintains that the movement of modern formalization (which culminates in Russell) and the movement of modern interpretation (which culminates in Freud) are not radically opposed but rather have a common origin and purpose. This explains (and presumably justifies) attempts to connect them – for example, phenomenology's effort to express the meaning contents of experience in precise discourse, structuralism's efforts to discover the pure forms of the unconscious. Foucault notes that these complementary enterprises reveal the "common ground" (299) of phenomenology and structuralism in the modern episteme.

The final – and, Foucault says, most important and most surprising – way in which modern thought has a special concern with language derives from the appearance of *literature*. Here "literature" does not mean just any sort of artistic writing but the peculiarly modern phenomenon of writing that presents the realm of language as an entirely autonomous domain. Literature in this sense (which has existed "from Hölderlin to Mallarmé and on to Antonin Artaud," 44) is "a manifestation of a language which has no other law than that of affirming – in opposition to all other forms of discourse – its own precipitous existence" (300). As such, literature is concerned solely with "the simple act of writing" itself. Here language is nothing but the "silent, cautious deposition of the word upon the whiteness of a piece of paper. . . , where it has nothing to say but itself, nothing to do but shine in the brightness of its being" (300). In sum, modern literature is language existing solely for its own sake, speaking in its own right and about nothing other than itself. Nietzsche said that, when confronted with a text, we should always ask: Who is speaking? Foucault notes that modern literature's (implicit) response to this question is given by Mallarmé: It is the words themselves.

In modern literature, according to Foucault, language returns to something like its status during the Renaissance. It has its own density, its own being, as opposed to the transparency of Classical representational language. But, whereas Renaissance language was ultimately controlled and limited by the primal Text of the world, given as God's creative word, the language of modern literature is totally ungrounded and wanders with "no point of departure, no end, and no promise" (44).

Foucault points out that, in spite of these important areas of modern interest in language, it has not until recently had the kind of importance that was earlier accorded life and labor, both of which were taken as the foundations of nineteenth-century efforts to probe the fundamental meaning of human existence. This, he suggests, was probably because, whereas life and labor were the objects of single scientific disciplines that gave them a unified and coherent intelligibility, the study of language was from the beginning of the modern era dispersed among a wide range of disciplines. Where life and labor were studied by biology and economics alone, the study of language was the concern of a wide range of intellectual enterprises, from philology and formal logic to hermeneutics and literature. But now, as we shall see, that the modern episteme itself seems to be failing, we have returned to language, thinking perhaps that, since modern thought arose with the dispersion of language, whatever is to replace it will require a rebirth of its unity (cf. 386). In any case, Foucault maintains that questions about language are once again central. We ask about the nature of signs, the scope and meaning of signification, the status of literature. All these questions can, perhaps, be summed up in the query (in which he says "the whole curiosity of our thought now resides"): "What is language

[and] how can we find a way round it in order to make it appear in itself, in all its plentitude?" (306). But, he says, we are unable to answer these questions and, what is more, cannot even assess the ultimate meaning of the fact that we are condemned to ask them. Our queries may be either the dawn of a new era (a new episteme) or just the completion of the modern breakup of Classical order. But, Foucault claims, his archaeological analysis of modern thought at least shows why we both can and must ask our questions about language.

Man and the analytic of finitude

Although we have surveyed the three axes of modern knowledge – the mathematical, the philosophical, and the empirical – we have not yet encountered the human sciences that are Foucault's ultimate concern. This is because, as he puts it, these sciences are not located on any of the three axes of modern knowledge but within the space of the three planes they define. Less metaphorically, the point is that the human sciences must be understood in terms of the special relations that they have to all the dimensions of modern knowledge. They have a constant aim of developing mathematical formalizations; they employ models taken from the empirical sciences; and their object is the "being of man" that is also, in a different way, the object of philosophy. We will return to the connection of the human sciences with mathematics and the empirical sciences of biology, economics, and philology. But our first step must be an understanding of how, on Foucault's view, modern philosophy (i.e., philosophy from Kant on) has dealt with the "man" that is also the object of the human sciences.

Foucault insists that "man" is a peculiarity of modern thought. He says that "before the end of the eighteenth century, *man* did not exist" (308) and that he will disappear with the (apparently imminent) collapse of the modern episteme. How are we to understand these odd pronouncements? There are two crucial points. First, we must realize that Foucault is here using *man* to refer to human beings precisely as those for whom representations exist. The term does not refer to human beings as a biological species nor even to their psychological and social reality except insofar as it involves representation. Second, when Foucault speaks of man "existing" or "not existing" in various eras, he means that the human power of representation is or is not an object of knowledge for that era. The claim that man did not exist in the Classical Age is merely a dramatic way of making the point, which we discussed above, that there was no way of representing representation itself and therefore no way of knowing representation as one object among others. As we saw, given the Classical conception of knowledge, representation could have been an object of knowledge only by treating it as one species of thought, related by a table of identities and differences to other such species. But this contradicts the Classical identification of all thought with representation. However, at the end of the eighteenth century, representation is no longer simply identified with thought, and questions can be raised about its origin as a specific form of thinking. Once this happens, representation becomes an object of knowledge – that is, "man exists." If, in some successor to the modern episteme, human beings are no longer conceived as those for whom representations exist, then man will have "ceased to exist," and we can speak of the "death of man."

The appearance of man within the modern episteme means that the subject of representational knowledge becomes, as such, an object of knowledge. Foucault recognizes the empirical sciences as one locus of such knowledge. They show how the representational capacities of humans as living organisms (e.g., perception), as economic agents (e.g., valuing), and as users of language (e.g., describing) are themselves the causal products of the forces of life, labor, and language that precede and mold man. But man cannot be merely an object produced by the world. He is also somehow the subject that constitutes that world and all that is in it as objects. Foucault maintains that the study of man, precisely as a constituting subject, is the central concern of modern philosophical reflection and, in another way, of the modern human sciences. He first examines the philosophical approach (in Chapter 9 of OT, "Man and his doubles") and then finally takes up the approach of the human sciences.

Man as an object – that is, of the empirical sciences – appears as a finite being, limited by the environment, forces of production, and linguistic heritage that have formed him. As Foucault sees it, the question for modern philosophy is how such a being can also constitute the world of objects in which it is included. He says that the general answer, first proposed by Kant, is that this is done precisely in virtue of the very finitude that characterizes man as an object. Kant argued that the very factors limiting our knowledge – its restriction to the forms of space and time and to the framework of the categories – are also the conditions for the possibility of knowledge. The constraints of having to experience objects as spatial and temporal, as implicated in a system of causality, and so on, are also the conditions that allow the appearance of objects in the first place. The idea of applying this sort of approach to the specific domains of life, labor, and language is to display particular characteristics of man's finitude as the bases of the objective reality of these domains. The forces of life that form me as an organism are given to me as objects by my body; the forces of production that form me as an economic being are given by my desire; the forces of language that form my speaking and writing are given by my expression (cf. 314–15).

The philosophical effort to show how this is possible is carried out in what Foucault calls an "analytic of finitude" – that is, a reflection on the conditions of possibility of human finitude. The goal of this analytic is to present man's finitude as providing its own foundation. In Foucault's terminology, finitude as *founding* is "the fundamental"; finitude as *founded* is "the positive" (315). The project of modern philosophy has been to discover a relation between the fundamental and the positive that will support a coherent account of human finitude's self-foundation. The difficulty of the project lies in the fact that the relation must somehow be both one of identity (since man is one being) and differences (since nothing can literally precede and produce itself). Foucault thinks that the efforts of modern philosophy to develop an analytic of finitude have taken three main forms, corresponding to three different ways of taking the fundamental-positive pair. One relates man as a transcendental subject to man as an empirical object; another relates man as the thinking *cogito* to man as the unthought the *cogito* tries to grasp; a third relates man as a return of his origin to the present to man as a retreat of his origin into the past. We will discuss each of these efforts in turn.

The empirico-transcendental doublet

Kant gave us the distinction between man as a transcendental subject, constituting the objects of his experience, and man as himself an empirical object of that experience. But, on Foucault's view, he was not able to give an adequate account of the relationship between man as transcendental and man as empirical. One approach to this problem taken by philosophers after Kant was to reduce the transcendental to the empirical. Foucault suggests that this approach was developed in two different ways. One took our (empirical) biological knowledge of the human body as the basis of a positivistic rendition of a transcendental aesthetic. The result was the discovery that "knowledge has anatomo-physiological conditions, that it is formed gradually within the structures of the body" (319). This was taken to show that human knowledge had an (empirical) nature that determined its character and, at the same time, made it an object of our empirical knowledge. Another development of the approach was based on historical rather than biological knowledge about the human condition. This led, for example, to a Marxist version of a transcendental dialectic, showing "that knowledge had historical, social, or economic conditions; . . . in short that there was a *history* of human knowledge which could both be given to empirical knowledge and prescribe its forms" (319).

Foucault notes that, although this reductionist approach, in both of its forms, purports to work entirely at the level of empirical objects, it presupposes epistemic distinctions that seem to require a reference to man as an irreducibly transcendental subject. Particularly important, he says, is the distinction between the empirical truth involved in our biological and historical knowledge of empirical objects and the truth of our philosophical discourse about this knowledge. To accept these as two irreducibly different kinds of truth would of course immediately reinstate a sharp distinction between the empirical and the transcendental. The reductionist approach must, therefore, find some way of giving a single account of both empirical and philosophical truth, basing the latter on the former or vice versa.

The alternative of basing philosophical truth on empirical truth Foucault calls "positivist," and that of basing empirical truth on philosophical truth he calls "eschatological" (320). The positivist alternative says that our philosophical discourse about knowledge is itself true in virtue of truths about empirical objects (presumably biological or historical truths about human beings). The eschatological alternative says that our scientific and historical accounts of empirical objects are true in virtue of the truth (once it is achieved) of our philosophical discourse about knowl-

edge. (Presumably, Foucault calls this alternative "eschatological" because for it the philosophical truths that are fundamental
are nonetheless established only as the culmination of the less
fundamental process of empirical understanding.) But Foucault
regards both alternatives as self-defeating. On the positivist approach we set out to give a philosophical account of the possibility of empirical truths but wind up grounding this very account
on the empirical truths that are in question. On the eschatological approach we base empirical truth on philosophical truth and
thereby abandon our initial project of working solely on the level
of empirical objects. Foucault notes that efforts (by, e.g., Comte
and Marx) to carry out the reductionist project typically fluctu-
ate between positivism and eschatology. But no matter how it is
developed, he concludes, the project is one in which "pre-critical
naïveté holds undivided rule" (320).

More recently, phenomenological philosophers (Husserl and,
especially, Merleau-Ponty) have tried to treat man as an "empirico-transcendental doublet" (322) without reducing either
term to the other. The idea is to develop "a discourse whose
tension would keep separate the empirical and the transcendental, while being directed at both" (320). Such discourse has appropriately undertaken the analysis of our concrete actual experience, which seems to be a locus of man both as transcendental
subject and as empirical object. "Actual experience is . . . both
the space in which all empirical contents are given to experience and the original form that makes them possible in general" (321). Foucault notes that the phenomenological description of actual experience has two absolute starting points that
provide the basis of its account of man: the body as experienced in its "irreducible spatiality"and culture as experienced
"in all the immediacy of its sedimented significations" (321).
However, according to Foucault, the body and culture are simply man's empirical reality as part of nature and of history,
respectively; this, he says, means that phenomenology in fact
understands man in terms that are ultimately empirical. For all
the care and subtlety of its descriptions, "it is doing no more . . .
than fulfilling with greater care the hasty demands laid down
when the attempt was made to make the empirical, in man,
stand for the transcendental" (321). Phenomenology is, therefore, at root the same sort of reductive project as, for example,

Marxism. Because of this, Foucault says, we should not be surprised at their recent *rapprochement.*

The cogito *and the unthought*

Viewing man as irreducibly both empirical and transcendental also requires resisting reduction of the empirical to the transcendental. Foucault argues that this means, in particular, renouncing the Cartesian notion of the *cogito,* which identifies man with the "sovereign transparency" of a pure consciousness (322). Any genuinely modern *cogito* must be one that sees human consciousness as inextricably tied to an *unthought* that cannot be entirely incorporated into the clarity of the *cogito*'s thought. For Kant, the unthought lay in a transcendence on the "other side" of nature. But for modern thought after him, the unthought is a dimension of our own reality, an otherness in which we must find ourselves. The *cogito*/unthought duality expresses the fundamental reality of man as both an experiencing subject and the never fully understood (indeed, always somehow misunderstood) object of that experience.

Foucault acknowledges that, in one sense, even Descartes presented his *cogito* as confronted by an unthought – that is, by dimensions of thought (e.g., illusions, dreams, madness) that escaped the control of reflective consciousness. But for Descartes, the uncontrolled status of certain thoughts was merely temporary. Ultimately, he claimed, they were controlled by being reduced to the clarity of reflective consciousness. The *cogito* of modern philosophy, however, must be understood in a way that respects and preserves the irreducible distance between it and the unthought in man. A modern philosophy of the *cogito* cannot, like Descartes, present "the sudden and illuminating discovery that all thought is thought"—that is, that all deviant thoughts (illusions, and so on) can be reduced to reflective control. It can merely continue to pose, without answering it, the question of "how thought can reside elsewhere. . . ; how it can *be* in the form of non-thinking" (324). For this modern *cogito,* therefore, there is no indubitable inference from "I think" to "I am" – that is, no unproblematic connection between man's reality as a reflective consciousness to his reality as an object in the world. For there is no unambiguous sense in which I can say, for example, that I (as a reflective consciousness) am "this language I speak, . . . this labour I perform, . . . this life I sense deep in me. . . . I can say, equally well, that I am and that I am not all this" (324, 325). Accordingly, "the [modern] *cogito* does not lead to an affirmation of being, but it does lead to a whole series of questions concerned with being . . . [e.g.] What must I be, I who think and who am my thought, in order to be what I do not think, in order for my thought to be what I am not?" (325). (Note the strongly Sartrean tone of these formulations.)

Foucault maintains that appreciating the distinction between the modern and the Cartesian *cogito* is important for assessing the significance of Husserl's transcendental phenomenology. It might seem, for example, that the phenomenological reduction shows how the empirical ego – like the entire empirical realm – is constituted (as meaningful) by the transcendental ego, even though the two are not ontologically distinct entities. If so, hasn't Husserl linked man as a transcendental subject and man as an empirical object in a coherent account of human finitude as its own ground? Foucault agrees that this indeed might be Husserl's achievement if the transcendental ego revealed by the epoche were a pure Cartesian consciousness. But, in fact, in the modern era, there is no basis for positing any such pure consciousness. Even transcendental consciousness must be understood in the manner of the modern *cogito* – that is, as intimately tied to an opaque unthought that is its own reverse side. This means that even the reduction cannot have effected a sharp distinction between man as a transcendental subject and man as an empirical object, so that even the Husserlian transcendental ego is an instance of, rather than a solution to, the problem of man's double status. Like every other instance of the modern *cogito*-unthought distinction, Husserl's merely poses and does not answer the question of man's being. Foucault concludes by noting that this explains the tendency of phenomenology to collapse into either the empirical analyses of psychologism (as we noted in Merleau-Ponty's existential analysis) or into a transcendental ontology.

In sum, then, Foucault allows that philosophical reflection on man in terms of the *cogito* and the unthought avoids the incoherence of attempts to reduce the transcendental to the empirical (and vice versa) and preserves the tension between man as constituting subject and man as constituted object. But he argues that it does not provide an understanding of the basic relationship underlying this tension. It effectively poses but is not able to answer the fundamental question of the analytic of finitude.

The retreat and return of the origin

Modern thought's final way of approaching the problem of man's double nature is in terms of the notion of his origin (i.e., by reflecting on man as a historical reality). Foucault suggests that from this point of view, the "positive" aspect of human finitude is found in the fact that man is, from the very first instant of his existence, burdened (even constituted) by a history that is not of his own making. In one sense, of course, this is true of anything, since there is nothing in the world that begins to exist without arising from something other than itself. But presumably Foucault's point is that the ordinary things of the world originate as members of a series of homogeneous elements. The "other" from which they arise is another of the same sort. Man, however, as the unique reality capable of knowing the world of which he is nonetheless a part, originates from what is *essentially* other than him. It is as though his origin is the limit of a series of terms (man's history) to which it does not belong. If, then, man tries to discover his essential nature and identity by tracing back his history to its origin, he will be continually frustrated. Any point of apparent origin that lies on the line of *human* history will be found not to be the true origin. On the other hand, the true origin (the point of application of the conditions that in fact produced man) will be a point at which man as such is not present; it will not, strictly speaking, be *his* origin. This is the sense in which man's origin constantly retreats from him. It is a limit that he can never reach by going back through the series of events that make up his history.

However, Foucault notes that reflection on the origin of man also reveals the "fundamental" dimension of his finitude. The world is, after all, constituted as a historical reality only through human consciousness. Apart from man, there is merely a succession of *events* that may possess the unity and intelligibility of a "natural history" but that are not part of the temporal series of meaningful *actions* that make up history properly speaking. History begins only with the projects of human consciousness; the world of events becomes historical only when consciousness interprets it in terms of these projects. Man, by constituting himself as a historical reality, also constitutes the world as historical. From this second point of view, then, man's origin does contain his essential identity. It is precisely the point at which he constitutes himself and his world. The path of our history has no doubt led us far away from this origin in which resides the fundamental meaning of our humanity. It is also true, as we have seen, that if we pursue it in terms of our positive finitude, the origin will always recede from us. But from the standpoint of fundamental finitude, even this retreat of the origin is part of the historical reality constituted by man. Consequently, it would seem that we can overcome the retreat of our origin by reapprehending the original project whereby man constituted history. Such a reapprehension would be a return of the origin through which man would recover his original, essential reality as man. Foucault interprets a number of modern thinkers from Hegel to Heidegger as having taken this return as their primary task, a fact which explains the modern age's "preoccupation with recurrence . . . its concern with recommencement" (334). There are, he thinks, two different ways in which modern thought has regarded the return of the origin. Some (e.g., Hegel, Marx, Spengler) see it as a restoration of a plentitude, a completion of what has been lacking in us as we wandered from the origin. Others (e.g., Hölderlin, Nietzsche, Heidegger) see it as the opening of a void, a collapse of all the meanings of our history back into the nothingness from which they sprang. These two construals of the origin correspond to two construals of man's essential identity, either as a fullness or a negation of being. But in both cases, the return of the origin is a return to the authentic and original meaning of human existence.

Foucault thinks that the approach to the analytic of finitude through reflection on the origin of man and his history does operate at a deeper level than do the other two approaches. Specifically, it leads us to the important realization that human finitude is rooted in "the insurmountable relationship of man's being with time" (335). However, he does not think that any of the modern projects for return are successful. The origin remains "ever-elusive" (336). This means that even the effort to think finitude in terms of history and time, for all its profundity, fails to understand the being of man, the mysterious relation between man as a transcendental subject and man as an empirical object.

The death of man

Foucault does not propose some further, more subtle or more profound, approach to the understanding of man. He claims, rather, that modern philosophy's quest for man, which has led it to take the form of "anthropology," has come to a dead end. The unquestioned acceptance of man as the ineluctable focus of philosophy is a new form of dogmatic slumber ("the anthropological sleep," 340). Our awakening from it requires the uprooting of anthropology through the elimination of man as a ruling category of our thought. Foucault sees this "death of man" – heralded by Nietzsche as the inevitable consequence of the death of God – as both imminent ("the . . . ground . . . is once more stirring beneath our feet," xxiv) and promising. The "void left by man's disappearance" is "the unfolding of a space in which it is once more possible to think" (342).

As to the new possibilities of thought opened up by the death of man, Foucault's main suggestion is that they are connected with the nature of language. As we noted above, he sees language as the major concern of current thought and as a concern that is particularly appropriate for those witnessing the end of the modern episteme. Since this episteme scattered our thinking about language through several disciplines, its demise seems connected to the return of a unified and coherent reflection on the nature of language. Here there are two possibilities (cf. 338–39). One is that our new unified account of language will be somehow integrated with an account of man. By this, Foucault presumably means that conditions of possibility for the existence of man would be derived from a new unified account of language, with the result that in a postmodern episteme man (like representation in the modern episteme) would have a derived rather than a fundamental status. In this case, the death of man would mean the loss of his central role, but not his total elimination. On the other hand, Foucault notes that up until now the incompatibility of unified conceptions of both man and language "has been one of the fundamental features of our thought" (339). Perhaps, then – though Foucault insists we have no way of knowing – a new episteme will involve a conception of language that has no place at all for man. In any case, Foucault is quite certain that the dominance of our philosophy by man and "all these warped and twisted forms of reflection" on him is at an end. "To all those who still wish to talk about man . . . we can answer only with a philosophical laugh" (342–43). But, presumably since the new philosophy that will replace reflection on man does not yet exist, this laugh must be "to a certain extent, a silent one" (343). Foucault's final suggestion is that whatever new philosophy develops will find its origin in the legacy of Nietzsche: "Nietzsche marks the threshold beyond which contemporary philosophy can begin thinking again; and he will no doubt continue for a long while to dominate its advance" (342).

The human sciences

However, Foucault does not think that the fortunes of man and the modern episteme that he dominates are identical with those of philosophy. Man is also the central concern of the human sciences (the sciences of man), to which we at last turn. These sciences deal with man as living, producing, and speaking but not in the manner of the empirical sciences of biology, economics, and philology. The latter treat man as part of nature, as an empirical object, presenting his powers of representation as products of the external world. The human sciences, like philosophy, are concerned with man as a subject, as a knower whose representations constitute his world and are not just products of it. "The human sciences are not . . . an analysis of what man is by nature." They are rather an analysis that moves from man's nature as a living, producing, speaking being "to what enables this same being to know (or seek to know) what life is, in what the essence of labour and its law consist, and in what way he is able to speak" (353). In contrast to biology, for example, a human science concerned with human life (e.g., psychology) is not interested in man as a "living being with a very particular form (a somewhat special physiology and an almost unique autonomy)." It is interested in him as a "living being . . . who constitutes representations by means of which he lives, and on the basis of which he possesses the strange capacity of being able to represent to himself precisely that life" (352).

But how then do the human sciences differ from philosophy, which is also centered on the active role of man's representations in the constitution of his world? Foucault thinks that the essential difference is that, whereas philosophy treats man's representations as they appear in his interior consciousness, the human sciences treat them as part of unconscious structures and processes (or at best as on the outer boundaries of consciousness). We will return to his account of how the human sciences deal with representations after a brief sketch of what he regards as their general methodological features.

Psychology, sociology, and literary analysis

Foucault thinks that we can, without too much imprecision, divide the domain of the human sciences into three "epistemological regions" (335), each corresponding to one of the empirical sciences of biology, economics, and philology. Linked with biology is a "psychological region" concerned with man as a living being that "opens itself to the possibility of representation" (355). Linked with economics is a "sociological region" concerned with the way "the labouring, producing individual offers himself a representation of the society in which this activity occurs. . ." (355). Finally, linked to philology is a region of "the study of literature and myths" concerned with "the analysis of the verbal traces that a culture or individual may leave behind them" (355–56).

Foucault develops his account of the methodology of the human sciences (i.e., of the "sort of concepts and the kind of rationality" they involve) in terms of this threefold division (356). An overarching point is that the difficulties and controversies surrounding the methodology of the human sciences do not derive, as is often claimed, from the peculiar complexity of their object. Rather, methodological difficulties – for example, do the human sciences employ genetic or structural analysis? do they aim at explanation or understanding? – arise primarily because of the peculiar position of the human sciences in the modern episteme. Specifically, most of the standard methodological difficulties derive from the human sciences' employment of models from the empirical sciences to which they are linked. The models Foucault has in mind are "constituent models," which he distinguishes from "models of formalization" and merely metaphorical models (e.g., organic models in nineteenth-century sociology). Constituent models constitute the objects of the human sciences.

"They make it possible to create groups of phenomena as so many objects for a possible branch of knowledge. . . . They play the role of 'categories' in the area of knowledge particular to the human sciences" (357).[2] Foucault holds that each of the three divisions of the human sciences employs a model taken from the empirical science to which it is particularly linked. Moreover, each model involves a key pair of concepts in terms of which the human science's objects are understood. Psychology, for example, takes from biology the model of *functions* regulated by *norms*. Through this model, man is viewed as reacting to stimuli (both physiological and social) in ways geared to maintain an adequate level of adjustment to his environment. Sociology borrows the economic model of *conflict* governed by a body of *rules,* thus presenting individuals in opposition to one another in the pursuit of their needs and trying to regulate the opposition socially. The study of literature and myths employs a philological model through which every form of human expression is understood as having *meaning* within the context of a *system* of signs.

Although Foucault believes that each of these models has a primary role and significance in one particular human science, he recognizes that all the models (and their associated pairs of concepts) operate in all the human sciences.[3] Because of this, "all the human sciences interlock and can always be used to interpret one another," and as a result, their boundaries blur and "composite disciplines multiply endlessly" (358). Foucault uses this interlocking to explain the methodological controversies endemic to the human sciences. They arise, he says, from disagreements about which constituent model is most appropriate for a given area of inquiry. For example, the opposition of genetic to structural explanation is an opposition between the diachronic biological model of function and norm and the synchronic models of

2. Compare Canguilhem's discussion of models in "The role of analogies and models in biological discovery" in A. C. Crombie, ed., *Scientific change* (London: Heineman, 1963). (The French original was published later in E.)

3. In BC (35–36) Foucault notes the importance of the connection of biology with medicine in the former's role as a model for the human sciences. He particularly emphasizes the role of the norms that characterize the modern medical understanding of man. "When [in the human sciences] one spoke of the life of groups and societies . . . or even of the 'psychological life,' one did not think first of the internal structures of *the organized being,* but of *the medical bipolarity of the normal and the pathological*" (35). Here, of course, Canguilhem's influence is particularly apparent.

conflict and rule and of meaning and system. Similarly, methodological disputes between proponents of understanding and proponents of explanation are about whether priority should be given to the philological model over those borrowed from biology and economics.[4]

Foucault maintains that we could write the entire history of the human sciences in terms of their relation to their three models. One key feature of such a history would be the primacy assumed by each of the models in turn. The dominance of the biological model in the Romantic period was followed by the reign of the economic model (Comte and Marx) and then by the rule (from Freud to the present) of the philological model. Another key feature of this history has been a gradual shift in priority from the concepts of basic elements (functions, conflicts, and meanings) to the concepts of organizing principles (norms, rules, and systems). (Foucault specifically locates this shift in Goldstein's work in psychology, Mauss's in sociology, and Dumézil's in interpretation of myths.) This is a particularly important development because it alters the role of norms in the human sciences. As long as the concepts of basic elements dominated, each domain of the human sciences accepted a fundamental division of the normal from the abnormal – that is, between the normal and the pathological in psychology, between the rational and the irrational in sociology, and between the meaningful and the meaningless in language analysis. But with the dominance of the concepts of organizing principles, each of which defines a normative domain, this division is eliminated. Because everything treated by the human sciences has a place in a domain of norms, rules, or principles of systematic ordering, the human sciences are no longer based on a fundamental "dichotomy of values" (361).

Given this brief survey of the methodology of the human sciences and its historical development, Foucault turns to the central question of exactly how the methods of the human sciences are deployed to provide knowledge of man as a representing subject. Modern philosophy has sought such knowledge through analyses of human consciousness (ranging from positivist reductions of it to an empirical object to the Heideggerian discovery of

4. The English translation speaks of "explanation and comprehension" (e.g., p. 356). But the standard contrast in Anglo-American discussions of methodology is between explanation and understanding, so the latter seems a better translation for *compréhension*.

its profound relation with time). But, according to Foucault, none of these efforts has been able to provide a coherent understanding of how man can be both an object in the world and a subject constituting that world. As we have seen, he thinks that a stumbling block for some approaches (those based on the *cogito*) has been the unthought encountered by modern thought as the essential obverse of human consciousness. He locates the originality of the human sciences in the fact that they seek the basis of man's active role as a subject (i.e., his power of representing objects) in this very unthought – in what has come to be called the unconscious.

We may ask why philosophy itself never took this direction. Foucault never raises this question. But he might respond that philosophy regarded consciousness as the only possible locus for man's representations of the world. It had, in moving out of the Classical episteme, rejected the idea that there was no consciousness without representation, but it had not been able to give up the converse claim, that there were no representations without consciousness. In any case, Foucault thinks the human sciences are able to do this through the three key pairs of concepts, borrowed from the empirical sciences, on which they are based. Meanings (signs), functions, and conflicts can all be represented without appearing to consciousness, merely through their organization by norms, rules, or systematic principles. In this way, the human sciences have been able, for example, to speak intelligibly of the function of a social practice, of a conflict within an individual psyche, or of the meaning of a myth, even though the society, individual, or culture in question has no awareness of it.

Through unconscious functions, conflicts, and meanings, the human sciences are, according to Foucault, able to develop an account of how man represents (though not consciously) the fundamental realities of life, labor, and language, which appear in the empirical sciences as determinants of man as an object. They now appear, on the level of the unconscious, as objects constituted by man as a subject. Moreover, this constitution itself is represented in the unconscious through the structuring of functions, conflicts, and meanings by norms, rules, and systems. Thus, the human sciences are able to show how man represents the very forces that determine him as an empirical object, and, in this way, they provide a coherent representation of man as a representing subject. He therefore concludes that they succeed where philosophy failed in constituting man as a coherent object of his own thought.

According to Foucault, this achievement of the human sciences belongs to the domain of knowledge but not of science. The human science are forms of knowledge because, just as much as physics or biology, they have a legitimate position defined in the modern episteme. "They are . . . not merely illusions, pseudo-scientific fantasies" existing merely "at the level of opinions, interests, or beliefs" (365). Rather, they successfully employ epistemically sound methodologies to yield bodies of objective knowledge. On the other hand, they "do not possess the formal criteria of a scientific form of knowledge" (365). Foucault does not elaborate on this theme, but presumably he has in mind the standard points concerning the differences of the human sciences from the natural sciences in standards of testing and formalization. He does, however, emphasize that the differences between the human sciences and "the sciences in the strict sense" is due to neither "the presence of some obstacle [no doubt in Bachelard's sense] nor some internal deficiency" but simply to the distinctive place of the human sciences in the modern episteme (366). In virtue of this place, they define a body of knowledge about man that lies between mere opinion and rigorous science. But their assumption of the title *sciences* comes only from the fact that they employ models taken from the sciences of biology, economics, and philology.

History

Psychology, sociology, and the analysis of literature and myth are, in an important sense, the central human sciences for Foucault; but they do not exhaust the domain. There are also history and a triad of disciplines that Foucault calls the human "counter-sciences" (psychoanalysis, ethnology, and linguistics) that play an essential role. Foucault holds that history has a special position because the object of the human sciences – man – is a historical being of which they treat only a single set of "synchronous patternings" (370). In other words, the "man" treated by any human science will in fact be man only through a particular range of his history. Because of this, Foucault thinks that history is needed to describe the historical range in which any given psychological, sociological, or literary analysis is valid. For each human science, history "determines the cultural area – the chrono-logical and geographical boundaries – in which that branch of knowledge can be recognized as having validity" (371). But precisely because of this – and because each human science is itself a historical entity – history also limits the scope of the human sciences and destroys any claim they might make to universality. Thus, the perspective of history results in fundamental limitations on the knowledge of the human sciences. (Foucault adds, that, as a human science itself, history too is subject to these limitations.)

The countersciences

Whereas history sets the central human sciences within temporal boundaries, Foucault sees psychoanalysis and ethnology as relating them to a deeper level of analysis. For example, while these sciences go no further than the unconscious representations through which man constitutes himself and his world, psychoanalysis uncovers, through a direct analysis of the nature of the unconscious, the conditions for the possibility of these representations. (Here Foucault has primarily in mind Lacan's structuralist version of psychoanalysis.) Earlier, Classical systems of representation (described by natural history, analysis of wealth, and general grammar) were found by the modern empirical sciences to depend on the forces of life, labor, and language. Similarly, the unconscious representations of these forces are now found to depend on the deeper "metapsychological" principles of Death, Desire, and Law (Lacan's formulations of Freud's death instinct, libido, and incest taboos). These are, for the modern episteme, the profoundest roots of human finitude, the conditions of possibility for the reality of man and for our knowledge of him. However, Foucault insists that we must not think of psychoanalysis as some sort of empirically grounded "general theory of man" (376). Precisely because it reveals conditions of possibility for all knowledge of man, it cannot have even the degree of systematicity and objectivity proper to the central human sciences. Its only access to its fundamental knowledge is through a therapeutic praxis that excludes the theoretical distance of these sciences. We should not, therefore, expect from psychoanalysis "anything resembling a general theory of man or an anthropology" (376).

Psychoanalysis reveals the general conditions for unconscious representations of life, labor, and language. Ethnology (cultural anthropology) deals with the conditions of possibility of such representations for individual cultures. (Here Foucault has in mind Lévi-Strauss's structuralist anthropology.) It shows, in particular, the precise form that a given culture gives to the norms, rules, and systems, which, by organizing functions, rules, and meanings, effect unconscious representations. In so doing, it describes a culture's distinctive form of historicity. This is not to say that ethnology treats cultures historically. Foucault accepts the common view that it is a study of stable structures, not of temporal series of events. But he maintains that its structural analyses yield an understanding of the form (cumulative, circular, fluctuating, and so on) taken by history in a given culture. In this way, ethnology provides the foundation for history's simultaneous validation and limitation of the human sciences. Finally, Foucault notes that, like psychoanalysis, ethnology arises out of concrete relations between human beings. Where psychoanalytic knowledge flows from the doctor–patient relation, ethnological knowledge arises from the special relationships that exist between the dominant Western culture and all other cultures. Consequently, we should not expect ethnology, any more than psychoanalysis, to yield a general scientific account of the nature of man.

In fact, Foucault argues that, instead of developing a general concept of man and putting the human sciences on a firm foundation, psychoanalysis and ethnology call the very concept of man into question. His point seems to be that, precisely because they probe the conditions outside man that make his reality as a representing subject possible, they offer ways of thinking that do not take man as a fundamental category and even offer alternative ways of conceiving ourselves. Just as Kant's raising of the question of the conditions for the possibility of representation led to the decline of representation, so the raising of a similar question about man by psychoanalysis and ethnology is a sign of the collapse of his hegemony in our thought. For this reason, we may say of both these disciplines "what Lévi-Strauss said of ethnology: that they dissolve man" (379). Psychoanalysis and ethnology are foundational in relation to the human sciences in the sense that they excavate the ground on which they are built. But Foucault thinks the result is not ultimately to strengthen their position but to undermine them by depriving the concept of man of its fundamental role. In relation to the human sciences, psychoanalysis and ethnology are not supporting but "countersciences" (379). Accordingly, both the failure of philosophy and the success of the human sciences in trying to develop an understanding of man lead equally to the breakup of the modern episteme, to the "death of man."

Foucault finally suggests the possibility, not yet realized, of a third counterscience: linguistics. It can be located epistemically by imagining future developments of psychoanalysis and ethnology whereby ethnology would, like psychoanalysis, pay explicit attention to the unconscious and psychoanalysis would employ ethnological methods of formal structural analysis. If this happened, Foucault suggests, it would be possible to establish a fundamental relation between these two countersciences by connecting the experience of the individual (the focus of psychoanalysis) to the structure of his culture (the focus of ethnology). Specifically, he seems to be thinking of a situation in which an individual's experiences are understood as a formal system of signification deployed in the same conceptual space as that of a culture's structure; and, conversely, in which this structure is, like that of the individual's experiences, construed as that of an unconscious. Then, the choices available (and those not available) to the individual at each point in his life history could be read as due to the structure of the culture in which he lives. Conversely, the development of social structures in one direction rather than another could be read as corresponding to a specification of the sorts of individuals that can (and those that cannot) exist in the culture.

A necessary condition of the interaction Foucault envisages is that both psychoanalysis and ethnology be developed as formal sign systems. The understanding of their nature and relations as such systems would have to be achieved through a new counterscience of linguistics. This linguistics could not be developed in the context of modern philology, which presupposes the fundamental role of man that is being questioned by the countersciences. It would rather be a study of language in a pure state, not as the product and the vehicle of man's power of representation. Such a linguistics (of which Foucault no doubt thought recent work in structuralist linguistics was an adumbration) would, he thinks, greatly strengthen the connection of the human sciences to formal methods and make the issue of formalization much more central than it has been so far. But even more important is the fact that the new linguistics would play an essential role in the reflection on language that, as we have seen, Foucault regards as a crucial part of the development of a new, postmodern episteme. In this reflection, the formalism of linguistics would, he suggests, be the counterpart of the "formalism" of modern literature, which also undermines the place of man by treating language as a self-contained, self-referring system that is not essentially tied to the human project of representing the world. What literature develops as an experience of "the end of man" linguistics would develop as a structural analysis that undermines man's central place in language.

Foucault concludes that all the developments of modern thought, its successes, its failures, and its immediate prospects point to the imminent collapse of the modern episteme. He admits that he may be wrong in his suggestions as to how the final collapse will occur and what may be the nature of a postmodern episteme. Specifically, his idea that the end of man will be essentially tied to a new vision of language can, he says, be expressed only as a question, not an affirmation. Similarly, implicit suggestions about the fundamental role of "structuralism" (Lacan's psychoanalysis, Lévi-Strauss's cultural anthropology, recent developments in linguistics) in a new episteme are only conjectures (and ones Foucault later backed away from). In the final paragraph of OT, Foucault even hedges a bit from his earlier declarations that the end of man is imminent, saying only that "if some event of which we can at the moment do no more than sense the possibility" were to alter the fundamental structures of knowledge, "then one can certainly wager that man would be erased, like a face drawn in sand at the edge of the sea" (387). But what remains entirely certain for him is the crucial fact that the modern episteme, dominated by its peculiar conception of human reality as "man," is merely one, relatively recent, way of thinking ourselves. Its constraints are not absolute and may one day be broken.

The order of things: methods and results

OT is much more explicit than Foucault's two previous historical studies in its formulation and deployment of the archaeological method. It claims from the outset to offer a new approach ("[my]

analysis does not belong to the history of ideas or of science," xxi) and, as we have seen, frequently pauses to explain just how, on a particular issue, it breaks with standard practices and results. However, to a very significant extent, Foucault's methods in OT are applications and extensions of Canguilhem's history of concepts. Certainly, his accounts of particular empirical disciplines of the eighteenth and nineteenth centuries are straightforward histories of concepts. In every case, Foucault's effort is to search beneath the play of theoretical formulations for more basic conceptual similarities and differences. For example, his treatment of natural history presents *structure* and *character* as the two organizing concepts of the Classical study of living things, spanning even the most important theoretical divisions (e.g., between the system and the method). Similarly, his discussion of economics is concerned to show the formation (from Smith to Ricardo) of *labor* as an original concept that distinguishes economics from the Classical analysis of wealth and as the common background of all nineteenth-century accounts of economic history. Further, in the typical fashion of a history of concepts, Foucault's work undermines the standard identification of precursors, based on superficial resemblances of terminology or theoretical form. Thus, he rejects eighteenth-century "developmentalists" and even Lamarck as precursors of Darwin on the grounds that they did not in fact have the concept of *evolution*. In sum, in OT's application of "archaeological" analysis to individual empirical disciplines, there is nothing that goes beyond the methodology of Canguilhem's history of concepts.

Foucault also extends the history of concepts to interdisciplinary contexts. There is, for example, his linking of apparently diverse disciplines by exhibiting similarities in their basic concepts. Thus, the three Classical empirical disciplines are all seen to have the "quadrilateral" structure of attribution, articulation, designation, and derivation found in the Classical analysis of language. Further, and more importantly, Foucault is able to show how philosophical concepts such as *resemblance, representation,* and *man* pervade the thought of an entire period. This enables him to introduce the notion of an episteme as the system of concepts that specifies the nature and structure of knowlege for an intellectual era.

These extensions of Canguilhem's approach also transform it. The key point is that, in analyzing concepts that span diverse modes of inquiry, Foucault moves to a level where individual disciplines are no longer allowed to define the terms in which the historian must understand them. As a historian of biology, Canguilhem focuses on the concepts that are in fact deployed by the biologists whose work he is analyzing. He writes the history of the reflex because this is a central concept in current description and explanation of biological phenomena. Foucault, however, deals not only with first-order biological concepts but also with concepts that define the conditions of possibility for formulating such concepts. He shows, for example, how concepts such as *structure* and *character, organic function* and *evolution* are themselves grounded in more general conceptions of representation and of historicity.

This is an important development, first, because it allows Foucault to write the history of disciplines such as the human sciences that are defined through essential relations to other disciplines. A history of, say, psychology that dealt only with the descriptive and explanatory concepts employed by contemporary psychologists would present a contradictory tangle of competing approaches and would not be able to exhibit psychology as an essentially unified application of the biological model of function and norm.

But far more important is the fact that Foucault's extension of the history of concepts undermines the privileged role of disciplines in the history of thought and knowledge. For Bachelard and Canguilhem, each particular domain of knowledge (e.g., chemistry, biology) emerged at some point from prescientific confusion and has, since that point, developed progressively as a unified body of scientific knowledge. There may be sharp conceptual breaks, but subsequent concepts are rectifications of earlier ones and contain them as special cases of a broader and more adequate explanation of the world. Accordingly, the history of science is written from the normative standpoint of current science, which provides the historian with standards for judging past scientific work by the extent to which it is preserved in today's science. For Foucault, however, the possibility of the entire conceptual development of any given discipline is based on deeper concepts, shared by other disciplines, and themselves subject to transformations over time that are not controlled by any discipline. The Classical empirical domains, for example, were grounded (along with Classical philosophy) in the concept of representation. When this concept was fundamentally transformed at the beginning of the modern era, the basis of all the Classical disciplines was eliminated and a whole new system of knowledge instituted. Such changes have constituted the grounds for the possibility of current disciplines; therefore, the history of such changes cannot be written in terms of the concepts of these disciplines and the norms of knowledge their concepts define. By extending Canguilhem's methods, Foucault discovered a level of conceptual history more fundamental than that of the first-order concepts of scientific (and other) disciplines.

The significance of the move to this level can be more fully appreciated by noting how it modifies some of the basic conceptions of Bachelard's philosophy of science. Consider, for example, the central notion of epistemological break. Bachelard used this in two different contexts: first, to characterize the move from nonscientific to scientific modes of thought and, second, to characterize major shifts within the progressive development of an established discipline. For Foucault, however, the notion further applies to transitions whereby one discipline is disestablished and replaced by another as the locus of knowledge of a given domain of reality. An epistemological break in this sense implies a radical change in how knowledge in the given domain is conceived; concepts previously regarded as embodying important truths are disregarded as inadequate, irrelevant, or, at best, peripheral.

Foucault's new level of analysis also involves a transformation of Bachelard's notions of epistemological obstacle and of the psychoanalysis of knowledge. Bachelard, after all, did recognize epistemological factors that work below the level of the first-order concepts of scientific disciplines and, unknown to those working in a given discipline, influence the formation of these concepts. However, for Bachelard such factors are entirely negative, the residues of outdated modes of thought that obstruct the path of scientific development by hindering the development of new concepts. By contrast, Foucault's deeper epistemological level is one that has positive significance, embodying the conditions that make possible the formation of new concepts. For him, therefore, the level beneath first-order scientific concepts is itself one of knowledge, not of obstacles to it. Foucault places less emphasis than Bachelard on the diachronic progress of knowledge but much more on its synchronic depth. The latter is the object of archaeological analysis, which, unlike Bachelard's psychoanalysis of knowledge, is concerned not with the elimination of negative epistemic factors but with the description of positive ones.

In summary, the archaeology that Foucault deploys in OT operates at two levels. The first, corresponding to his analyses of particular Classical and modern empirical sciences, is essentially that of Canguilhem's history of concepts. The second, corresponding to his analyses of the epistemes that ground the possibility of a variety of empirical disciplines, fundamentally transforms the conception of knowledge employed by Bachelard and Canguilhem.

We have already discussed, at the end of Chapter 4, criticisms of OT's specific and constructive histories of the Renaissance and Classical Age. The general points made there also apply to Foucault's treatment of the modern episteme. His interpretations of particular authors (particularly Cuvier and Marx) have drawn some criticism, but the primary objection is to the lack of detailed evidence for the sweeping claims of his constructive history. This must be admitted but, as before, it can be pointed out that the primary value of constructive history lies in fruitfulness rather than accuracy.

In any case, Foucault's account of the modern episteme is primarily important as the basis of his critical history of the human sciences. OT differs from FD in that it does not merely provide a heuristic basis for such a critique but actually endeavors to carry it out through an analysis of the nature and limitations of both recent philosophy and the central contemporary disciplines of psychology, sociology, and literary studies. In the case of both philosophy and the human sciences, the basis of his critique is the centrality of the concept of man in these disciplines. Given this, he goes on to argue that philosophy has been unable to provide an adequate account of how man can be both constituting subject and constituted object and so has never really made man an object of knowledge. The human sciences have been more successful. Approaching man not through a self-reflective analysis of consciousness but through an analysis of his unconscious, they have managed to make him an object of knowledge, even though this knowledge lacks the rigor of a science. However, Foucault further claims that this focus on the unconscious has led to the structuralist countersciences (psycho-analysis, ethnology, and – on the horizon – linguistics) that undermine the concept of man on which the human sciences are based.

Foucault's critique seems open to at least three lines of fundamental criticism. First, there are difficulties associated with his claim that philosophy and the human sciences are based on the concept of man (as he understands it). With regard to philosophy, for example, the claim may well be acceptable for the sort of philosophy Foucault discusses under the rubric of the "analytic of finitude" – for example, phenomenology and its existential progeny. But what of the rich variety of Anglo-American philosophical projects that we assign the vague label "analytic philosophy"? The only ways in which they can be plausibly thought of as covered by Foucault's discussion of the modern episteme are in his comments on formalization (à la Russell) for the sake of linguistic clarity and on positivism as a naive rejection of the modern problematic of man. But it is highly implausible to think that anything close to the whole of current analytic philosophy could be reduced to either Russellian formalism or positivism. At a minimum, then, there is a major gap in Foucault's case for regarding philosophy as dominated by the modern concept of man.[5] Moreover, even if Foucault can show that analytic philosophy too is directed toward the understanding of man, he must also show that it has not been able to achieve this understanding. Perhaps, for example, the turn of many analytic philosophers from consciousness to language as their fundamental category makes the problem of man's status more tractable. The linguistic turn may have the same sort of virtues that Foucault sees in the human sciences' move to the unconscious.

Second, Foucault is far from successful in showing that even the sorts of philosophy he does discuss in the analytic of finitude cannot reach an adequate understanding of man. Consider, for example, his treatment (in his discussion of the empirico-transcendental doublet) of Merleau-Ponty's attempt to understand man through an existential phenomenology of "actual experience." He notes that this experience is doubly focused: on the body that defines the perspective of our perceptions and on the

5. On the other hand, Thomas Nagel's discussion of the root of major problems in analytic philosophy might support Foucault's conclusion. Cf. Nagel's *The view from nowhere* (Oxford: Oxford University Press, 1986).

culture that defines the perspective of our social practices. From this, he abruptly concludes that Merleau-Ponty's project of understanding man by describing his fundamental bodily and cultural experiences is an empirical one. But this conclusion follows only on the assumption that Merleau-Ponty is wrong in his central claim that our actual experience of bodily and cultural meanings occurs at a level prior to the distinction of transcendental subject and empirical object. Foucault gives no reason at all for questioning this claim, which Merleau-Ponty would hold is justified by a rich variety of phenomenological analyses; he simply denies it. At the best, Foucault offers an indication of the direction in which he would carry out a critique of Merleau-Ponty's approach (presumably by actually exhibiting the empirical character of his phenomenological descriptions). But there is no such critique presented in OT.

Foucault's critiques of Husserl's transcendental phenomenology and of Heidegger's ontology of time are similarly unsatisfactory. The former is based on the unsupported assertion that the Cartesian ideal of total reflection is impossible and the latter on the likewise unsupported assertion that a genuine return to the origin of man is impossible. In both cases, Foucault's "critique" is once again merely a matter of gratuitously denying the possibility of what the philosophers he is criticizing present as the ultimate achievement of their mode of analysis. Since Foucault's discussions of the three "doubles" include some of the most convoluted and obscure passages in OT, readers can be easily fooled into thinking that there is a level of profound criticism they have failed to penetrate. In fact, however, whatever profundity there is in these analyses concerns only Foucault's way of understanding the major projects of recent Continental philosophy and relating them to one another. On this interpretative level he may be making an important contribution. But the contortions of his interpretative analysis serve only to hide the weakness of his criticism.

The third difficulty concerns the significance of Foucault's conclusion that the structuralist "countersciences" undermine the concept of man and hence the human sciences based on it. Lacan's psychoanalysis and Lévi-Strauss's ethnology provide, he maintains, an analysis of the unconscious conditions that enable us to understand how man can be both constituting subject and constituted object. (Just how they do this is not made clear in

OT, but let us grant the point for the sake of the argument.) In this sense, they ground the concept of man. But, precisely because they explain man in terms of something more basic (his unconscious), they deprive the concept of man of its place as a fundamental epistemic category. In this sense, they undermine it. The idea here seems to be that the countersciences show how such a thing as man is possible, but only by moving to a level of analysis at which he appears as just one possibility. They therefore also show that there are alternatives to thinking of ourselves under the category of man, thereby freeing us from the tyranny of this concept.

But the question naturally arises, What tyranny? Granted that the human sciences are based on the concept of man and that this concept has been somehow undermined, what differences does this make for human liberation? The problem is that the concept of man, as articulated in OT, is an epistemological concept. It encapsulates a view of man as both a knower and an object of knowledge. The elimination (or decentering) of this concept will no doubt significantly alter our conception of knowledge. But why should such a change bring with it the sort of social and moral transformations relevant to human liberation? The evident joy with which Foucault heralds the "death of man" strongly suggests that he thinks something more than a change in the epistemic wind is at stake. But there is little in OT to explain why this should be so.

At the root of this crucial gap in Foucault's critique is the fact that OT almost entirely ignores nondiscursive practices, which, in his work both before and after OT, are the essential means of controlling human freedom. There is nothing corresponding to the asylum in FD, the clinical hospital in BC, or the prison in DP. The entire analysis is of bodies of discourse. The reason, as Foucault explains in an interview shortly after the publication of OT, was his realization that "discursive domains did not always obey the structures that they share with their associated practical and institutional domains, but rather [sometimes] obey the structures shared with other epistemological domains."[6] Accordingly, contrary to his approach in FD and the beginning of BC, OT treats discourses as relatively independent of nondiscursive structures.

Foucault was not, admittedly, abandoning his earlier concern

6. Bellour, 195–96.

with the relations of discursive and nondiscursive structures but merely bracketing it until he had a better understanding of the former in their own terms. Thus, in the interview cited above, he says that archaeology must pursue "two perpendicular axes of description: that of the theoretical models common to several discourses, [and] that of the connections between the discursive domain and the nondiscursive domain."[7] This view is also reflected in his remark, noted above, that questions about the causes of changes in episteme require reference to nondiscursive factors that we will be able to discuss only after we have more fully developed archaeology as discursive analysis.

It is, however, not just that the lack of nondiscursive analysis in OT makes it impossible for Foucault to explain *there* how the concept of man is tied to restrictions on human freedom or why its elimination would be a blow for human freedom. Even when, in DP and HS, he integrates nondiscursive structures into his analysis of the human sciences, it remains unclear what OT's epistemic concept of man has to do with domination. There is a brief reference in DP to the notion of *man* invoked by Enlightenment legal reformers (74). But here "man" refers to a notion of "humanity," common to all human beings and the locus of their inviolable moral worth. Foucault offers no account of how, if at all, this moral concept of humanity is to be connected to man as an epistemological concept.

It is, of course, true that DP and HS connect knowledge with the social and political power that restricts freedom. Moreover, DP shows how people are dominated by being made objects of knowledge, while HS shows how they are dominated (through systems of self-surveillance) by becoming subjects possessing and employing knowledge. In this sense, Foucault does eventually connect domination with the epistemic categories of subject and object. However, the conception of knowledge at work in DP and HS requires merely that human beings have knowledge about themselves – a situation that would obtain at any period in human history. Even the Classical Age, for example, had no difficulty with the idea of human beings as objects of their own knowledge. The modern concept of man further requires the notion of human beings as somehow constituting themselves as objects of their knowledge and knowing themselves precisely as

7. Ibid., 196.

knowers. Foucault offers no account of how this distinctively modern concept of man is connected with modern systems of power.

In view of the above difficulties, we must conclude that Foucault's critique of the human sciences in OT is unsuccessful. Not that the objections I have raised show the key claims of his critical history to be false. But there are major gaps at crucial points in the argument that must be filled if these claims are to be adequately supported.

6

THE ARCHAEOLOGY OF KNOWLEDGE

It would be too much to claim that the histories of thought Foucault wrote before the methodological reflections of AK were, from the beginning, part of a single coherent project. He himself remarks[1] that it was only after finishing OT that he saw the possibility of construing the earlier works as part of a unified enterprise. But, as our discussions of the methods at work in the three books has confirmed, there is an important sense in which this series of studies gradually develops a distinctive approach to the history of thought. AK was Foucault's effort to articulate this approach in an explicit methodology.[2]

The leitmotiv of AK is its connection of the archaeological method developed in Foucault's three historical studies to the primary substantive thesis of OT: the death of man. The book's

1. "La naissance d'un monde" (interview with J-M. Palmier on AK), *Le Monde*, 3 mai, 1969.
2. Foucault gives an interesting preliminary sketch of some of the main ideas of AK in his reply to questions posed by students at the Ecole Normale Supérieure, "Sur l'archéologie des sciences: response au cercle d'épistémologie," *Cahiers pour l'analyse* 9 (1968), 5–44. This has been translated (in a slightly condensed form) as "On the archaeology of the sciences," *Theoretical Practice* 3/4 (1971), 108–27. Cf. also Foucault's "Response à une question," *Esprit* 36 (1968), 850–74, translated by R. Boyers and C. Gordon as "Politics and the study of discourse," *Ideology and Consciousness* 3 (1978), 7–26.

main effort is to define archaeology as an approach to the history of thought that eliminates the fundamental role of the human subject. Archaeology would thus operate as the historical counterpart of the structuralist countersciences (psychoanalysis, ethnology, and linguistics) in the postmodern move away from a conception of man as the object that constitutes the world of objects.

This explains both the close link of Foucault's work with structuralism and his insistence that he is not a structuralist. The link derives from the fact that, like structuralist work on language, culture, and the unconscious, archaeology displaces man from his privileged position. As Foucault said in a 1969 interview, both archaeology and structuralism operate "within a great transformation of the knowledge of the human sciences" that has "put into question . . . the status of the subject, the privileged place of man."[3] But, as he goes on to say, although archaeology works "alongside" structuralism in this transformation, it is not part of it. This is simply because archaeology is a historical method of inquiry, concerned not with structural possibilities but with actual occurrences and their effects. As Foucault remarked to Raymond Bellour regarding his relation to structuralism: "I am not so much interested in the formal possibilities offered by a system like a language. Personally, I am, rather, obsessed by the existence of discourses, by the fact that words have happened, that these events have . . . left traces behind them."[4]

As a historical method that decenters the human subject, archaeology is, according to Foucault, similar to that practiced by the historians of the *Annales* school (and by the Cambridge and the Soviet schools).[5] He notes that history has been the last bastion of those who insist on the primacy of man. Even if structuralism has eliminated the originative role of the subject in the study of language and the unconscious, still, they maintain, man rules over his own history. "For them, there is an absolute subject of history, who makes history, who assures its continuity, who is the

3. "Michel Foucault explique son dernier livre" (interview with J.-J. Brochier on AK), *Magazine littéraire* 28 (1969), 25.
4. Raymond Bellour, "Deuxième entretien avec Michel Foucault," in Bellour's *Le livre des autres* (Paris: L'Herne, 1971), 201. (The interview first appeared in *Lettres françaises*, 15 juin, 1967.)
5. Cf. Bellour, 189–91, and Brochier, 23–24.

author and the guarantee of its continuity. As to structural analyses, they are merely part of a synchronic slice of this continuity of history, which is thus submitted to the sovereignty of man."[6] (Foucault says that those holding this view include not only Sartre but also Goldman, Lukàcs, Dilthey, and the nineteenth-century Hegelians.) But Foucault argues that contemporary historiography, as practiced by the *Annales* group and others, belies this claim. It has, for example, focused on periods of such great length (*la longue durée*) that they cannot be the loci of the activities of any individual or social subject; the relevant factors become instead slowly altering material conditions such as geography and climate.

In the history of thought (e.g., history of science, of philosophy, of literature), the move away from the constituting subject has, by contrast, been associated with an emphasis not on long-term continuities and gradual change but on sharp discontinuities, on radical breaks and dislocations. This is because in the history of thought, unlike other history, the subject has primarily been a principle of continuity, transmitting (through mechanisms such as influence and tradition) ideas from one mind to another. Foucault mentions the work of both Bachelard and Canguilhem on the history of science as examples of the new approach. He also refers to Martial Guéroult's work in the history of philosophy and that of Michel Serres in the history of mathematics. But his own studies in FD, BC, and OT are clearly the main examples he has in mind in undertaking to formulate a methodology for a non-subject-centered history of thought.

The very idea of such a history may seem incoherent. How can there be a history of thought that is not essentially a history of thinkers? To begin undermining this notion, so deeply entrenched in standard history of ideas, Foucault undertakes a critique of the "subjective unities" (i.e., the various products of the intellectual activities of human subjects) that are the objects of the standard history. Such unities fall into a hierarchy depending on their closeness to the immediate activity of the individual subject. Thus, at the most fundamental level, there is the particular *book* (or poem, essay, or what have you) by a given writer; next there is the *oeuvre*, the assemblage of all the works of a writer. At a higher level, there are such things as *periods* and

6. Brochier, 24.

traditions (works of authors related by way of interests and influences). Finally, there are *disciplines* (each itself part of a disciplinary hierarchy, ranging, for example, from science in general to subspecialties of microbiology) that include different traditions through different periods. Within the framework of traditional history of ideas, these various subjective unities are related by a number of subjective *means of transmission*. Thus, there is the *development* of an author from work to work, the *influence* of one author on another, and that generalized influence of all on all that is called the *spirit of an age*.

Foucault marshals a variety of considerations to question the coherence and intelligibility of these subjective unities and subjective means of transmission. The former – particularly the fundamental unities of book and oeuvre – are often taken as self-evident, unproblematic starting points for the history of thought. A little reflection reveals, however, that we are hard put to define the extension of either *book* (does it include an "anthology of poems, a collection of posthumous fragments, . . . a volume of Michelet's *Histoire de France* . . . , a Catholic missal"?) or *oeuvre* (does it include "pseudonymous texts, unfinished drafts, letters, reported conversations"? [AK, 23]).[7] As to the subjective means of transmission, it is apparent that intellectual histories tracing the "influence" of writers on one another often yield uninformative juxtapositions of parallel texts and that explanations in terms of the "spirit of the age" are often virtually tautologous. Foucault reacts with understandable impatience to much garden-variety "research" in the history of ideas:

> To seek in the great accumulation of the already-said the text that resembles "in advance" a later text, to ransack history in order to rediscover the play of anticipations or echoes, . . . to say that the Port-Royal grammarians invented nothing, or to discover that Cuvier had more predecessors than one thought, these are harmless enough amusements for historians who refuse to grow up. (AK, 144)

Here, of course, he is echoing Canguilhem's critique of "precursors."

7. On the same subject, cf. Foucault's essay, "What is an Author?" in Colin Gordon, ed., *Language, Counter-memory, and Practice* (Ithaca, N.Y.: Cornell University Press, 1977).

Such difficulties do not, of course, show that the subjective unities and subjective means of transmission are incoherent or unusable, but they do suggest that they are not unproblematic, entirely self-evident starting points and may be challenged and replaced as basic categories of the history of thought by alternative, non-subject-centered categories. Foucault sees his archaeology of thought as doing precisely this.

The elements of archaeology

Like any historical inquiry, Foucault's archaeology begins with *documents,* collections of statements that we have received from our ancestors. Ordinary history – and especially the history of ideas – sees documents as clues to the intentional acts (beliefs, thoughts, desires, feelings) of those who produced them. It uses the objective linguistic data of statements to reconstruct the inner life of subjects. Foucault, by contrast, proposes to take statements as objects of study in their own right, making no effort to use them as means to revive the thoughts of the dead. He treats them as *monuments* rather than documents (AK, 7).[8] We are, of course, already familiar with two (nonhistorical) areas of inquiry that treat statements in their own right: grammar, which defines the conditions under which a statement is meaningful, and logic, which specifies what can and cannot be consistently added to a given set of statements. But it is obvious that the set of statements actually made in a given domain and epoch is a very small subset of those permitted by grammar and logic. Ordinarily, we explain the vast number of grammatically and logically possible statements that are not made on the basis of the experiences, beliefs, and intentions of subjects. We do not speak of Jupiter hurling thunderbolts because we do not believe in him; the ancient Greeks did not speak of space travel because they had no experience of it; the Victorians suppressed certain aspects of sexuality out of shame. Foucault suggests that in many fundamental cases the explanation for such linguistic gaps is rather that statements are subject to a further set of rules (neither grammatical nor logical) to which speakers unwittingly conform. Such a set of statements belongs to what he calls a *discursive formation.*

8. Foucault credits Canguilhem with suggesting to him this use of the term *monument.* Cf. "Sur l'archéologie des sciences," 127.

More fully, Foucault regards a discursive formation as involving four basic elements: the *objects* its statements are about, the kinds of cognitive status and authority they have (what Foucault calls their *enunciative modality*), the *concepts* in terms of which they are formulated, and the *themes* (theoretical viewpoints) they develop. However, he does not think of a given discursive formation as defined by a unique system of objects, a single enunciative modality, a distinctive conceptual framework, or a consistent set of themes or theories. The same discursive formation will be a vehicle for discourse about different systems of objects, categorized in terms of different conceptual frameworks, and its statements will have a variety of enunciative modalities and may develop very diverse theoretical viewpoints.

Accordingly, Foucault does not regard a discursive formation as distinguished by any unity (of, e.g., objects, concepts, method) provided by its elements. Rather, a discursive formation is a "system of dispersion" for its elements: It defines a field within which a variety of different, even conflicting, sets of elements can be deployed. Thus, the unity of a discursive formation is due entirely to the *rules* that govern the formulation of statements about different systems of objects, exhibiting different enunciative modalities, employing different conceptual frameworks, and expressing different theoretical viewpoints.

Examples of discursive formations that Foucault treated in his historical studies are the three Classical empirical sciences, general grammar, natural history, and analysis of wealth as well as the modern sciences of philology, biology, and economics. Further, the sharp break between Classical and modern thought is reflected in the fact that the nineteenth-century empirical sciences are each separate discursive formations, not part of the discursive formations of the corresponding Classical disciplines. But these examples should not mislead us into thinking that discursive formations are always coterminous with scientific (or quasi-scientific) disciplines. A scientific discipline may, for example, be just one part of a discursive formation that also includes various sorts of nonscientific (e.g., legal, literary, philosophical, and commonsense) statements. As we will see below, this is Foucault's view of nineteenth-century psychiatry. His archaeological analyses before AK did almost always start from scientific (or would-be scientific) disciplines and often enough (especially in BC and OT) did not go much beyond them. But in his general characterization of discursive formations, he wants to emphasize that the scope of archaeological analysis is much broader than some of his practice might suggest. Moreover, it is clear that this broader construal is operative in his earlier work, especially FD and the beginning of BC.

There are two other important ways in which Foucault's preceding historical practice does not correspond exactly to the general conception of discursive formations put forward in AK. For one thing, none of his analyses deal with all four of the elements of a discursive formation on anything like an equal level. In all three of the earlier books, there is a very strong emphasis on the history of concepts, either in Canguilhem's sense of the concepts of a particular scientific discipline or in the deeper archaeological sense of the concepts underlying various disciplines and/or nondiscursive practices. The question of the objects of discursive formations is extensively considered only in FD, in, for example, its discussion of criteria for the recognition of the mad. The topic of the cognitive status (enunciative modality) of statements is important primarily in BC, because of its concern with the emergence of a medicine that claims to be based on empirical scientific knowledge. Alternative theoretical viewpoints are emphasized primarily in OT, where Foucault is concerned to show the relative superficiality of what other historians take to be fundamental disagreements. Foucault's own suggestion (AK, 65) – that FD operates primarily on the level of objects, BC on that of enunciative modalities, and OT on that of concepts – seems quite an oversimplification. It may be that in retrospect these seemed to him the areas in which the three studies made their most important or most original contribution. But, particularly in its downplaying of concern with concepts in FD and BC, the suggestion is very misleading.

Secondly, Foucault's earlier treatments of discursive formations do not highlight their role as "systems of dispersion" nearly so much as AK does. The idea is occasionally present but distinctly muted, since the primary emphasis is on the common ground rather than the diversity it supports. OT does, of course, emphasize the role of the various empirical disciplines as common grounds uniting those engaged in theoretical disagreements, and these disagreements surely also involve differences in views about the locus of scientific authority (e.g., reason versus experience) and about the conceptualization and objectification of empirical domains. But there is no suggestion that under-girding such diversity is the primary function of discursive formations such as general grammar and nineteenth-century economics. The reason for this is perhaps that most of the discursive formations of OT are scientific disciplines, which are much more homogeneous than formations that also embrace a variety of nonscientific discursive practices.

None of the above points show that the notion of discursive formation developed in AK is not present in Foucault's historical studies. But they do suggest that his explicit methodology emphasizes aspects of the earlier works that are often only implicit and/or subordinated to other concerns. Rereading them from the perspective of AK involves a construal of their intention and results that in some ways deepens our understanding of them and in others distorts it. AK not only elucidates Foucault's past achievements but also appropriates them for his present and future purposes.

Foucault's general analysis of discursive formations consists of his detailed classification of the rules governing them. These fall into four types, each corresponding to one of the elements of a discursive formation. First, there are *rules for the formation of objects*, which are themselves of three sorts. The first sort includes rules associated with the social loci ("surfaces of emergence") from which the objects of a discursive formation emerge. Such rules derive from the social norms whereby objects characterized in a certain way are separated off from a social context and transferred to the domain of the discursive formation. For example, in modern society, children whose behavior is sufficiently deviant from social (e.g., familial) norms are judged mentally disturbed and hence become an object of concern for psychopathology. Thus, the family is a surface of emergence for objects of the discursive formation of contemporary psychopathology. A second sort of rules for the formation of objects is associated with those to whom a society gives the authority of deciding what objects belong to a given discursive formation. (Here Foucault speaks of "authorities of delimitation.") Thus, even if a person's behavior has not been sufficiently deviant from social norms, doctors may decide, after careful tests and examinations, that he or she is mentally disturbed and requires their care. Finally, entirely apart from social norms and authoritative judgment, people may merit classification as mentally disturbed simply in virtue of having certain symptomatic properties. Here they will be objects of psychopathology because of where they are located on what Foucault calls "grids of specification," the systems whereby discursive formations classify and relate different kinds of objects. In nineteenth-century psychopathology, for example, the "soul," conceived as a specific system of interrelated faculties, and the "body," conceived as a specific system of interrelated organs, were grids of specification. Thus, someone with a certain sort of chemical imbalance or inherited disposition might, by that very fact, be an object of psychopathology. Foucault emphasizes that these three sorts of rules for the formation of objects are not independent of one another. For example, in some typical cases, a social unit's (say, a family's) decision that certain deviant behavior shows that a child is mentally disturbed can be overruled by a psychiatrist's judgment, and the latter judgment is itself subject to the rules of psychopathological classification. But it would be an oversimplification to say that the only relation between the three types of rules is this one of hierarchical subordination. There will, for example, be cases in which the rules of psychopathological classification yield to the rules associated with social deviancy. Thus, a president's assassin might be judged sane even if this judgment is not supported by the rules of classification. More generally, the formation of objects depends on a complex variety of interactions among the three sorts of rules.

A second general type of rule governing the statements of a discursive formation concerns the formation of enunciative modalities. A statement's modality is a function of the context from which it originates. One key determinant of modality is the right of certain people to use a given mode of speech. Thus, only those properly trained and certified may make authoritative medical statements. Another factor is the "institutional site" from which a statement originates – whether, for example, it is the report of a hospital laboratory test, an article in *The New England Journal of Medicine,* or the advice to a patient of a physician in private practice. A third consideration is the position of the subject making the statement vis-à-vis the objects of discourse – for example, whether the statement is a direct perceptual report, a conclusion drawn from evidence by theoretical calculation, or a restatement of such a conclusion, on a theoretician's authority, by a classroom teacher. To each of these three sorts of factors there correspond different sorts of rules for the formation of enunciative modalities.

The third type of rules of a discursive formation comprises

those that govern the formation of concepts. On Foucault's account, concepts are specified by a complex set of rules regarding our treatment of statements. Once again, he distinguishes three sorts of such rules. First, there are those that establish relations (e.g., logical or methodological) of ordering and succession among statements. In Classical natural history, for example, there are rules that govern how we move from direct observational descriptions of a plant to a characterization of its essential properties and then to a classification of it in a taxonomic table. Similarly, certain statements of natural history will be related to others as premises to conclusions, hypotheses to verifications, or laws to applications.

Second, there are rules for the formation of concepts that establish various attitudes of acceptance or rejection toward classes of statements. Such rules define, first, *a field of presence* – that is, a range of statements in the discursive formation in question that are accepted, a range that are rejected, and a range that are regarded as needing critical evaluation. They also define a *field of concomitance,* a range of statements from *other* discursive formations that are, in various ways, "active" (e.g., as models or analogical confirmations) in the given discursive formation. Finally, these rules define *a field of memory,* a range of statements that are no longer accepted or even discussed in their own right but that have various historical connections with accepted statements. Foucault illustrates these sorts of rules by referring once again to Classical natural history (AK, 58). But his account of the modern sciences of man is also a good example. Their field of presence corresponds to the distinctive set of statements about man that are accorded serious disciplinary consideration by psychology, sociology, and literary analysis. Their field of concomitance includes, most prominently, the empirical sciences (biology, economics, and philology) that provide their models. And their field of memory includes the Renaissance and Classical disciplines for which, as OT shows, they are the modern replacements.

Third, the formation of concepts is governed by rules specifying various *procedures of intervention* that may be applied to a discursive formation's statements to produce new statements. Thus, there are techniques for rewriting statements (from, e.g., linear to tabular form), of transcribing them (e.g., into a formalized language), or of translating them (e.g., into quantitative or

qualitative form). Also included here are methods of approximation, techniques for limiting the domain of a statement's validity,
procedures for applying a statement to a new domain, and methods of systematizing statements.

The fourth and last type of rule governing the statements of a
discursive formation concerns the formation of strategies. By a
strategy Foucault means a specific theory (or theme) that develops
within a discursive formation (e.g., a theory of evolution in biology, the idea of an original language from which all others derive
in philology). Foucault notes that, for standard history of ideas,
theories develop from "chance encounters between ideas . . . ,
influences, discoveries, [and so on] . . . that the genius of individuals arranges into more or less well constituted wholes" (AK, 64).
His own view, by contrast, is that the range of possible theories in a
discursive formation is specified by rules that underlie and implicitly control the efforts of individual thinkers.

The range of theoretical alternatives is defined, first of all, by
the various *points of diffraction* found in a given discursive formation. Such points exist where there are two or more statements,
existing on the same level and equally permitted by the discursive
formation's rules, that are incompatible with one another. They
thus represent forks within the discursive formation from which
different theoretical turns can be taken, leading to very different
theoretical developments. Alternative theories are *equivalent* in
the sense that the rules of the discursive formation do not prefer
one over the other, but they are *incompatible* in the sense that both
cannot be accepted at once. In OT, for example, the split in biology between Cuvier's fixism and Darwin's evolutionism occurs at
a point of diffraction, as does the separation of Marx's from Ricardo's economics.

Foucault notes, however, that we do not in fact find points of
diffraction everywhere that the rules of the discursive formation
allow them. This is because there are further factors (he calls
them "authorities") that limit the number of alternatives. One is
the economy of the discursive constellation to which the discursive
formation in question belongs. By this Foucault means the relation of the discursive formation to other contemporary discursive formations. The various discursive formations within a constellation will be analogous or complementary to one another
and will serve one another as models for application; and such
relations may lead to the elimination of points of diffraction that

would otherwise exist within a discursive formation. Another limiting factor is the fact that a discursive formation exists in a field of nondiscursive practices. Thus, an economic discursive formation will be employed in government decision making, a grammatical discursive formation in pedagogy, or – to cite another order of example – the discursive formation of a certain kind of pornography may be an object of forbidden desire. In all such cases, a nondiscursive authority may affect the theoretical options allowed within the discursive formation. Further, Foucault insists that such authorities should not be regarded as "disturbing elements," altering the structure of an intrinsically complete discursive formation; rather, they are "formative elements" (AK, 68) of the discursive formation.

Foucault lays special emphasis on the importance of the interconnections among the various systems of rules that govern a discursive formation. He says, for example: "One might say, then, that a discursive formation is defined (as far as its objects are concerned, at least) if one can establish . . . a group of relations . . . between authorities of emergence, delimitation, and specification" (AK, 44). Similarly, speaking of the "elements" (i.e., the various systems of rules of ordering, coexistence, and intervention) that govern the formation of a discursive formation's concepts, Foucault says: "What properly belongs to a discursive formation and what makes it possible to delimit the group of concepts, disparate as they may be, that are specific to it, is the way in which these different elements are related to one another" (AK, 60). Similar points hold for the rules for the formation of enunciative modalities and of theoretical strategies. Foucault also emphasizes the interrelations among the four kinds of rules of formation themselves. Thus, the possibility of strategic choices "is determined by points of divergence in the groups of concepts" (AK, 72) and, conversely, "theoretical choices exclude or imply . . . the function of certain concepts" (AK, 73). Similarly reciprocal relations hold among other pairs of systems of rules of formation. Because of this emphasis on interconnections of systems of rules, Foucault often speaks of a discursive formation being specified by *discursive relations* (i.e., relations among its rules of formation). Different discursive formations may have many of (even, in theory, all) the same rules, but different discursive relations among their rules will differentiate them.

Statements

Foucault presents discursive formations as groups of statements. But just what does he mean by *statement?* Since archaeological analysis is distinct from both grammar and logic, Foucault refuses to identify statements with either sentences – that is, the units of grammatical analysis – or propositions – that is, the units of logical analysis. Indeed, he finally concludes that a statement is not really any kind of linguistic *unit* at all but is rather a *function.* To understand what Foucault has in mind here, we need to get some perspective on his way of thinking about language. A language, he says, echoing Saussure, is "a collection of signs defined by their contrasting characteristics and their rules of use" (AK, 85). From such a collection we can, of course, form numerous particular series of signs. A given series will be a sentence or a proposition depending on whether it conforms to the grammatical and logical rules that govern these linguistic units. Further, whether a series of signs is a sentence or a proposition is *entirely* determined by reference to the relevant set of rules; it does not require that the series have any relation to other series of signs (on the same linguistic level). There could in principle be a language with only one sentence or one proposition. By contrast, a series of signs is a *statement* only if it is related to other series of signs, which series constitute the statement's *associated field* (cf. AK, 96). Indeed, the fact that it is a statement and the precise statement that it is are entirely determined by the complex set of rules whereby it is related to other series of signs (which, by virtue of this same set of relations are themselves statements). Thus, a statement is not a linguistic unit, as are sentences and propositions, since it has no reality as a statement prior to its inclusion within a rule-governed system. Thus, like a mathematical function, a statement is entirely defined by the relations between a set of elements. The other meaning of *function* is also relevant: a series of signs is a statement precisely because it has a place – a role or a function – within a system.

Linguistic units such as sentences and propositions (and other entities such as graphs, diagrams, and formulas) will also typically be statements – not, of course, simply because they are sentences, propositions, and so on, but because they are parts of sign systems. As such, they will be open to analysis not only at the standard levels of logic and grammar but also at the *enunciative* level – in terms of their enunciative function (*enunciative* since *statement* translates the French *énoncé*). The enunciative level is not unconnected to other semantical levels. Indeed, in important respects it is presupposed by them. Consider, for example, the case in which we say that a proposition – for example, "The present king of France is bald" – is false or meaningless because it has no referent. This will be so only if "The present king of France is bald" is a statement that belongs to a factual, historical discursive formation. If it instead belongs to a fictional discursive formation (say of a novel written about the days of Charles the Bald), then the corresponding proposition will have a referent (in the fictional domain) and indeed be true. Similarly, when we say that a certain string of words (say, "a way a lone a last a loved a long the") is meaningless, this is so only if we are assuming that the string occurs in some ordinary context and is not part of an experimental literary work. Thus, a group of signs' status as a statement is relevant to whether or not it is (as a sentence or a proposition) true or even meaningful. Specifically, questions of truth and meaning depend on the nature of the relevant discursive formation's domain of objects and relations (which Foucault calls its *referential*): "The referential of the statement . . . defines the possibilities of appearance and delimitation of that which [objects, states, relations] gives meaning to the sentence, a value as truth to the proposition" (AK, 91).

The nature of Foucault's statements can be clarified by comparing them to the speech-acts that are the concern of language analysts such as Austin and Searle. Although Foucault initially maintained (in AK) that statements cannot be identified with speech-acts, he later admitted, in correspondence with Searle, that "I was wrong in saying that statements were not speech-acts."[9] But exactly what are we to make of this admission? One point Foucault may have had in mind is that statements are "things done with words" (moves in a language game). From this point of view, the analytic category of speech-act is extensionally equivalent to that of the statement. Both are general linguistic categories that include not only expression of sentences and propositions but also of other linguistic units such as graphs, tables, and gestures. But, as Foucault also suggests in his correspon-

---

9. Cf. H. Dreyfus and P. Rabinow, *Michel Foucault: beyond structuralism and hermeneutics*, 2d ed. (Chicago: University of Chicago Press, 1982), 46, note.

dence with Searle, his concern with statements is very different from the concern a language analyst has with speech-acts. In my view this difference can be best put this way.[10] The analyst works at the level of meaning – that is, the level of the implicit under-standing of a language possessed by those who use it. (Hence the standard method of asking "What do we say when. . . ?" or "What would we say if. . . ?") Such analysis is concerned with distinguish-ing and describing the functions that speech-acts have within a language. But Foucault, as an "archaeologist," is rather con-cerned with a structure of relations between statements that is not available to speakers' reflections on the meaning of what they say. He wants to look at statements from the outside and describe the relations that define the field in which various sorts of statements are able to perform their linguistic functions and hence have various meanings.

The rules and relations that constitute a statement have, as we would expect, nothing to do with the beliefs and projects of human subjects:

> The analysis of statements operates . . . without reference to a cogito. It does not pose the question of the speaking subject . . . it is situated at the level of the "it is said" – and we must not understand by this a sort of communal opinion, a collective rep-resentation that is imposed on every individual . . . but we must understand by it the totality of things said, the relations, the regularities, and the transformations that may be observed in them. (AK, 122)

Of course, all statements are made by individual speakers, but in making a statement a speaker takes up a position that has al-ready been defined – quite apart from his mental activity – by the rules of the relevant discursive formation. Foucault does hold that every statement has a *subject* (not in the grammatical sense but in the sense of a discursive source). But this subject is not any "speaking consciousness" (which will at most be the au-

10. Dreyfus and Rabinow, 47–48, suggest that, unlike Searle et al., Foucault is interested in "serious speech-acts" (those that have a special institutional status and autonomy) rather than "everyday speech-acts." This is not entirely correct, since Foucault explicitly says that archaeology is concerned with the *savoir* underlying "les opinions de tous les jours" (everyday opinions). (Cf. Raymond Bellour, 138.) His archaeological analyses do in fact deal almost exclusively with serious speech-acts. But I do not think that this is the funda-mental difference between Foucault's work and that of speech-act theorists.

thor of a particular formulation of the statement) but rather "a position that may be filled in certain conditions by various individuals" (AK, 115). This position is, of course, established by the rules of the discursive formation.

It is important to be clear about Foucault's view of the relation of the statements of a discursive formation to the rules that govern them. The rules do not have a transcendental status; that is, they are not "principles of construction" or "conditions of possibility" that exist somehow prior to statements and constitute them. If this were so, we could distinguish between a discursive formation as an "ideal form" and its exemplification in a particular set of historically existing statements. But for Foucault there is nothing more than the historically existing statements and the relations that obtain among them. The rules of the discursive formation are simply the description of the existing relations. Thus, he says: "The regularity of statements is defined by the discursive formation itself. The fact of [a statement's] belonging to a discursive formation and the laws [rules] that govern it are one and the same thing" (AK, 116). Hence, "discourse in this sense is not an ideal, timeless form that also possesses a history . . . ; it is, from beginning to end, historical" (AK, 117).

To emphasize that archaeological analysis treats statements merely as given historical facts, without concern about any transcendental origin, Foucault calls the groups of statements he is concerned with (the statements of discursive formations) *positivities*. And he says that if rejection of a transcendental approach means that "one is a positivist, then I am quite happy to be one" (AK, 125). Similarly, to express the role of discursive formations as conditions on the thought that goes on within them, he introduces the admittedly "rather barbarous" term *historical a priori* (AK, 127). This is to make clear that a condition "imposed" by a discursive formation is "not a condition of validity for judgments, but a condition of reality for statements." A discursive formation provides "an a priori not of truths that might never be said, or really given to experience, but an a priori of a history that is given, since it is of things actually said" (AK, 127). At a yet higher level, Foucault speaks of the *archive* as the complex of all the discursive formations that exist in a given "society, culture, or civilization" (AK, 130). The archive is, for a given society or culture, "the law of what can be said, the system that governs the appearance of statements as unique events" (AK, 129). But, like discursive formations and their historical a prioris, the archive is not a transhistorical condition on history; it is merely the compendium of existing discourse. Foucault also takes pains to make clear the precise level on which analyses of statements and discursive formations (archaeological analyses) take place. On the one hand, archaeology is not concerned with textual analysis, with specific questions about what particular words mean or how particular statements are logically or rhetorically connected. It "remains anterior to this manifest level" of specific linguistic usage and does not account for the specific details of a particular text. "It leaves the final placing of the text in dotted outline" (AK, 75). Foucault also makes this point by distinguishing the *discursive relations* with which archaeology is concerned from the *secondary relations* (grammatical, logical, rhetorical) that govern the concrete uses of language. But he is even more insistent that archaeological analysis is not an access to a nondiscursive reality that lies outside and grounds the discursive formation. It does not operate at the level of the *primary relations* that, "independently of all discourse or all objects of discourse, may be described between institutions, techniques, social forms, etc." (AK, 46). Put another way, if archaeology does not deal with concrete *words,* neither does it deal with *things themselves* (AK, 48).[11] It remains within discourse, but at its borders (which it is concerned to define as clearly and precisely as possible) rather than at its interior. Foucault also makes it clear that his commitment to an archaeological approach does not mean that he rejects the alternative approaches (which we might label "linguistic" and "ontological"). He allows that there is place for the linguistic analysis of a term (of, e.g., what *melancholia* meant in the seventeenth century) and even that one might write a "history of the referent" that would aim to "uncover and free . . . prediscursive experiences from the tyranny of the text" (AK, 47). But whatever the value of these sorts of enterprises, Foucault's archaeology deals neither with prediscursive experience of things nor with the verbal forms produced by discourse. It focuses on "a group of rules . . . [that] define not the dumb existence of a reality nor the canonical use of a vocabulary, but the ordering of objects" (AK, 49). Without denying that discourse is composed of signs or

11. In view of this, the title *Les mots et les choses* is, as Foucault notes, ironic, since archaeology operates at the level of neither words nor things. Cf. "Michel Foucault explique son dernier livre," 24.

that signs can be used to designate things, he insists that there is more to discourse than this. "It is this 'more' that we must reveal and describe" (AK, 49).

Archaeology and the history of ideas

As we have seen, Foucault's archaeology is meant as an alternative to the traditional approach, which sees the history of thought as constituted by the human subject. By focusing on systems of statements in their own right, archaeology turns away from the subject and toward the conditions that define the discursive space in which speaking subjects exist. This fundamental difference from standard history of ideas has a number of consequences that further clarify the distinctiveness of archaeological analysis. These consequences concern attitudes toward tradition and innovation, the handling of apparent contradictions, and the problem of change and discontinuity.[12]

Tradition and innovation

History of ideas is dominated by the two poles of the old and the new: "In every *oeuvre*, in every book, in the smallest text, the problem is to rediscover the point of rupture, to establish, with the greatest possible precision, the division between the implicit density of the already-said, a perhaps involuntary fidelity to acquired opinion, the law of discursive fatalities, and the vivacity of creation, the leap into irreducible difference" (AK, 142). As a result, such history is concerned with ordering the thoughts of individuals in a single great chronological series, with each member of the series characterized by its degree of resemblance to previous members. Thus, a primary concern is finding out who was the true originator of a given thought and who merely repeated or creatively modified it; or, as Foucault wryly puts it, "determining those degrees of nobility that are measured here by the absence of ancestors" (AK, 143). However, he insists, for the archaeology of knowledge "the originality/banality opposition . . . is not relevant" (AK, 144). The archaeologist is con-

12. Foucault also presents archaeology as having a distinctive approach to the comparison of different systems of thought, particularly in its concern with regional rather than global analyses. We have already discussed his views on this topic at the end of Chapter 4.

cerned only with what Foucault calls the "regularities" of discursive practices (enunciative regularities). These are the patterns defined by the relation of any given statement to other statements. These patterns (expressed in the rules of the discursive formation discussed above) define the field in which all statements, from the most creative to the most banal, emerge. The archaeologist is, therefore, concerned only with what statements can reveal about the rules of discursive formations. Since the most original statement embodies the relevant rules no more and no less than its hackneyed repetitions, the question of innovation is of no interest to archaeology.

In this way, Foucault provides a basis in principle for the disdain of hunts for precursors we noted in his preliminary critique of subjective means of transmitting ideas. This moves beyond Canguilhem's point that such hunts are frequently based on overinterpretation of superficial (e.g., verbal) similarities. If this were the only problem, then the search for precursors might still form an integral part of the archaeology of knowledge, provided it was carried out (as by Canguilhem himself in his work on the reflex) with sufficient sensitivity and acuity. Foucault allows (AK, 143–44) that studies like Canguilhem's are legitimate approaches to history of science, but even so they have no place in the realm of archaeological analysis, which operates on a level where questions of who thought what first are simply irrelevant.

Contradictions

The search for an underlying coherence beneath apparent contradictions is basic to historians of ideas' methodology. Within a given book, an author's oeuvre, or an intellectual tradition, they seek to view conflicts and disagreements as illusory or accidental when seen in the light of the fundamental principles of the discourse in question. Sometimes, the search for an underlying coherence fails and instead leads to a discovery of the discourse's basic contradiction, a "secret law that accounts for all minor contradictions and gives them a firm foundation" (AK, 150–51). In either case, history of ideas never accepts conflicting statements on their own terms; it must either reconcile them or understand their conflict as a manifestation of a deeper contradiction. Consider, for example, the case of the apparent conflict in Classical natural history between fixist and developmentalist views of spe-

cies. Historians of ideas either try to show that "beneath this opposition . . . everyone accepted a number of fundamental theses (the
continuity and plentitude of nature, the correlation between
recent forms and climate, the almost imperceptible transition
from the non-living to the living)"; or else they try to show that
the "opposition reflects, in the particular domain of Natural History, a more general conflict that divides all eighteenth-century
thought (the conflict between the theme of an ordered creation,
acquired once and for all . . . and the theme of a prolific nature . . . gradually deploying itself through history)" (AK, 151–
52). But the archaeologist of knowledge takes neither of these
approaches: "For archaeological analysis, contradictions are neither appearances to be overcome, nor secret principles to be un-
covered. They are objects to be described for themselves. . . ."
(AK, 151). Archaeology is concerned rather with describing the
discursive structures that make the conflict possible. Thus, in the
case of Classical fixism and developmentalism, it will show (as
Foucault did in OT) how the disagreement corresponds to a
"point of diffraction" in the discursive formation of Classical natural history – how, that is, the formation rules for describing species allow for these two incompatible views of their origin. Instead
of explaining (or explaining away) the contradiction, the archaeologist describes the discursive conditions of its possibility.

Change and discontinuity

Foucault (and, even more, some of his commentators) has emphasized the central role that discontinuity plays in his approach
to the history of thought. At the beginning of AK, he says:

> One of the most essential features of the new history is probably
> this displacement of the discontinous: its transference from the
> obstacle to the work itself; its integration into the discourse of the
> historian, where it no longer plays the role of an external condi-
> tion that must be reduced, but that of a working concept. . . . It is
> no longer the negative of the historical reading . . . but the posi-
> tive element that determines its object and validates its analysis.
> (AK, 9)

This insistence on discontinuity has led many of Foucault's readers to think that his archaeological approach allows no place for

gradual transformations or continuous developments, that it sees the history of thought as a series of quantum leaps from one self-contained discursive formation to another. (Compare the similar reaction of readers of Thomas Kuhn to his notion of the incommensurability of paradigms.[13]) But such an idea is clearly a misrepresentation, as we can appreciate by seeing the precise role discontinuity plays in Foucault's conception of history. First of all, as we noted above, the emphasis on discontinuity has special importance as a current strategy for writing the history of thought. Traditional history of ideas has emphasized the continuity of human thought through the centuries by reading it as "homogeneous manifestations of a single mind or of a collective mentality." Undermining this sort of continuity has been a necessary part of the new history of thought that questions the privileged role of the human subject. Accordingly, "beneath the great continuities of thought . . ., one is now trying to detect the incidence of interruptions" (AK, 4). For such an enterprise, "the great problem is not how continuities are established, . . . how for so many different, successive minds there is a single horizon . . . – the problem is no longer one of tradition, of tracing a line, but one of division, of limits" (AK, 5). But such an emphasis on discontinuity is merely a strategy presently appropriate for the history of thought. As we have seen, other sorts of history have, on the contrary, eliminated the central role of the subject by emphasizing long-term continuities that are independent of the flux of human action. "For many years now historians have preferred to turn their attention to long periods. . . , the movements of accumulation and slow saturation, the great, silent, motionless basis that traditional history has covered with a thick layer of events" (AK, 3). Thus, in principle, non-subject-centered history can (depending on the strategic situation) emphasize either continuity or discontinuity.

Foucault further makes it clear that an archaeology of thought is concerned with changes from one discursive formation to another and that these changes may occur against a background of significant continuities. He agrees that in certain senses archaeo-

13. The question of similarities between Foucault and Kuhn is potentially fruitful but can easily trick us into making too much of superficial resemblances. For an excellent start on a comparison of the two thinkers, cf. Ian Hacking, "Michel Foucault's immature science," NOUS 13 (1979), 39–51. There are also some remarks on this topic in G. Gutting, "Continental philosophy of science" in P. D. Asquith and H. E. Kyburg, eds., Current research in philosophy of science (East Lansing, Mich.: Philosophy of Science Association, 1979), 94–117.

logical analysis works synchronically: Rules of discursive formations may remain the same for long periods, and the order the
archaeologist discovers in a set of statements may not correspond to the order in which the statements appeared temporally.
But, he insists, though "there is a suspension of temporal succession . . ., this suspension is intended precisely to reveal the relations that characterize the temporality of discursive formations"
(AK, 167). Further, these relations will typically involve the continuity of various discursive elements through a given change:

> To say that one discursive formation is substituted for another . . .
> is to say that a general transformation of relations has occurred,
> but that it does not necessarily alter all the elements; it is to say
> that statements are governed by new rules of formation, it is not
> to say that all objects or concepts, all enunciations or all theoretical
> choices disappear. . . . We must not forget that a rule of forma-
> tion is neither the determination of an object, nor the characteriza-
> tion of a type of enunciation, nor the form or content of a con-
> cept, but the principle of their multiplicity and dispersion. One of
> these elements – or several of them – may remain identical . . .,
> yet belong to different systems of dispersion, and be governed by
> distinct laws of formation. (AK, 173)

This concern with continuities through change is evident, for
example, in OT's discussions of Adam Smith's treatment of labor
and Lamarck's of character in the transition from Classical to
modern empirical sciences.

So archaeology does not differ from traditional history of
ideas by ignoring change and continuity. But it does differ by
taking difference and discontinuity as seriously as it does continuity. According to Foucault, traditional history of ideas tries to
reduce all apparent discontinuity to a series of incremental
changes, all contributing toward a finally achieved enlightenment. Here he seems to have specifically in mind the long-
dominant tradition of "Whiggish" history, which presents a
cumulative progression of achievements, with the numerous
errors and misdirections that undeniably occurred as unimpor-
tant background noise. Like Braudel, Foucault rejects this project of "total history," which assumes that the phenomena it
deals with are unified around a single center (the progress of
mankind, final scientific truth) in favor of "general history"
(AK, 9–10). The latter allows that its phenomena may form

disparate series that cannot be reduced to a unity, but without insisting that these series are entirely independent. General intellectual history seeks to describe the complex interrelations of mutually irreducible discursive formations.

Given that archaeology is concerned with change, the question arises of how to explain it. What sort of causes does Foucault see as driving forces of the history of thought? As we have seen, he has little regard for the influences, spirits of the times, *Weltanschauungen,* and so on, that are commonly appealed to by historians of ideas. For one thing, their status is often little short of magical; they are so amorphous and ubiquitous as to explain almost any intellectual development at all (cf. OT, Foreword to the English Edition, xiii). More importantly, even when such causal factors are properly invoked, they will explain the development of thought only on the level of the subject and so will have no archaeological significance.

From Foucault's earlier excursions into causal questions (in FD, BC, and even MMP), it seems clear that his inclination is to look for answers in the relations of thought and discourse to factors that lie outside them (e.g., institutional structures). Even though OT deliberately avoids questions of causality, Foucault says there that the discontinuous change that produces a new episteme "probably begins with an erosion from outside, from that space which is, for thought, on the other side" (OT, 50). And, as we shall see, AK insists on a close tie between the discursive and the nondiscursive. However, in both OT and AK, he is reluctant to say much about the way nondiscursive causal factors operate. (Some hints of the direction of his thinking are apparent in his comments on the relation between discursive formations and nondiscursive practices, which we discuss below). His view is that we need to develop archaeology more fully as a description of the transformations that have occurred in the history of thought before we move to questions of their causal explanation (cf. OT, xii and 51). Foucault later returns to the question of causality when, in DP and later works, he focuses explicitly on the connection of knowledge and power.

Archaeology and the history of science

In principle, Foucault's archaeological approach is applicable to any sort of discourse at all – literary, philosophical, political, and so on. In fact, however, he had, up to the time he wrote AK, applied the approach only to sciences (or would-be sciences). For this reason, we need to pay special attention to the relation of archaeology to one part of traditional history of ideas: the history of science. Foucault approaches this question by reflecting (AK, 178ff) on the connection between the sciences and the discursive formations (positivities) that are the concern of archaeology. We might think that positivities simply are sciences or, at least, what Foucault calls "disciplines" – that is, "groups of statements that borrow their organization from scientific models, which tend to coherence and demonstrativity, which are accepted, institutionalized, transmitted, and sometimes taught as sciences" (AK, 178). But Foucault denies that discursive formations are in general disciplines of any sort, whether scientific, pseudoscientific, or prescientific. He cites as an example his early work (in FD) on madness. Here the relevant discipline was clearly the psychiatry that emerged at the beginning of the nineteenth century. Foucault's archaeological analysis did reveal that psychiatry was based on a discursive practice and a corresponding discursive formation. But this practice "is not only manifested in a discipline possessing a scientific status and scientific pretensions; it is also found in operation in legal texts, in literature, in philosophy, in political decisions, and in the statements made and the opinions expressed in daily life" (AK, 179). Further, Foucault found that, in the seventeenth and eighteenth centuries, although there was no single discipline that dealt with madness (no precursor of psychiatry), "there were a discursive formation and a positivity perfectly accessible to description" (AK, 179). So, though discursive formations may be intimately related to sciences, they cannot be identified with them. Nor can they be identified as "prototypes of future sciences," so that we can think of a discursive formation as a grouping of "all the heterogeneous and dispersed elements whose complicity will prove to be necessary to the establishment of a science" (AK, 180). For a single science may be formed from elements of a wide variety of discursive formations. Thus, the science of biology, which first appeared in the nineteenth century, combines elements derived not only from Classical natural history but also from the seventeenth- and eighteenth-century analysis of reflex movement, theory of germs, and explanation of animal and vegetal growth – all of which were developed in discursive forma-

THE ARCHAEOLOGY OF KNOWLEDGE 251

tions very different from that underlying the taxonomic classifications of natural history. Foucault accordingly concludes that
"discursive formations can be identified . . . neither as sciences,
nor as scarcely scientific disciplines, nor as distant prefigurations
of the sciences to come, nor as forms that exclude scientificity
from the outset" (AK, 181).

Foucault's positive account of the relationship of discursive
formations to sciences is based on the special sense he gives to
the distinction between *connaissance* and *savoir*. By *connaissance*
he means (in accord with ordinary French usage) any particular
body of knowledge such as nuclear physics, evolutionary biology, or Freudian psychoanalysis; thus, *connaissance* is what is
found in what Foucault characterized as disciplines. *Savoir*, on
the other hand, refers to the discursive conditions that are necessary for the development of *connaissance*, to, in Foucault's
words, "the conditions that are necessary in a particular period
for this or that type of object to be given to *connaissance* and for
this or that enunciation to be formulated" (cf. AK, 15, transla-
tor's note 2). In Foucault's view, a particular science (or, more
generally, a discipline) is the locus of *connaissance* whereas a
discursive formation is the locus of *savoir*. As such, the *savoir* of
a discursive formation provides the objects, types of cognitive
authority (enunciative modes), concepts, and themes (theoretical strategies) that are necessary for a body of scientific *connaissance*. Or, we might say, a discursive formation provides the pre-
knowledge (*savoir*) necessary for the knowledge (*connaissance*)
achieved by a science. This latter locution is justified by Foucault's talk of *savoir* as the "basis" or "precondition" of *connaissance*. But it is important that we not think of *savoir* in this role
as an epistemological given (*donnée*), "a lived experience, still
implicated in the imagination or in perception" (AK, 182). Foucault's *savoir/connaissance* distinction is not a version of the phe-
nomenologist's idea that we begin with uncritical "immediate
knowledge" that is transformed by rigorous method into apodic-
tic scientific knowledge. The *savoir* presupposed by a science is
not "that which must have been lived, or must be lived, if the
intention of ideality proper to [the science] is to be established."
Savoir is rather "that which must have been said – or must be
said – if a discourse is to exist that complies . . . with the experimental or formal criteria of scientificity" (AK, 182). *Connaissance* is an achievement of an individual or a group con-

sciousness and so is naturally the focus of a subject-centered enterprise such as traditional history of science. *Savoir*, by contrast, is the concern of Foucault's archaeology: "Instead of exploring the consciousness/knowledge (*connaissance*)/science axis (which cannot escape subjectivity), archaeology explores the discursive practice/knowledge (*savoir*)/science axis" (AK, 183).

Archaeology's concern with *savoir* rather than *connaissance* means not only that it operates on a different epistemic level from that of traditional history of science but also that it has a wider scope. History of science will rightly deal only with disciplines that are scientific; a "scientific domain" (the object of the history of science) excludes literary and philosophical texts that do not meet the accepted scientific norms of their periods. But an "archaeological territory" will extend to texts of all the disciplines, scientific and nonscientific, that are conditioned by the *savoir* it analyzes. "Knowledge [*savoir*] is to be found not only in [scientific] demonstrations, it can also be found in fiction, reflexion, narrative accounts, institutional regulations, and political decisions" (AK, 183–84).

Thus, from an archaeological view, a science is just one, localized formation in the "epistemological site" that is a discursive formation. Science neither supersedes nor exhausts the discursive formation that is its background. Further, the process whereby a science is "articulated" on a discursive formation is just one of several possible episodes in the history of a discursive formation. Foucault in fact distinguishes four stages or *thresholds* relevant to the historical reality of discursive formations. Prior (logically, though not necessarily temporally) to the "threshold of scientificity" are the "threshold of positivity" and the "threshold of epistemologization." The former is simply the emergence of the discursive formation as an individual, autonomous system governing the formation of statements; the latter involves the development of epistemic norms (e.g., for coherence and verification) that claim to provide standards of validity for knowledge. The threshold of scientificity is crossed when to the basic epistemic norms of the discursive formation there are added specific rules for constructing propositions in accord with the canons of a scientific methodology. These canons introduce standards of precision and rigor beyond those of mere epistemologization and define the "objectivity" and the "systematicity" proper to a science (OT, 365). Finally, there is the "threshold of formalization," which is crossed when the scientific dimension of a discursive formation is able to exhibit its structures in axiomatic form. Foucault does not want these thresholds to be taken as regular, successive stages in the inevitable development of discursive formations. True, there may be cases in which all four stages of positivity, epistemologization, scientificity, and formalization follow one another in that order, and it makes no sense for logically subsequent stages to occur before prior ones (e.g., formalization before epistemologization). But different discursive formations develop at different and very irregular rates and some may not have the capacity to reach all four thresholds. Further, a discursive formation may pass through two or more thresholds at the same time. Foucault cites the extreme case of mathematics, which, he says, simultaneously crossed all four thresholds. More common are cases in which a new discursive formation emerges with norms of epistemic valuation and perhaps even canons of scientific method. Then the discursive formation passes at once the thresholds of positivity, epistemologization, and perhaps scientificity. Foucault thinks this happened when the discursive formation of modern biology succeeded the discursive formation of Classical natural history (AK, 188). Foucault emphasizes the complex variety of ways his threshold schema applies to specific discursive formations. It is not a univocal model, applying in the same way to all discursive formations.

The *connaissance/savoir* distinction and the distinction between the threshold of scientificity and the threshold of epistemologization provide Foucault with the means of clearly separating archaeological analysis from history of science as practiced by Bachelard and Canguilhem. Whereas the latter deals only with *connaissance*, with bodies of scientific knowledge, archaeology studies the *savoir* that provides the conditions of possibility for such knowledge. Because of its concern with *savoir*, archaeology is not, like history of science, restricted to the domains of knowledge defined by past and present scientific disciplines but can reveal structures common to various disciplines. Moreover, it can even map the ground common to scientific and nonscientific forms of discourse, as Foucault did in FD and at the beginning of BC.

With regard to the distinction of thresholds, Foucault points out that Bachelard and Canguilhem are concerned only with disciplines that have passed the threshold of scientificity. They accept as normative the concepts and rational standards of current scientific disciplines and write the history of how these concepts and standards won out over prescientific prejudices and misunderstandings. Their purpose is "to discover how . . . a science was established over and against a prescientific level, which both paved the way and resisted it in advance, how it succeeded in overcoming the obstacles and limitations that still stood in its way" (AK, 190). Such history evaluates past scientific work as true or false, rational or irrational, progressive or regressive in terms of the best judgment of current science.

Foucault labels the history of Bachelard and Canguilhem "epistemological history," since it begins from the norms provided by an epistemological analysis of the concepts and methods of current science. These norms are not themselves critically evaluated but are applied to judge past scientific work. By contrast, archaeological history of science is primarily concerned with discursive formations that have passed the threshold of epistemologization but not that of scientificity. Its purpose is to describe in a neutral way the process whereby cognitive norms (whether genuinely scientific or not) are formed. Consequently, "at this level [that of archaeological history], scientificity does not serve as a norm" (AK, 190). This is no doubt what Canguilhem had in mind when he said, in his review of OT, that "there is today no philosophy less normative than that of Foucault."[14] But such a claim is true only in the sense that archaeology does not, like the history practiced by Bachelard and Canguilhem, judge the past on the basis of the norms of current science. On the other hand, archaeological analysis is centrally concerned with norms as themselves the products of historical developments. "Such an analysis sets out . . . to outline the history of the sciences on the basis of a description of discursive practices; to define how, in accordance with which regularity, and as a result of which modifications, it was able to give rise to the processes of epistemologization, to attain the norms of scientificity, and, perhaps, to reach the threshold of formalization" (AK, 190–91).

Here we find what is no doubt the most fundamental way in which Foucault moves beyond the approach of Bachelard and

14. Georges Canguilhem, "Mort de l'homme ou épuisement de *cogito?" Critique* 24 (1967), 612.

Canguilhem. For him the norms found in (purportedly) scientific disciplines are not unquestioned givens for historical reflection but themselves the outcome of contingent historical processes. Unlike Bachelard and Canguilhem, he undertakes the writing of the history of science (or what claims to be science) without presupposing the norms of the domains he is dealing with. Bachelard had criticized philosophical claims, based on outdated science, about necessary limitations on knowledge. Foucault opens the way to a historical critique of current scientific norms themselves as something less than absolute conditions for the possibility of knowledge. In this way, Foucault transforms the history of science in accord with his ultimate goal of dissolving constraints on human freedom.

However, even here the move away from Bachelard and Canguilhem is not as decisive as it might seem. Foucault's critiques of norms are not directed at the "noble" sciences of physics and chemistry that were Bachelard's concern. Nor does he raise any questions about the standards of modern biology in itself as distinct from certain of its applications in medical practice. Foucault does not move his archaeological critique of scientific norms in the direction of a debunking of scientific rationality as such. Rather, his critique is exclusively directed toward the dubious disciplines of psychiatry, medicine, and the human sciences. (And even here he is willing, as we have seen, to allow a certain level of objectivity and truth.) With regard to the well-established natural sciences, Foucault seems content to accept the approach of Bachelard and Canguilhem.

Nevertheless, archaeology does suggest a new way of looking at the question of the justification of the norms of even the most well-established sciences. As we saw, neither Bachelard nor Canguilhem was able to offer a satisfactory account of the basis of scientific norms. From the viewpoint of archaeology, it might be suggested that this is because they seek such an account on the level of the subject, whether construed as an individual or as a social group. Thus, as we saw in Chapter 1, Bachelard speaks of objective norms deriving from the move from the individual *cogito* to the collective *cogitamus*. For Foucault, by contrast, norms presumably derive from archaeological structures antecedent to the cognitive activities of subjects. Specifically, they no doubt originate at the point of interaction between discursive formations and the nondiscursive factors (e.g., social institutions, economic causes) that, along with discourse, constitute our practical involvement with the world. We will return to this topic in the next section.

Discourse and the nondiscursive

The focus of AK is on *discursive* formations – that is, on knowledge as the outcome of linguistic practices. However, the book also frequently asserts a close connection between discourse and nondiscursive practices. Here Foucault resumes a theme that is, as we saw, prominent in FD but increasingly muted in BC and, especially, OT. He presents archaeology as providing a distinctive approach to the relations between discourses and nondiscursive domains such as "institutions, political events, economic practices and processes" (AK, 162). History of ideas explains such relations via either symbolic or causal analysis. The former sees a discourse (e.g., that of clinical medicine in the late eighteenth century) and nondiscursive factors (e.g., the political, economic, and institutional developments of the eighteenth century) as sharing a common form or meaning in virtue of which each reflects the other. The latter tries to "discover to what extent political changes, or economic processes, could determine the consciousness of scientists" (AK, 163) – for example, how nineteenth-century industrial capitalism's need for large numbers of workers caused the medical profession to think and speak of the origin and cure of diseases in social terms. Archaeology, as we would expect, is concerned rather with the discursive formation as a condition of the possibility of such symbolic and causal connections. Specifically, with respect to the latter, this means that archaeology "wishes to show not how political practice has determined the meaning and form of . . . discourse, but how and in what form it takes part in its conditions of emergence, insertion, and functioning" (AK, 163). Thus, BC's archaeology of early nineteenth-century medicine shows how social phenomena such as conscripted armies and public-assistance hospitals for the poor provided the context for the emergence of the statistical norms of health discussed by clinical medicine. On another level, the special authority of the doctor (as "virtually the exclusive . . . enunciator of [medical] discourse" – AK, 164) is connected with the nineteenth-century institutions of hospitalization and private practice.

Foucault's archaeological approach to the relation of scientific discourse to nondiscursive factors differs in two very important ways from that of most contemporary sociology of science (e.g., the Edinburgh "strong program"). For one thing, as we have already noted, he is not concerned with the influence of social factors on the content of scientific theories (e.g., the influence of seventeenth-century political institutions on Newton's laws of mechanics); archaeology works on the more fundamental level of the definition of basic objects and concepts, the cognitive authority of the scientist, and the social function of science. More importantly, Foucault is reluctant to characterize science as straightforwardly determined by social causes. Rather, he speaks of social factors as "open[ing] up new fields for the mapping of [scientific] objects" (AK, 163) and of a scientific practice as "articulated on [social] practices that are external to it" (AK, 164). But this idea is not developed since, as we have seen, Foucault is not yet prepared to extend archaeology to causal questions. Nonetheless, he is clearly trying to make intellectual room for a discussion of science and society that will somehow connect the two on fundamental levels but not require the reductionists' presupposition of social determinism.

In any case, it is precisely at this point of connection that the issue of the origin and basis of scientific norms might be fruitfully raised. Perhaps, for example, we could show how such norms are essentially connected with social practices so fundamental that, at least for a given culture, they define the essential nature of human reality. Of course, Foucault would be suspicious on principle of any norms that claim such a basic status. But not all suspicions turn out to be well-founded, and his acceptance of the objectivity of at least the natural sciences seems to require the admission that some norms are genuinely regulative of our knowledge. If so, nondiscursive social practices that express, at least for the time being, the nature of our fundamental engagement with the world would be plausible candidates as the ground for scientific norms. The sort of practices relevant here might, for example, be Foucault's parallel to Habermas's cognitive interests. Perhaps our fundamental practical orientations toward controlling nature, understanding one another, and emancipating ourselves from arbitrary psychological and social constraints provide the basis for the norms of scientific objectivity.

Such suggestions are, of course, only speculations about how

Foucault might respond to questions that in fact he never directly addressed. His own interest was clearly much more in undermining illegitimate normative claims than in grounding legitimate ones.[15] However, there is one important problem facing any account of scientific objectivity that Foucault does (briefly) discuss. This is the question of the relation of science to ideology. On the one hand, he says that archaeology enables us to see ideology as a natural accompaniment of any science. A science's origin from a discursive formation that also provides intellectual space for nonscientific (e.g., political, religious) practices makes it inevitable that there will be deep similarities and important practical connections between the sciences and the political, economic and religious ideologies of an era. Thus, to cite a standard example, it should come as no surprise that "political economy has a role in capitalist society, that it serves the interests of the bourgeois class, that it was made by and for that class, and that it bears the mark of its origins even in its concepts and logical architecture" (AK, 185). But, on the other hand, archaeology enables us to see that even strong ideological connections need not exclude the scientificity of a discipline: "Ideology is not exclusive of scientificity. Few discourses have given so much place to ideology as clinical discourse or that of political economy: this is not a sufficiently good reason to treat the totality of their statements as being undermined by error, contradiction, and a lack of objectivity" (AK, 186). A given scientific discipline will have a certain ideological significance and function precisely because of the way it is related to other discourses rooted in its discursive formation. But this need not alter the fact that the discipline in itself is governed by norms of scientific objectivity. (Note how Foucault consistently rejects a *teleological* interpretation of the role of ideology in science. It is not a question of, for example, some class *using* the science for its purposes but of a common presubjective origin for both the science and the ideology.) It may even be (though Foucault does not explicitly say so) that the ideological function of a science requires it to meet certain standards of objectivity. For example, history designed to further the claims of a religious institution competing

15. Moreover, as we shall see in Chapter 7, there is another approach to the problem of norms – one denying the need for a philosophical grounding – that is more in accord with Foucault's own inclinations. But it is still worth noting that his archaeological approach does not exclude in principle some sort of philosophical basis for norms.

for allegiance in a pluralistic society may need to be objective to obtain the ideological goal of gaining the respect and attention of nonbelievers. Of course, ideology may also cause defects of objectivity in a science. But, Foucault holds, eliminating the defects need not destroy the ideological connections: "The role of ideology does not diminish as rigour increases and error is dissipated" (AK, 186). Thus, he moves away from the standard view that there is a deep gap between valid science and ideologically influenced inquiry and leads us to see scientific objectivity and ideological bias as two intertwined aspects of a discipline's rootedness in a discursive formation.

We arrived at Foucault's analysis of ideology from a discussion of the connections between discursive and nondiscursive factors in knowledge. It is striking, however, that his analysis makes no mention of the nondiscursive sources of ideology but seems to treat it as an autonomous discursive phenomenon. Later, Foucault expressed strong reservations about the concept of ideology, saying "this is a notion that cannot be used without circumspection." Among his reasons is that "ideology stands in a secondary position relative to something which functions as its infrastructure, as its material, economic determinant, etc."[16] His point here is clearly directed against AK's treatment of ideology.

This treatment of ideology is, moreover, an example of one of AK's major flaws. Although the book insists in principle on the intimate tie between discursive formations and nondiscursive factors such as institutions, there is no serious discussion of the nature of the nondiscursive factors and of the influence they exert. AK offers a full-blown methodology for a history of thought that, like OT, treats it as a set of autonomous systems of discourse. But it does not do justice to histories (like FD and the beginning of BC) that deal with the interrelations of discourse and nondiscursive practices. It recognizes the existence of such interrelations and even (in its treatment of the formation of objects, concepts, enunciative modalities, and theoretical options) notes some specific points of interaction. But there is no elucidation of the fundamental nature and ultimate significance of the link between the discursive and the nondiscursive.

This issue (and the closely related one of the source of change

16. "Truth and power," in Colin Gordon, ed. *Power/knowledge* (New York: Pantheon, 1980), 118.

in the history of thought) becomes central for the next stage of Foucault's work. From DP through the first volume of HS, he supplements the archaeological analysis of discourse with a complementary analysis (dubbed "genealogical") of the relation of discursive knowledge to the power structures of society. This focus on "power/knowledge" takes Foucault considerably beyond his earlier work. But in many ways it remains an explicit development of what is implicit in the books from FD through AK. The next chapter, which is primarily a philosophical evaluation of the archaeological method, will also offer a few further comments on its relation to Foucault's later genealogical work.

Conclusion

It is clear that, at a minimum, AK is important as an explicit formulation of the approach to the history of thought that Foucault developed in FD, BC, and OT. As we have seen, its methodology does not entirely accord with the practice of the preceding case studies; but it is a reconstruction faithful to the central features of that practice. Beyond this, although AK's methodology is primarily oriented toward the description of discursive formations, the book does point – with many unclarities and hesitations – toward Foucault's later efforts to come to terms with nondiscursive causal factors in the history of thought. AK thus appears as a methodological essay that both sums up Foucault's previous historical work and moves haltingly toward his later, genealogical work.

It may, however, seem that AK is something more than a historian's articulation of his methodology. In particular, we may be inclined to regard it as an effort to provide a philosophical basis or justification for this methodology. On such a view – implicit, for example, in Dreyfus and Rabinow's discussion of AK – Foucault's goal is to ground his historical practice in a philosophical account of knowledge and language. I will express my reservations regarding this interpretation of AK in the course of my evaluation of his archaeological approach in the next, concluding chapter.

7

REASON AND PHILOSOPHY

Readers of Foucault are likely to question the value of his work on at least three levels. First, alternatively befogged by the tortuous opacities of his prose and dazzled by the seeming gratuitousness of his audacious claims, they may well ask if there is anything at all here worth their while. Do his writings, beneath all the fireworks and attendant billows of smoke, in fact express a position of sufficient clarity, plausibility, and interest to merit sustained attention? The preceding chapters represent my own effort to provide an affirmative answer to this question. By careful analysis of all the major books Foucault wrote through the 1960s, I have tried to show that they do express a coherent and challenging approach to the history of Western thought. The next sort of question likely to confront Foucault's readers is that of his historical accuracy. Here an adequate response would require detailed specialist investigations beyond both the scope of this book and the competence of its author. However, I have offered a general framework for the historical evaluation of Foucault's work, based on a distinction of the levels of specific history, constructive history, and critical history. Moreover, I have discussed some typical difficulties raised by historians concerning the first two levels and have offered fuller evaluations of the critical history of FD and OT. My tentative overall assessment is that, at all levels, Foucault's history is sufficiently responsible and challenging to be worth serious attention, but it is also often greatly oversimplified and lacking in evidential support.

But, at least for the philosophically minded reader, there remain serious evaluative questions. For Foucault does not claim merely to offer interesting and plausible accounts of some data in the history of Western thought. He also suggests that his accounts support a new view of reason as a historical phenomenon and, correspondingly, a new conception of philosophical reflection. The question is whether this account of reason and this conception of philosophy are ones we ought to accept.

At the heart of his view of reason and philosophy is Foucault's distinctive appropriation of Kant's conception of philosophy as the critical use of reason. As we saw in the Introduction, he ultimately presented his intellectual enterprise as a self-critical continuation of the Enlightenment project of seeking autonomy through reason. Like Kant, he accepts reason as the key to freedom and autonomy. But, in characteristic postmodern fashion, he also sees the ways in which reason itself can tyrannize rather than liberate and sets himself the task of employing reason to overcome its own destructive tendencies.

Given this understanding of Foucault's project, two central critical questions directly arise. First, is the archaeological method that Foucault developed from the implicit practice of FD through the explicit methodological reflection of AK, in fact consistent with and an appropriate vehicle for his philosophical project? We may suspect, for example, that Foucault's late formulation of what he was trying to do does not fit well with what he in fact did from fifteen to twenty-five years earlier. Second, even given the internal compatibility of Foucault's explicit philosophical telos and his archaeological practice, is the telos itself viable? Some of the most acute and challenging criticisms of Foucault (e.g., those formulated by Jürgen Habermas and by Charles Taylor) suggest that his philosophical telos is itself incoherent, that it embodies a fatal self-referential inconsistency.

Archaeological method and Foucault's philosophical project

One source of tension between archaeological method and Foucault's Enlightenment conception of liberating philosophy is his fascination with madness – the foil of reason – as the locus of the ultimate truth of human reality. As we saw in Chapter 2, although most of FD deals with conceptions of madness developed from the standpoint of reason, there is also a recurring "countertheme," dominant at the end of the book, of the mad's own experience of their madness. Here Foucault strongly suggests that this experience has access to a privileged truth about the reality of madness. He further suggests that this truth, particularly as expressed through the literature of madness, is the key to an understanding of human reality that will lead us beyond the arbitrary restrictions of mere reason. Thus, he speaks of the works of such writers as Hölderlin, Nerval, Roussel, Nietzsche, and Artaud as "lightning flashes" that reveal the "sovereign enterprise of unreason" and effect a "total contestation" of Western culture that promises an escape from the "gigantic moral imprisonment" that is the life of reason (FD, 530; MC, 278).

Such a view maintains the project of human liberation but, contrary to Foucault's position in "What Is Enlightenment?", makes this project not the work of but a revolt against reason. Foucault's goal appears to be not a self-critical continuation of the Enlightenment struggle for rational autonomy but, in the manner of romantic irrationalism, an infrarational vision of ultimate truth. Further, in the original Preface to FD (omitted in the second edition), Foucault seems to suggest that the historical method employed in that book (i.e., archaeology) is itself meant to function as an instrument of this enterprise, establishing contact with the "pure" experience of madness in its own right. He does not go so far as to say that archaeology can simply restore this experience: "The wild state [of madness] can never be restored in itself" but remains an "inaccessible primitive purity" (FD, vii). But he does claim that through a "structural study of the historical ensemble – notions, institutions, juridical and police measures, scientific concepts – " we can "get back to the decision that simultaneously connects and separates reason and madness" and "discover the perpetual exchange, the obscure common root, the original confrontation that gives meaning [sens] to both the unity and the opposition of sense [sens] and the senseless [l'insensée]" (FD, vi). This at least suggests that archaeology is meant to excavate the oracle of madness.

If this were the true significance of Foucault's archaeological method, then it would obviously not be an appropriate instru-

ment for his later project of a self-critique of autonomous reason; it would be rather a means of reaching a fundamental truth
buried far beneath the realm of reason. But however much the
Foucault of FD was taken with this naive idea of a privileged
experience of madness, such an experience cannot be plausibly
regarded as the primary object of that book's historical analysis.
Despite the claims of the Preface, these in fact focus almost
exclusively on the ways the nonmad view the mad. Only in brief
reflections on De Sade's writings and Goya's paintings is there
any serious effort to evoke madness as the mad live it. Accordingly, even though Foucault does hold in FD that there is a
privileged experience of madness that provides fundamental
infrarational truth, his archaeological history of madness is not a
history of this experience.

As a matter of fact, the idea of finding the truth in some
special infrarational experience is one that lingers for a considerable time in Foucault's thought. At the end of OT, for example,
he evokes the figure of "madness as it is posited in the modern
experience, as its truth and alterity." In this figure, he says, we
encounter "the very hollowness of our existence . . ., the finitude
upon the basis of which we are, and think, and know, is suddenly
there before us: an existence both real and impossible" (OT,
375). This view may also be connected with OT's quasi-mystical
effusions suggesting a postmodern salvific return of language,
not as an instrument of reason but as an autonomous reality.

The same theme emerges even in AK, which in other ways is
the high tide of Foucault's flirtation with rationalist structuralism. There he does insist that archaeology is not a matter of
"writing a history of the referent" and that, for example, "we are
not trying to reconstitute what madness itself might be, in the
form in which it first presented itself to some primitive, fundamental, deaf, scarcely articulated experience" (AK, 47). And, in
a footnote to this passage, he says: "This is written against an
explicit theme of my book [FD], and one that recurs particularly
in the Preface" (AK, 47, n.1). However, even here Foucault's
point is merely that archaeology is concerned only with discursive systems, not with the real referents of these systems, such as
"madness itself." He does not deny that there are such referents
or even that we may have some access to them. In fact, immediately after saying, "we are not trying to reconstitute what madness might be," he adds: "Such a history of the referent is no

doubt possible; and I have no wish at the outset to exclude any effort to uncover and free these 'prediscursive' experiences from the tyranny of the text" (AK, 47).

It is, nonetheless, important that in AK Foucault explicitly recognizes that, whatever prospects there may be for a discovery of pure, prediscursive madness in itself, this has nothing to do with his work as an archaeologist of thought. Presumably, whatever revelation may be in store for us will derive from art, not Foucault's archaeology.[1] In this regard, it is significant that Foucault mentions the Preface but not the concluding sections of FD in his self-critical footnote. Even though the latter have much more to say about madness in itself, it is only the Preface that suggests that Foucault's own historical investigations – not only the "lightning flashes" of great art – may reveal the truth of madness. Accordingly, even though Foucault seems to have long nurtured a romantic irrationalism, he eventually realized (what his actual historical work bears out) that it had no essential connection with the philosophical project of his archaeology.

Nevertheless, Foucault's prolonged fascination with the idea of an infrarational truth does have a significant – and, in my view, negative – influence on his work from FD through AK. It accounts, I think, for much of the obscure and self-indulgent writing we find in these books. Even though the purpose of archaeological method is to analyze madness, disease, life, labor, and language as intellectual and social constructs, Foucault all too often befogs his discussion with an incantatory rhetoric striving to evoke a sense of the realities in themselves that he thinks lie beneath the rational constructs. The result is to obscure the clarity and blunt the precision of which his archaeological analyses are capable. Significantly, after Foucault definitely shook off the charm of infrarational ultimate truth, his writing (in DP and HS – especially the second and the third volumes of the latter) becomes much leaner and more lucid.

Foucault's philosophical project is rationalist in the sense that it involves an acceptance of reason as the primary means of human liberation. This is why what I have called the temptation of romantic irrationalism is a *temptation*. But the project is also historical and critical; that is, it is based on the idea that reason

1. For an excellent discussion of Foucault's changing views on art (particularly modernist literature), cf. John Rajchman, *Michel Foucault: the freedom of philosophy* (New York: Columbia University Press, 1985), Chapter 1.

itself is a historical phenomenon whose norms are always open to challenge through critical analysis. Since such analysis is itself an exercise of reason, it follows that, from the standpoint of Foucault's philosophical project, it too must be regarded as historically situated in the discursive and nondiscursive practices of a particular age. As such, it corresponds to a specific, historically limited perspective and is not a disengaged "view from nowhere" that offers an absolute, ahistorical body of theoretical truth. In view of this, it may well seem that the archaeological approach Foucault develops from FD through AK cannot be the vehicle of the critical analysis his philosophical project requires. For it seems that archaeology claims to be precisely the sort of neutral, ahistorical theoretical knowledge to which Foucault's later philosophical project allows no place.

Here we find Foucault encountering what I will call the *structuralist temptation*. There is no doubt that his increasingly explicit development of the archaeological approach in the 1960s was very closely tied to his fascination with and enthusiasm for structural analysis. We know that he was particularly impressed by the work of Dumézil on ancient religions, of Lévi-Strauss on primitive cultures, and of Lacan on psychoanalysis. Also, as we saw in Chapter 6, he thought of his archaeology as a historical counterpart of structuralism, effecting in the history of thought the kind of decentering of the subject that the structuralists had achieved in other domains. Structuralist analyses generally presented themselves as scientific results, and the structuralist approach as a whole was widely regarded as fulfilling the hope for an objective theoretical understanding of human beings (genuine human sciences). As a result it was easy for Foucault (and his readers) to think of his archaeology as one further step along this path to objective, theoretical knowledge of ourselves.

Such a view of archaeology is further reinforced by Foucault's tendency in AK to present his work as a more adequate successor of major philosophical efforts, in the phenomenological and hermeneutical traditions, to provide a fundamental understanding of human reality. He deploys the full apparatus of a traditional "discourse on method," delimits the domain of his research via a complex categorization of the "rules" governing discourse, and, through his account of the statement and discursive formations, seems to offer a grounding of his entire enterprise in a philosophy of language. All of this strongly suggests that archaeology is meant to take its place in the imposing series, from Plato to Husserl, of philosophical theories designed to catch once and for all the essential features of human existence.

It is, then, both tempting and possible to read Foucault's archaeological method – especially as he articulates it in AK – as directed toward the very sort of general theoretical understanding of human beings (social scientific or philosophical) that his later philosophical project is committed to undermining. If we do this, we will conclude that Foucault's archaeology succumbs to the structuralist temptation and is indeed incompatible with his philosophical project. Moreover, archaeology so construed is open to the sort of devastating philosophical criticisms that Dreyfus and Rabinow develop in their study of Foucault.[2]

What is not so clear, however, is whether archaeology need be – or is best – construed along the theoretical lines corresponding to the structuralist temptation. Such a construal is perhaps inevitable if, like Dreyfus and Rabinow, we present Foucault's work as essentially a response to the efforts of twentieth-century philosophers and social scientists to achieve a theoretical understanding of human beings. There is no doubt that this is an important perspective for understanding some aspects of Foucault's enterprise. But, even where the force of the structuralist temptation is at its strongest (at the end of OT and in AK), there is reason to think that Foucault never entirely succumbs to it. Moreover, our study of his development of the archaeological approach has shown that it is primarily a method of concrete historical analysis, not of general social scientific or philosophical theorizing.

There is no doubt that the concluding chapter of OT is a very strong endorsement of structuralist human science. Lévi-Strauss's cultural anthropology, Lacan's psychoanalysis, and a (hoped-for) new form of structuralist linguistics are presented as the engines that will finish off the modern episteme's central concept of man and clear a new space for constructive thought. It is striking, however, that even here Foucault insists that the new structuralist countersciences cannot be regarded as bodies of neutral scientific knowledge. As we saw, he maintains that both of the currently existing countersciences are essentially

2. H. Dreyfus and P. Rabinow, *Michel Foucault: beyond structuralism and hermeneutics*, 2d ed. (Chicago: University of Chicago Press, 1983), Chapter 4.

tied to practices specific to our current social, cultural, and political situation. Psychoanalysis depends on the special relationship between doctor and patient, and ethnology on the dominant world-role of the Western democracies. As a result, Foucault holds that the knowledge generated by these countersciences has an even lower status than that of the human sciences, which themselves fall far short of the standards of full scientific objectivity. He particularly emphasizes that the structuralist countersciences must not be taken to provide anything like general theories of human nature.

Accordingly, even if archaeology is viewed in relation to Foucault's enthusiasm for structuralism, it can at best be regarded as another counterscience, just as limited as the others in its scientific significance. In fact, it seems likely that, in terms of the account of OT, archaeology would find its natural place as a counterscience to the modern discipline of history. As we saw in Chapter 5, Foucault presents the latter as the discipline that shows how all the human sciences, including itself, have validity only within a restricted temporal and cultural domain. Archaeology can be plausibly regarded as the non-subject-centered counter to this history, performing a parallel function for the likewise non-subject-centered structuralist countersciences. As a counterscience, archaeology would have the same kind of limitations as history itself and the other countersciences. It would have to give up its "claim to validity within the element of universality" (OT, 371). This would make it quite impossible for Foucault to present it as a neutral, universally valid body of theoretical knowledge.

With regard to AK itself, it is important to remember that all the theoretical analyses of the statement and of the rules of discursive formations are explicitly presented as part of an effort to articulate an alternative to certain standard approaches to the history of thought. Since these approaches have been often based on philosophical accounts (Hegelian, Sartrean) of the human subject, it makes sense for Foucault to sketch an alternative philosophical picture corresponding to his new approach to history. But the primary focus of the book, as the entire second half makes clear, is to distinguish Foucault's way of doing the history of thought from standard approaches, not to justify it on philosophical grounds. In reply to the question (posed at the end of AK), Is he doing history or philosophy?, Foucault responds that he is certainly not doing philosophy in the sense of providing a foundation for his archaeological practice: "For the moment, and for as far ahead as I can see, my discourse . . . is avoiding the ground on which it could find support" (AK, 205). The justification offered for archaeology – as Foucault's constant references to his previous case studies suggest – is rather the fruitfulness of its specific applications. What might appear to be foundational philosophical theories (of language, for example) are better construed as no more than attempts to show that the archaeological approach can be coherently formulated without relying on the modern philosophical category of the subject. The role, therefore, of AK's theoretical discussions is not to prove that archaeology is the right method of history, much less to establish a finally adequate theory of human reality. Their purpose is merely to exhibit the appropriateness of archaeology as the method of a history that will move us beyond the modern concept of man.

This interpretation not only fits the predominantly historiographical, rather than philosophical, emphasis of AK; it also explains the ironic, self-distancing tone the book often exhibits toward its enterprise.[3] This tone is particularly evident in the introductory and concluding dialogues with an imagined critic (AK, 17, 199–211), which put the main body of the text in self-questioning brackets. Such passages are a device for backing away from the high philosophical seriousness that might be suggested by the book's technical and systematic character. They suggest that the philosophical analyses are not in fact an effort at final theoretical understanding but merely instruments for clarifying a specific approach to the history of thought.

The strongest support for the conclusion that Foucault's archaeological method does not succumb to the structuralist temptation lies in its close connection with Canguilhem's history of concepts. As we have seen in detail, the method develops as an extension and transformation of Canguilhem's methodology as a historian of science. Faced with the problems of writing histories of madness, disease, and the human sciences that would do justice to features ignored by standard histories of ideas, Foucault

3. Allan Megill has particularly emphasized the irony of AK. Cf. his "Foucault, structuralism, and the ends of history," *Journal of Modern History* 51 (1979), 451–503 and *Prophets of extremity* (Berkeley: University of California Press, 1984), Chapter 4. In my view, however, he is incorrect in reading the irony as a sign of radical irrationalism.

adapted and revised Canguilhem's method to meet specific histo-riographical needs.[4] Thus, the archaeological method derives much more from Foucault's efforts to deal with concrete histori-cal data than from general philosophical theory. Moreover, as we have seen, the historiographical needs that formed Foucault's archaeology are intimately tied to the project for a historical critique of reason formulated much later. Archaeology is, from the beginning, an instrument of a critical history that accords with the philosophical telos laid down in the essay "What Is Enlightenment?" Accordingly, we can confidently conclude that Foucault's archaeological method does not represent a yielding to the structuralist temptation of pure, ahistorical theory and does work as an appropriate instrument of his critical philosophi-cal project.

A remaining question concerns the relation of archaeology to the genealogy that figures so prominently in Foucault's work af-ter 1970. An adequate response to this question would require a thorough study of Foucault's practice of genealogy (especially in DP) and of his many scattered – and not obviously mutually con-sistent – comments about it in essays and interviews. I think, how-ever, that a careful analysis would support an account roughly along the following lines. Archaeology, as the preceding chapters have characterized it, continues to play a key role in Foucault's later work. It is, however, applied not only (as in OT) to discursive practices but also to nondiscursive practices. Thus, reflection on DP's account of the modern practice of punishing criminals by imprisonment reveals it to involve the four key features of discur-sive formations. It constitutes new classes of objects (e.g., delin-quents), characterized in terms of a set of distinctive concepts (e.g., criminal character); it distinguishes practices with different sorts of authority (that of the judge, of prison officials, of parole boards); and it defines alternative lines of strategic action (for example, different approaches to the use of solitude and of work in the treatment of prisoners). This application of archaeological analysis is not an innovation but rather a return to the approach of FD, where, for example, archaeology showed the common structure of Cartesian philosophical discourse and the Classical

4. Cf. the discussions of Foucault's method at the ends of Chapters 2, 3, and 5 above.

nondiscursive practice of confinement and revealed the moral import of the nineteenth-century asylum.

The simultaneous application of archaeology to discursive practices (e.g., those, such as criminology, leading to the understanding of criminals) and to nondiscursive practices (e.g., those, such as the prison system, leading to the control of criminals) enables Foucault to establish an essential symbiotic relation between knowledge and power. This connection, of course, becomes the central leitmotiv of his work during the 1970s. Given this connection, Foucault was able to return to the question, bracketed in OT, of the cause of changes in discursive formations (and epistemes). Like other historians, he sees changes in nondiscursive practices as due to a wide variety of economic, social, political, and ideological causes. But, contrary to many standard accounts, he maintains that these causes cannot be fit into any simple unified teleological scheme (e.g., the rise of the bourgeoisie, the ambition of Napoleon). Rather, he holds that nondiscursive practices change because of a vast number of small, often unrelated factors (ad hoc adjustments of existing procedures, the chance discovery of a new implement or technology), the sorts of "petty causes" Nietzsche made the concern of his genealogy. Thus, changes in the nondiscursive practices that constitute a society's power structure must be understood as due to an immensely complex and diffuse variety of microfactors (a "micro-physics of power"). (This approach does for nondiscursive practices what archaeology did for discursive practices: It eliminates the role of a central, controlling "subject.") The action of the microcauses can eventually lead to fundamentally new sorts of discursive practices and to a corresponding revolution in the correlated discursive practices (a new episteme).

It seems, then, that Foucault's development of a genealogical approach to history is a matter of (1) returning archaeology to its role of describing both discursive and nondiscursive practices, (2) thereby exhibiting an essential tie between knowledge and power, and (3) exploiting this tie to provide a causal explanation of changes in discursive formations and epistemes. Accordingly, genealogy does not replace or even seriously revise Foucault's archaeological method. It rather combines it with a complementary technique of causal analysis.

If the above account is essentially correct, then archaeology continues to hold a central place even in Foucault's genealogical work. This would strongly support our claim that archaeology is compatible with Foucault's later formulation of his philosophical project.

Is Foucault's critique of reason self-refuting?

So far we have been discussing a question of relative consistency: Is the archaeological method compatible with the critique of reason for which Foucault wants to employ it? An even more fundamental line of criticism, developed in different ways by many writers, raises the question of the absolute consistency of Foucault's project: Doesn't his historical critique of reason wind up refuting itself? Isn't it a self-referentially inconsistent project?

The most straightforward formulation of this objection comes from critics who think Foucault is a universal skeptic or total relativist who denies that there are any objective truths at all and so must, if he is consistent, deny the objective truth of his own position. Thus, J. G. Merquior says: "So at bottom Foucault's enterprise seems stuck on the horns of a huge epistemological dilemma: if it tells the truth, then *all* knowledge is suspect in its pretence of objectivity; but in that case, how can the theory itself vouch for its truth? It's like the famous paradox of the Cretan liar – and Foucault seemed quite unable to get out of it."[5] Hilary Putnam offers a similar criticism, based on the idea that Foucault is a "modern relativist" who "should end up by regarding his own utterances as mere expression of feeling."[6] The much more elaborate and sophisticated critiques of Charles Taylor and Jürgen Habermas also make use of the self-refuting nature of what they take to be Foucault's relativism.[7]

Despite their popularity, such criticisms, based on the charge of global skepticism or relativism, are unfounded. They ignore three aspects of Foucault's work that definitely distinguish it from any universal assault on the notion of truth. First, there is

5. J. G. Merquior, *Foucault* (London: Fontana, 1985), 147.
6. Hilary Putnam, *Reason, Truth, and History* (Cambridge: Cambridge University Press, 1981), 163.
7. Cf. J. Habermas, *The philosophical discourse of modernity*, translated by F. Lawrence, (Cambridge, Mass.: MIT Press, 1987), Chapters 9 and 10; and Charles Taylor, "Foucault on freedom and truth," *Political Theory* 12 (1984), 152–83, reprinted in David Hoy, ed., *Foucault: a critical reader* (Oxford: Basil Blackwell, 1986).

the explicitly local or regional nature of his analyses. His histori-cal critiques of reason are always directed toward very specific applications (psychiatry, clinical medicine, the human sciences), with no suggestion that the inadequacies of any one domain can be extrapolated to others. Second, Foucault's focus is always on the domains of "dubious disciplines" dealing with human beings. There is no suggestion that he thinks his archaeological method could be applied to sciences like physics or chemistry to show that their claims to truth and objectivity are questionable. There is, in fact, strong reason to think that Foucault on the whole accepted the objectivist view of these disciplines held by Bache-lard and Canguilhem. Moreover, in OT, he accepts the modern empirical disciplines (biology, economics, and philology) as do-mains of objective scientific knowledge.

Third, even for the dubious disciplines that are the objects of his critique, Foucault does not deny all truth and objectivity. He says, for example, that, even though the human "sciences" (un-like the empirical disciplines on which they are modeled) do not meet "the formal criteria of a scientific form of knowledge," they nonetheless do belong "to the positive domain of knowledge" (OT, 365). He even allows, as we saw in Chapter 2, that modern psychiatry may have a degree of "scientific validity." More gener-ally, we saw how he insists (in AK) that even strong ideological bias is compatible with the attainment of objective truth.

So the short answer to these criticisms is simply that Foucault does not espouse the universal skepticism or relativism they suppose he does. It might, nonetheless, be maintained that, given other views he holds, Foucault ought to accept these self-destructive positions. Here critics have frequently cited three of Foucault's views that they think lead logically to skepticism or relativism: that there are no facts independent of interpreta-tion, that different periods of Western thought have been ruled by radically different epistemes, and that all knowledge is essen-tially tied to nondiscursive social structures (the connection be-tween knowledge and power).

Regarding the first point, critics frequently cite a passage in Foucault's Royaumont lecture, "Nietzsche, Freud, Marx," on the pervasiveness of interpretation: "If interpretation can never be completed, this is quite simply because there is nothing to inter-pret. There is nothing absolutely primary to interpret, for after all everything is already interpretation, each sign is in itself not the thing that offers itself to interpretation but an interpretation of other signs."[8]

Those who cite this passage as proof of Foucault's relativism fail to realize that, in it, Foucault is not speaking in his own name. He is engaged in an exposition of the "system of interpretation the nineteenth century founded,"[9] and the passage cited is a statement of the second of what he presents as the three fundamental principles of this system as it was developed by Marx, Nietzsche, and Freud. The discussion is a historical one (corresponding to the later remarks on modern hermeneutics in OT) and is not meant to express Foucault's own views. This, of course, is precisely what we should expect, given Foucault's rejections of hermeneutic interpretation, particularly in BC and AK. Indeed, if he did hold that there is nothing but interpretation "all the way down," there would be no place for his archaeological method, designed to describe discursive formations as objective structures quite apart from any meanings that subjects may give to them. This point is in fact implicit in the last paragraph of "Nietzsche, Freud, Marx," where Foucault points out that "hermeneutics and semiology are two fierce enemies," since semiology precisely denies the infinity of interpretations and "believes in the absolute existence of signs."[10] At a minimum, *semiology* here means the structuralist approach to language and other signs, for which Foucault at this time surely had more sympathy than he did for hermeneutics. But Foucault no doubt also has in mind his own archaeological method, which he characterizes (in AK) as a "pure description" of signs just as they exist in themselves. There is, accordingly, no basis in this text for thinking that Foucault denies a distinction between facts and our interpretations of them.

Foucault does hold – with Bachelard, Canguilhem, most current Anglo-American philosophers, and of course Kant – that there are no simply given facts (e.g., sense impressions) apart from concepts that fit them into some broader categorical scheme. In this sense, he would agree that there are no uninterpreted facts. But this surely does not entail the skeptical or relativist conclusion that there are no genuinely objective facts.

8. "Nietzsche, Freud, Marx," translated by J. Anderson and Gary Hentzi, *Critical Texts,* 3 (1986), 3.
9. Ibid., 1.
10. Ibid., 5.

Indeed, it may be, as Kant and many philosophers after him have maintained, that falling under a categorical scheme is a *condition* of objectivity.

But Foucault does not merely maintain, like Kant, that our thoughts and experiences occur only within fixed categorical boundaries. He also holds, contrary to Kant, that these boundaries are themselves contingent products of our history and that, in different epochs, there have been radically diverse systems (epistemes, in his terminology) governing thought and experience. Does this not, we may ask, entail that views held within one particular episteme (e.g., our own) can have validity only relative to that episteme? Here there are three key points to be made on Foucault's behalf. First, as we have seen, he is far from denying all continuity in changes from one episteme to another. In OT he explicitly presents the work of thinkers such as Lamarck, Smith, and Jones as having a transitional character. And his account in AK makes explicit room for objects, concepts, enunciative modalities, and theories that exist in different discursive formations. Second, Foucault can argue, like Bachelard, that discontinuity does not in itself exclude progress, that, in particular, discoveries made in one episteme may be permanent in the sense that they will have to be included (appropriately reformulated) in any subsequent episteme. Third, even if Foucault's specific studies of "dubious disciplines" were to show that, in these cases, there have been charges so radical that their results are entirely relative to their historical epochs, a parallel claim does not follow for other disciplines. There is no reason to suppose that the results of an archaeological analysis of the natural sciences, for example, would yield the same sorts of results as an archaeology of the sciences of man.

A final assessment of the alleged skeptical or relativist implications of Foucault's views on the connection between knowledge and power would require a full discussion of this connection that is beyond the scope of this book. However, there are two points worth noting. First, even though Foucault apparently sees all bodies of knowledge as originating from nondiscursive practices of social control, he also allows that some disciplines have been able to free themselves effectively from this connection. For example, the natural sciences, he maintains, arose in the sixteenth century from the methods of judicial investigation employed by the Inquisition. But, in the course of their development, they became autonomous modes of knowledge. "In becoming a technique for the empirical sciences, the investigation has detached itself from the inquisitorial procedure, in which it was historically rooted" (DP, 226). This specific account of the origins of modern natural science may be dubious. But the important fact for our purposes is Foucault's recognition that a body of knowledge may come to exist in essential independence of the social power structures that gave rise to it.

Second, there is surely no general objection to essential connections between bodies of objective knowledge and nondiscursive social practices. Certainly, even the least controversial instances of scientific knowledge are intimately connected with complex institutions and other social structures. As Foucault pointed out in one of his very last interviews, even "mathematics is linked, in a certain way and without impairing its validity, to games and institutions of power" (127). (Indeed, as we suggested in our discussion of AK, the very norms of scientific objectivity may be grounded in nondiscursive social practices.) Given this, the only question is what sorts of social structures and practices are compatible with some degree of objective knowledge. Foucault's studies in fact suggest that a significant degree of objective truth can be based on even major instruments of social control. This is why, as we have seen, he can allow that even psychiatry may have a certain degree of scientific validity.

It may be urged that, even if there is objective truth in some sense, its close association with power will always make it subservient to social mechanisms of power. Charles Taylor, for example, cites Foucault's assertion that "we are forced to produce the truth of power that our society demands, of which it has need, in order to function" and comments: "This regime-relativity of truth means that we cannot raise the banner of truth against our regime. There can be no such thing as a truth independent of its regime, unless it be that of another."[11]

In one sense, Foucault would agree with this. Our ways of knowing are always connected with social power structures, and we would not know the truths we do if these structures did not exist. But this does not imply, as Taylor seems to think, that Foucault regards the truths in question as somehow valid only

11. Taylor, 94. The citation from Foucault is from C. Gordon, ed., *Power/knowledge* (New York: Pantheon, 1980), 93.

within the regime in which they arise. We need to distinguish the relativity of the means whereby truths can be attained from the relativity of their validity. Foucault maintains that the methods and occasions of obtaining any truth will ultimately depend on some aspects of a society's power structure (though he would surely agree that there may be different structures in different societies adequate for the discovery of a given truth). But he does not hold that the truth thus obtained is inevitably valid only within the society in question. Some "truths" may be of this sort, but others may have an objective validity that transcends any particular regime. Admittedly, as the text Taylor cites says, a society will generate truths that function to support its power structures. But this does not imply that such truths by that very fact lack objective validity or that the society generates *only* truths that support it. A regime's system for the production of supportive truths may – precisely because the validity of a truth need not be restricted to the regime producing it – also lead to truths capable of undermining it.

There is, therefore, ample reason to deny that Foucault is a universal skeptic or relativist. Why then have so many critics, including some of the best, persisted in this view of him? Primarily, it seems, because they incautiously ascribe to Foucault an extreme version of Nietzschean perspectivism. Taylor, for example, says: "In the end, the final basis of Foucault's refusal of 'truth' and 'liberation' seems to be a Nietzschean one. This is not all of Nietzsche. . . . But at least in the *Fröhliche Wissenschaft* we have a doctrine that Foucault seems to have made his own. . . . Foucault espouses both the relativistic thesis from this view, that one cannot judge between forms of life/thought/evaluation, and also the notion that these different forms involve the imposition of power."[12] Similarly, Habermas maintains that "only in the context of his interpretation of Nietzsche does Foucault yield to the familiar melody of a *professing* irrationalism."[13]

There is, however, no basis for moving from Foucault's obvious admiration for Nietzsche to the conclusion that he espouses relativism or skepticism. The main locus of Foucault's treatment of Nietzsche is his 1971 essay, "Nietzsche, Genealogy, History." The first point to notice is that this essay is entirely devoted to

12. Ibid., 93.
13. Habermas, 278.

the exposition and interpretation of Nietzsche's views. At no point does Foucault express his own agreement with the position he is discussing. The specific passage Habermas cites as showing Foucault to be a "professing irrationalist" is quite explicitly a summary of Nietzsche's view of how the allegedly objective enterprises of history can be revealed to be based on "instinct, passion, the inquisitor's devotion, cruel subtlety, and malice." The passage ends with the striking claim "that all knowledge rests upon injustice (that there is no right, even in the act of knowing, to truth or foundation of truth)."[14] Not only is much of the language of this passage Nietzschean, but also a footnote cites specific passages in three of Nietzsche's books. Even though we know that Foucault was very sympathetic to Nietzsche, there is no basis for simply attributing the view expressed in this text to him.

Moreover, even if we do attribute the position stated in this passage to Foucault, it is by no means clear that the position itself amounts to relativism or skepticism. It can very plausibly be read as nothing more than the thesis, discussed above, that the origins of knowledge are always tied to power structures. An act of knowing may have no "right to truth" in the sense of some essential (nonaccidental) orientation to truth in virtue of its noble, disinterested origin. But it may nonetheless attain at least some degree of truth.

The fact remains, of course, that Foucault does undermine much of the authority of important domains of human knowledge, even if he does not assert a total skepticism or relativism. This suggests a more limited form of the objection we have been considering: that Foucault's archaeological analyses undermine the authority of precisely the sort of knowledge to which they themselves lay claim. His archaeological critiques are, after all, directed toward all modern efforts to know human beings. But surely archaeology itself is just such an effort. It offers accounts of specific features of our intellectual history (how we distinguish reason from unreason, how we think about disease, how we have conceived of ourselves as both subjects and objects of our knowledge). Moreover, taken as a whole, these accounts suggest an overall picture of what human reality is like: radically

14. "Nietzsche, Genealogy, History," in D. F. Bouchard, ed., *Language, Counter-memory, Practice* (Ithaca: Cornell University Press, 1977), 163.

historical, formed by structures beyond the control of subjectivity, subject to sharp epistemic breaks.

Of course, Foucault can point out that his approach differs from the modern human sciences because it is not based on the concept of man and so does not employ the conception of history connected with that concept. But surely he must admit that his enterprise, even if it has moved beyond the limitations of the modern episteme, is constrained and distorted by the limitations of another, postmodern episteme. Indeed, these limitations are the more insidious since we are not yet in a historical position even to begin to see what they might be. Perhaps Foucault can accept a broadly Bachelardian account that allows the natural sciences to be significantly independent of any particular episteme (in virtue of their progress and the permanence of their results over epistemic breaks). But his work is not in physics or chemistry but in the same historical line as the human sciences that are the objects of his critique. What reason is there to think that a twenty-first century successor to Foucault would not be able to carry out on archaeology the same sort of critical analysis that Foucault himself has carried out on the modern human sciences?

A similar point can be made regarding the connection of knowledge and power. Even though there may be knowledge (in the natural sciences) that has escaped its origins in social power structures, there is surely no reason to think that Foucault's own archaeological and genealogical studies have effected any such escape. No doubt they have a somewhat different relation to the current nexus of power than the human sciences they analyze and criticize. But it would be entirely arbitrary for Foucault to maintain that his own work does not have some significant relationship to power. It may, for all we know, be just another, as yet undetected, instrument of the very power mechanisms it seems to be undermining. Certainly, Foucault's own analyses of such enterprises as psychiatry and criminology show how knowledge that seems liberating can be actually dominating.

Foucault sometimes suggested that his effort is to recognize and develop marginal, alternative bodies of knowledge associated with resistance to current power structures.[15] But his own accounts show how systems of power can make use of even what

15. Cf. "Two Lectures," in Gordon, 82.

seems to be opposition to strengthen their position. And, in any case, if Foucault is right about the essential tie of knowledge to power, then alternative bodies of knowledge must be associated with alternative systems of power and so will bring their own sort of domination.[16]

Foucault can, of course, reply that, even if his own results are on the same epistemic level as those of the disciplines he is analyzing, this does not deny them all authority. As we have seen, he does not maintain that there is no objectivity or truth attained by the human sciences. They are, in spite of all their limitations, genuine bodies of knowledge; therefore the same can presumably be said of his own archaeology and genealogy. So even if Foucault must admit that there is an epistemic parity between his own analyses and those of the disciplines he is criticizing, this does not undermine the cognitive status of his results. In this sense, his position is still not self-referentially inconsistent.

This would be an entirely adequate response if Foucault's goal was simply a body of historical knowledge. Such knowledge could complement and correct similar bodies of knowledge even if it had no privileged status with respect to them. But Foucault's work is not directed toward the mere construction of yet another domain of knowledge. The knowledge he achieves is meant to be deployed to further the cause of human liberation, to remove arbitrary limitations and constraints imposed by other bodies of knowledge. But if his own knowledge can claim no privileged position over the disciplines it criticizes, why should we prefer the limitations and constraints that it no doubt brings to those that it opposes? Foucault may be perfectly right in maintaining that psychiatry, criminology, and the modern human sciences in general are major obstacles to human liberation. But it is also true – though he tends to ignore the fact – that these same disciplines have in other ways worked for human liberation.[17] The Classical treatment of the mad, for example, involved, on Foucault's own account, numerous restrictions (both conceptual and physical) that were in fact eliminated by modern psychiatry. Similarly, he could hardly deny that the modern decline of representation opened up possibilities for human thought and action that the Classical episteme had excluded. What reason does Foucault

16. Cf. Habermas, 281.
17. Taylor makes this sort of point very effectively.

have for thinking that archaeological and genealogical knowledge will not be similarly ambivalent between liberation and domination?

He might, of course, maintain that archaeology and genealogy will at least effect a net gain in liberation over domination. But it is hard to see how he could defend any such claim. His own studies suggest that each stage of development (from the Renaissance through the Classical Age to the Modern era) has involved greater, if more subtle, domination. If so, why should we expect the next stage to be any better? Here his neglect of the liberating role of modern disciplines is again relevant. What reason does he have for thinking that, from the standpoint of postmodern disciplinary systems, modern "humanitarianism" will not take on the sort of nostalgic glow that he seems to find in the Renaissance and the Classical Age?

The difficulty can also be formulated in terms of the problem of norms that we have seen to be so fundamental for Bachelard and Canguilhem as well as for Foucault. Archaeology is, as we have noted, a method for analyzing the historical development of norms. To this extent, it provides a neutral historical account of a society's norms that may reveal their contingent character. This serves the purposes of Foucault's philosophical project of historical critique by identifying unnecessary constraints on human freedom. But the mere fact that a constraint is historically contingent and hence can be eliminated does not entail that it should be eliminated. To draw this conclusion we need, first, the judgment that constraints on human freedom are wrong and, second, the judgment that the constraints we propose to eliminate are worse than those our action would put in their place. Consequently, Foucault's project for a critique of reason cannot simply criticize given norms; it must also propose norms of its own. As Nancy Fraser says, "Why is struggle preferable to submission? Why ought domination to be resisted? Only with the introduction of normative notions could he begin to tell us what is wrong with the modern power/knowledge regime and why we ought to oppose it."[18] The question is where Foucault's philosophical project finds the justification for its own norms and how it shows these norms to be preferable to those that it criticizes.

18. Nancy Fraser, "Foucault on Modern Power: Empirical Insights and Normative Confusions," *Praxis International* 1 (1981), 283.

One possible response to this question would be for Foucault to maintain, along the lines suggested in Chapter 6, that the relevant norms are grounded in fundamental social practices, practices that, at least for now, really do define boundaries that we cannot transgress. The idea would be that even the most rigorous and thorough historical critique might find some limitations on reason that do not turn out to be contingent (or, if they are contingent in some ultimate sense, nonetheless have the force of necessity for us). One way of developing this idea would be to undertake archaeological and genealogical studies of the natural sciences with a view to discovering the social basis for the norms that govern their privileged sort of truth and objectivity. The hope would be that such norms could also be shown to support the normative judgments of Foucault's critique of reason. Another line of development would be to show that the very project of a historical critique of reason (quite apart from any particular judgments it might make) requires an acceptance of certain norms (e.g., norms definitive of rational discourse itself). The first approach would effect a "quasi-naturalistic" grounding of Foucault's normative judgments, since it would (following Bachelard and Canguilhem) take for granted the objectivity and validity of the natural sciences. The second would be a Foucaultian version of Habermas's "quasi-transcendental" grounding of norms in the conditions of any rational discourse.

Although the above sort of response does not seem to be logically excluded as a possibility for Foucault, it does not fit well with the strongly antitheoretical and antifoundational direction of his thought. Another response, more in keeping with his spirit, is simply to deny the need for any sort of philosophical grounding for normative judgments. The idea here is not that normative judgments are arbitrary choices. It is rather that the specific evaluations defining the goals of our struggle for human liberation are grounded in our concrete experiences of oppressive institutions and practices, quite independent of any justification by philosophical theorizing. We do not need a philosophical theory to establish that the oppression and exploitation of factory workers, prisoners, or the mad are wrong or that the situation would be genuinely improved if specific changes could be made in the regimes governing them.

This sort of response does still, however, include a crucial role for philosophy. Projects of liberation are opposed by bodies of expert knowledge (psychiatry, criminology, economics) telling us that the changes we envisage are simply not possible because they violate established truths about human nature, society, and so on. The role of philosophy – that is, the historical critique of reason – is to examine such claims of impossibility, showing the extent to which they are bogus and thereby clearing the path to liberation. The generic normative judgment that liberation is worthwhile and the numerous specific normative judgments regarding the changes needed to achieve it are not provided by philosophy but rather define the context in which philosophy operates. Philosophy is not the foundation of the project of liberation but an underlaborer clearing the path for it.

This sort of response to the problem of the basis for normative judgments fits in well with Foucault's insistence, in his essay on enlightenment, that the project of the historical critique of reason must be "experimental" in the sense of continually putting itself "to the test of reality, of contemporary reality." This contact with contemporary reality, complementing "the realm of historical inquiry" that the project opens up, enables it "both to grasp the points where change is possible and desirable, and to determine the precise form this change should take."[19] What Foucault says here can be plausibly read as asserting the priority of the contemporary reality of struggles for liberation over philosophical reflection.

Such a reconception of the role of philosophy is not without its difficulties. If we simply accept, without critical scrutiny, the norms implicit in our struggles for liberation, what guarantee do we have that these norms are sound? And how are we to adjudicate conflicting normative judgments by those participating in these struggles? Foucault's own concrete judgments about what is oppressive and what not conform fairly well with the standard views of leftist intellectuals. For him the major threats to human freedom are such things as bourgeois morality and the exploitation of workers. But why should we prefer his judgments to those of rightists who think labor unions, pornography, abortion, and international Communism are the real problems? Surely we cannot just blindly assert our judgments in face of widespread challenges to them. And what alternative

19. "What is Enlightenment?" in P. Rabinow, ed., The Foucault reader (New York: Pantheon, 1984), 46.

to blind assertion is there other than the defense of our own views on the basis of a fundamental philosophical analysis of human nature and values?

The alternative for Foucault is precisely the grounding, mentioned above, of our normative judgments in our concrete experiences of domination. Instead of basing our normative judgments on general philosophical principles, we can ground them in our direct, practical encounters with alleged sources of domination. To find out if prisons and asylums or pornography and abortion are major obstacles to human liberation, we need to encounter them as concrete realities, not as instances of general philosophical principles or theories. There is surely reason to think that the intensity of Foucault's own commitment on these matters, which surfaces in even his most austere archaeological analyses, is rooted in such things as his own observations of asylums, investigations of the causes of prison riots, and experiences of society's attitude toward homosexuals.

There are, of course, many errors to which judgments formed from direct experience are susceptible. But these errors are much more limited and more readily corrected by further experience than are judgments rooted in general philosophical theories. Indeed, such theories have themselves proved to be among the greatest dangers to human freedom. "In fact we know from experience that the claim to escape from the system of contemporary reality so as to produce the overall programs of another society or another way of thinking . . . has led only to the return of the most dangerous traditions."[20] Normative judgments grounded only in direct practical experiences will not have the scope or radicality of those based on profound and comprehensive philosophical theories. As a result they will lead us only to very specific, local transformations of our society. "I prefer even these partial transformations that have been made in the correlation of historical analysis and the practical attitude, to the programs for the new man that the worst political systems have repeated through the twentieth century."[21]

It seems, then, that Foucault's preferred response to the question of the ground of his normative judgments is one that rejects the traditional role of philosophy as somehow providing the

20. Ibid.
21. Ibid., 47.

founding truths for our practical commitments. Just as, for Bachelard, scientific knowledge is not underwritten by philosophy, so, for Foucault, practical normative judgments are not justified by philosophical principles. In both cases, philosophy enters only in a context that has already been defined by another sort of activity.

Foucault proposes, in the end, a twofold transformation of the traditional concept of philosophy. First, he turns it away from the effort at an a priori determination of the essential limits of human thought and action and instead makes it a historical demonstration of the contingency of what present themselves as necessary restrictions. Second, he no longer asks it to provide the justification for the values that guide our lives but instead employs it to clear the path of intellectual obstacles to the achievement of those values. This reconception of philosophy is particularly significant for those of us who see scant prospects for a fulfillment of philosophy's traditional goal of legitimating knowledge claims and actions via a body of fundamental truths. While eschewing this goal, Foucault is still able to assign philosophy an important role in the enlightenment and liberation of human beings.

There are, nonetheless, two important questions that need to be raised regarding this tempting reconception. The first is whether it even makes sense to think of the historicocritical project Foucault proposes as "philosophy." It would seem to be nothing more than intellectual history carried out for the sake of very specific political and social goals. Why, then, should those who practice it be regarded as the legitimate successors of Plato, Aristotle, Aquinas, Descartes, Hume, Kant, and Hegel? Doesn't an enterprise that gives up on the grand and ultimate questions of human existence and contents itself with historical contingencies rather than eternal, necessary truths by that very fact cease to be philosophy?

To this objection I think there are two lines of response. First, although it is true that traditional philosophy aimed at knowledge of ultimate truth, the point of seeking such truth has traditionally been the freedom and happiness of human beings. From Plato's vision of the Forms, through Aquinas's contemplation of the divine essence, to Hegel's return to the Absolute, knowledge of fundamental truth has been pursued for the sake of liberation and fulfillment. Foucault's project can be regarded as a new, more modest (and realistic) way of seeking these traditional philosophical goals.

Second, even though the search for foundational truths has been abandoned, Foucault's enterprise requires many of the same intellectual skills and virtues as traditional philosophizing. Meticulous analysis of concepts, rigorous assessment of arguments, dialectical flair and imagination – these are all requisites for Foucault's critical philosopher as much as for the traditional constructive philosopher. There is, indeed, one respect in which Foucaultian philosophy is closer to the grand tradition than much current philosophizing. Whereas the latter frequently isolates itself in the narrow and rarified space of its specialized problems, the former requires the very sort of broad cultural and historical awareness that we find in the great figures of traditional philosophy.

But the fact remains that, in most cases, there would be very little overlap or similarity between the actual work of a Foucaultian and a traditional philosopher. Certainly, very few of those currently calling themselves philosophers have either the ability or the inclination to carry out the sort of historical inquiries that Foucault did. This leads to the second question we must ask regarding Foucault's reconception of philosophy: What place, if any, does it allow for the kind of work that in fact has traditionally occupied philosophers? Is there, for example, room for such standard fare as solutions to the mind-body problem, proofs of God's existence, refutations of skepticism, and so on? Aren't these precisely the sorts of efforts to answer fundamental questions that Foucault's project would have us abandon? Such an abandonment may well be understandable in face of the long and sad story of failed pretensions that is the history of philosophy. But surely a great deal would be lost by giving up the enterprise.

In my view, however, there is no reason to think that accepting Foucault's reconception of philosophy requires giving up the sorts of investigations that have occupied traditional philosophers. For one thing, I do not see how the Foucaultian can rule out in principle the possibility of our someday actually finding answers to the great, ultimate questions. He cannot base his skepticism about traditional philosophy on anything other than the historical fact that philosophers have for centuries failed to solve the deep problems they have set themselves. To go further and suggest that there is some fundamental feature of the mind or the world that excludes ultimate philosophical truth in principle would be itself a philosophical claim in the traditional mode. Since success in answering traditional philosophical questions is not excluded (however unlikely it may be) and would surely be of immense value, it is only reasonable to accept continuing work on these questions. Moreover, an important lesson of our philosophical past is that such work, even when unsuccessful, has many positive side effects. For example, it refutes inadequate theories and improves our intellectual resources by introducing new concepts and clarifying old ones. Such side effects will often be of great value for the Foucaultian philosopher's projects of historicocritical analysis.

It seems, then, that acceptance of Foucault's reconception of philosophy need not exclude traditional philosophical work. We can not only tolerate but encourage and even profit from such work, all the while, of course, maintaining a healthy skepticism regarding its ultimate success and being alert to its possibilities for constraining human freedom.

Conclusion

What, finally, are we to make of Foucault's work? A crucial preliminary point is that, despite many obscurities and deficiencies, it does deserve our serious attention. Foucault is not just another Left Bank magician, dazzling us with the latest versions of the standard intellectual tricks. He is prone to fads and gimmicks and sometimes displays the quirks and prejudices of the Parisian intelligentsia at its least attractive. More importantly, there are, as we have seen, major gaps in his arguments for many of his central historical and philosophical claims. Nevertheless, our close studies of his main writings through 1969 show that they offer a body of thought that is not only intelligible and coherent but also remarkably perceptive and challenging in its analyses of the last three hundred years of intellectual history. As such, it offers numerous insights into many specific domains of historical and philosophical inquiry.

Beyond this, I think that three general aspects of Foucault's achievement promise to be particularly fruitful for those who come after him. First, his idea of writing the history of thought on an archaeological level beneath that of human subjectivity opens up an important new dimension for understanding our past. It should not (as Foucault's rhetoric sometimes suggests) be regarded as a replacement for other, standard approaches to the history of ideas. But it does represent a particularly valuable means of developing new historical perspectives and for correcting and sharpening views from old ones.

Second, Foucault's use of histories of thought for the critical purpose of questioning the authority of major bodies of contemporary knowledge is a valuable counter to some of the best hidden and most effective mechanisms of domination in our society. Particularly important, in my view, is Foucault's insistence on the highly specific, regional character of his critiques. Unlike the typical revolutionary, he does not see one all-pervading enemy, whose existence corrupts everything and whose elimination will solve all our problems. Rather, he thinks the liberation of human beings requires an unending series of local battles against an ever-changing series of particular evils. "My point is not," he once said, "that everything is bad, but that everything is dangerous."[22] His techniques of critical history provide a model for how we can maintain our awareness of the dangers implicit in all bodies of knowledge and effectively oppose those that, at a given time, have become sources of evil.

Finally, his reconception of philosophy as a historical critique of reason in the service of human freedom enables us to maintain the ideals and utilize the distinctive intellectual virtues of traditional philosophizing, although we remain dubious regarding the grand claims of this enterprise. Through this new conception of philosophy he offers our skeptical age the hope that, even without the Truth, we may still be made free.

22. Afterword (1983) to Dreyfus and Rabinow, 231.

BIBLIOGRAPHY

The following list contains all of Foucault's and Canguilhem's books and all of Bachelard's on the philosophy of science. The list of secondary publications (and of Foucault's essays and interviews) is a representative selection, with particular emphasis on works relevant to topics discussed in this book. For more comprehensive bibliographies on Bachelard and Canguilhem, see J.-C. Margolin, *Bachelard*, B. Saint-Sernin, ed., *Canguilhem* (special issue of *Revue de métaphysique et de morale* 90 [1985], and C. M. P. M. Hertogh, *Bachelard en Canguilhem*. On Foucault, there is the splendid work of Michael Clark, *Michel Foucault: an annotated bibliography*, New York: Garland Press, 1983. This provides an essentially complete listing of primary and secondary sources through 1981, and the annotations are invaluable. For more recent comprehensive listings of just Foucault's publications, see J. Lagrange, "Les oeuvres de Michel Foucault," *Critique* 42 (1986), 942–62, and J. Bernauer and T. Keenan, "The Works of Michel Foucault: 1926–1984," *Philosophy and Social Criticism* 12 (1987), 230–69. Another useful bibliography of work by and about Foucault is J. Nordquist, *Michel Foucault: a bibliography*, Santa Cruz, Calif.: Reference and Research Services, 1986.

Bachelard

1. Books by Bachelard on philosophy of science

Essai sur la connaissance approchée. Paris: Vrin, 1928.
Etude sur l'évolution d'un problème de physique: la propagation thermique dans les solides. Paris: Vrin, 1928.
La valeur inductive de la relativité. Paris: Vrin, 1929.
Le pluralisme cohérent de la chimie moderne. Paris: Vrin, 1932.
L'intuition de l'instant. Paris: Stock, 1932.
Les intuitions atomistiques. Paris: Boivin, 1933.
Le nouvel esprit scientifique. Paris: Alcan, 1934. (*The New Scientific Spirit,* translated by A. Goldhammer. Boston: Beacon Press, 1984.)
La dialectique de la durée. Paris: Boivin, 1936.
L'expérience de l'espace dans la physique contemporaine. Paris: PUF, 1937.
La formation de l'esprit scientifique. Paris: Vrin, 1938.
La psychanalyse du feu. Paris: NRF, 1938. (*The psychoanalysis of fire,* translated by A. C. M. Ross. Boston: Beacon Press, 1964).
La philosophie du non. Paris: PUF, 1940. (*The philosophy of no,* translated by G. C. Waterston. New York: Orion Press, 1969.)
Le rationalisme appliqué. Paris: PUF, 1949.
L'activité rationaliste de la physique contemporaine. Paris: PUF, 1951.
Le matérialisme rationnel. Paris: PUF, 1953.
Bachelard: epistémologie. Textes choisies par D. Lecourt. Paris: PUF, 1971.
L'engagement rationaliste (a posthumous collection of texts with preface by G. Canguilhem). Paris: PUF, 1972.

2. Books and articles about Bachelard

Bhaskar, R., "Feyerabend and Bachelard: two philosophies of science," *New Left Review,* 94 (1975).
Bouligand, G., et al., *Hommage à Gaston Bachelard.* Paris: PUF, 1957.
Canguilhem, G., "Sur une épistémologie concordataire," in Bouligand, et al., *Hommage à Gaston Bachelard,* 4–12.
"L'histoire des sciences dans l'oeuvre épistémologique de Gaston Bachelard," *Annales de l'Université de Paris,* no.1, 1963. Reprinted in *Etudes d'histoire et de philosophie des sciences,* 173–86.
"Gaston Bachelard et les philosophes," *Sciences,* no. 24, 1963. Reprinted in *Etudes,* 187–95.
"Dialectique et philosophie de non chez G. Bachelard," *Revue internationale de philosophie* 4 (1963). Reprinted in *Etudes,* 196–207.
"Gaston Bachelard, psychanalyste dans la cité scientifique?" *Il Protagora* 24 (1984), 19–26.

Dagognet, F., "M. Gaston Bachelard, philosophe de l'imagination," *Revue internationale de philosophie* 4 (1960), 32–42.

"Le matérialisme rationnel de Gaston Bachelard," *Cahiers de l'institut des sciences économiques appliquées*, 126 (1962), 17–31.

Gaston Bachelard, sa vie, son oeuvre, avec un exposé de sa philosophie. Paris: PUF, 1965.

Gaukroger, S. W., "Bachelard and the problem of epistemological analysis," *Studies in History and Philosophy of Science* 7 (1976), 189–244.

Ginestier, P., *Pour connaître la pensée de Bachelard.* Paris: Bordas, 1968.

Grieder, A., "Gaston Bachelard – 'phénoménologue' of modern science," *Journal of the British Society for Phenomenology* 17 (1986), 107–23.

Gutting, G., "Gaston Bachelard's philosophy of science," *International Studies in the Philosophy of Science* 2 (1987), 55–71.

Hertogh, C. M. P. M., *Bachelard en Canguilhem.* Amsterdam: VU Uitgeverij, 1986.

Hyppolite, J., "Gaston Bachelard ou le romantisme de l'intelligence," *Revue philosophique*, 1954, 85–96. Reprinted in G. Bouligand, et al., *L'hommage à Gaston Bachelard.*

"L'epistémologie de Gaston Bachelard," *Revue de l'histoire des sciences et de leurs applications*, 12 (1964).

Lalande, M., *La théorie de la connaissance scientifique selon Gaston Bachelard.* Montreal: Fides, 1966.

Lecourt, D., *Bachelard, le jour et la nuit.* Paris: Grasset, 1974.

Pour une critique de l'épistémologie (Bachelard, Canguilhem, Foucault). Paris: Maspero, 1972. (*Marxism and epistemology: Bachelard, Canguilhem, and Foucault,* translated by B. Brewster. London: NLB, 1975.)

Loi, M., "Bachelard et les mathématiques," *Il Protagora* 5 (1984), 45–57.

Margolin, J.-C., *Bachelard.* Paris: Seuil, 1974.

Quillet, P., *Gaston Bachelard.* Paris: Seghers, 1964.

Smith, Roch C., *Gaston Bachelard.* Boston: Twayne Publishers, 1982.

Tiles, Mary, *Bachelard: science and objectivity.* Cambridge: Cambridge University Press, 1984.

Vadée, M., *Bachelard ou le nouvel idéalisme épistémologique.* Paris: Editions sociales, 1975.

Canguilhem

1. Books by Canguilhem

Essai sur quelques problèmes concernant le normal et le pathologique. Strasbourg: Publications de la Faculté des Lettres, 1943.

Le Normal et le pathologique. (the preceding thesis, along with an essay, "Nouvelles reflexions sur le normal et le pathologique"). Paris:

PUF, 1966. (*On the normal and the pathological*, translated by C. Fawcett. Dordrecht: Reidel, 1978.)

La connaissance de la vie, 2nd ed. Paris: Vrin, 1969.

La formation du concept de reflex aux XVIIe et XVIIIe siècle, 2nd ed. Paris: Vrin, 1977.

Idéologie et rationalité. Paris: Vrin, 1977.

Etudes d'histoire et de philosophie des sciences, 5th edition. Paris: Vrin, 1983.

2. Writings about Canguilhem

Foucault, M., "Introduction" to G. Canguilhem, *On the normal and the pathological*, translated by C. Fawcett. Dordrecht: Reidel, 1978. A somewhat different French version appeared in *Revue de la métaphysique et de morale* 90 (1985), 3–14.

Hertogh, C. M. P. M., *Bachelard en Canguilhem*. Amsterdam: VU Uitgeverij, 1986.

Lecourt, D., *Pour une critique de l'épistémologie (Bachelard, Canguilhem, Foucault)*. See complete listing under "Books and articles about Bachelard."

Macherey, P., "La philosophie de la science de Georges Canguilhem," preceded by a "Presentation" by Louis Althusser, *La Pensée* 113 (1964), 54–75.

Saint-Sernin B., ed., *Canguilhem* (special journal issue), *Revue de la métaphysique et de morale* 90 (1985).

Spicker, S. F., "An introduction to the medical epistemology of Georges Canguilhem: moving beyond Michel Foucault," *The Journal of Medicine and Philosophy* 12 (1987), 397–411.

Foucault

1. Books written by Foucault

Maladie mentale et personnalité. Paris: PUF, 1954.

Folie et déraison: Histoire de la folie à l'âge classique. Paris: Plon, 1961. Second edition (with new preface and appendices): *Histoire de la folie à l'âge classique*. Paris: Gallimard, 1972. Second edition reprinted without appendices, 1976. (*Madness and civilization*, translated by R. Howard. New York: Pantheon, 1965. A greatly abridged translation.)

Maladie mentale et psychologie. Paris: PUF, 1962. Revised version of *Maladie mentale et personnalité*. (*Mental illness and psychology*, translated by A. Sheridan, foreword by H. Dreyfus. Berkeley, Calif.: University of California Press, 1987.)

Naissance de la clinique: une archéologie du régard médical. Paris: PUF,

1963. (*The birth of the clinic*, translated by A. Sheridan. New York, Vintage, 1973.)

Raymond Roussel. Paris: Gallimard, 1963. (*Death and the labyrinth: the world of Raymond Roussel*, translated by C. Ruas. Garden City, N.Y.: Doubleday & Company, 1986. Also includes an interview with Foucault.)

Les mots et les choses: une archéologie des sciences humaines. Paris: Gallimard, 1966. (*The order of things*, translated by A. Sheridan. New York: Random House, 1970.)

L'archéologie du savoir. Paris: Gallimard, 1969. (*The archaeology of knowledge*, translated by A. Sheridan. New York: Pantheon, 1972.) Also includes "The Discourse on Language," a translation of *L'ordre du discours*, Foucault's inaugural address at the Collège de France. Paris: Gallimard, 1971.

Ceci n'est pas une pipe: deux lettres et quatre desseins de René Magritte. Montpellier: Fata Morgona, 1973. (*This is not a pipe*, translated and edited by J. Harkness. Berkeley, Calif.: University of California Press, 1981.)

Surveiller et punir: naissance de la prison. Paris: Gallimard, 1975. (*Discipline and punish*, translated by A. Sheridan, New York: Pantheon, 1977.)

Histoire de la sexualité. I: la volonté de savoir. Paris: Gallimard, 1976. (*The history of sexuality, Vol. I: An introduction*, translated by R. Hurley. New York: Pantheon, 1978.)

L'usage des plaisirs: histoire de la sexualité, tome 2. Paris: Gallimard, 1984. (*The Use of Pleasure*, translated by R. Hurley. New York: Pantheon, 1985.)

Le souci de soi: histoire de la sexualité, tome 3. Paris: Gallimard, 1984. (*The care of the self: history of sexuality*, Vol. 3. Translated by R. Hurley. New York: Pantheon, 1986.)

2. Books edited by Foucault

Moi, Pierre Rivière, ayant égorgé ma mère, ma soeur et mon frère: une cas de parricide au XIXe siècle. Paris: Gallimard-Julliard, 1975. Includes a Foreword and an essay by Foucault. (*I, Pierre Rivière, having slaughtered my mother, my sister and my brother: a case of parricide in the 19th century*, translated by F. Jellinik. New York: Pantheon, 1975.)

Herculine Barbin, dite Alexina B. Paris: Gallimard, 1978. (*Herculine Barbin: being the recently discovered memoirs of a nineteenth-century French hermaphrodite*, translated by R. McDougall. New York: Pantheon, 1980. Includes an Introduction to the English edition and a note by Foucault.)

(With A. Farge) *Le désordre des familles: lettres de cachet des Archives de la Bastille*. Paris: Gallimard-Julliard, 1982.

3. Collections of essays by and interviews with Foucault

Language, counter-memory, practice, edited and with a foreword by D. Bouchard. Ithaca, N.Y.: Cornell University Press, 1977.

Michel Foucault: power, truth, and strategy, edited by M. Morris and P. Patton. Sydney, Australia: Feral Publications, 1979. Also includes some essays about Foucault.

Power/knowledge: selected interviews and other writings, 1972–1977, edited and with an Afterword by C. Gordon. New York: Pantheon, 1980.

The Foucault reader, edited by P. Rabinow. New York: Pantheon, 1985.

Politics, philosophy, and culture: interviews and other writings, 1977–1984. New York: Routledge, 1988.

4. Selected articles and other essays

"Introduction" to L. Binswanger, *Le rêve et l'existence,* translated by J. Verdeaux. Bruges: Descleé de Brouwer, 1954, 9–128. ("Dream, imagination, and existence," translated by F. Williams, *Review of Existential Psychology and Psychiatry* 19 (1984–85), 29–78.)

"La recherche psychologique et la psychologie," in *Des chercheurs français s'interrogent,* edited by J-E. Morère. Paris: PUF, 1957, 171–201.

"La folie, l'absence d'oeuvre," *La table ronde,* no. 196, May, 1964, 11–21. Reprinted in the second edition of *Histoire de la folie,* 575–82.

"Nietzsche, Freud, Marx," in *Nietzsche: cahiers de Royaumont,* Philosophie, Tome VI. Paris: Seuil, 1967, 183–200. ("Nietzsche, Freud, Marx," translated by J. Anderson and Gary Hentzi, *Critical Texts* 3 (1986), 1–5.)

"Sur l'archéologie des sciences: reponse au cercle d'épistémologie," *Cahiers pour l'analyse* 9 (1968), 5–4. ("On the archaeology of the sciences," *Theoretical Practice* 3/4 (1971), 108–27.)

"Reponse à une question," *Esprit* 36 (1968), 850–74. ("Politics and the study of discourse," translated by R. Boyers and C. Gordon, *Ideology and consciousness* 3 (1978), 7–26.)

"Qu'est-ce qu' un auteur?" *Bulletin de la Société française de Philosophie* 63 (1969), 73–95 (followed by a discussion, 96–104). ("What is an author?" in *Language, counter-memory, practice.*)

"Mon corps, ce papier, ce feu," *Paideia,* Sept., 1971. A revised version is reprinted in the second edition of *Histoire de la folie,* 583–603. ("My body, this paper, this fire," translated and introduced by G. P. Bennington, *Oxford Literary Review* 4 (1979), 5–28.)

"Nietzsche, la généalogie, l'histoire," in *Hommage à Jean Hyppolite.* Paris: PUF, 1971, 145–172. ("Nietzsche, genealogy, history," in *Language, counter-memory, practice.*)

"Gaston Bachelard, le philosophe et son ombre: 'piéger son propre culture,'" *Le Figaro littéraire,* Sept. 30, 1972, 16.

"Governmentality," translated by R. Braidotti, *Ideology and consciousness* 6 (1979), 5–21.

"Omnes et singulatim: towards a criticism of 'political reason'," in S. MacMurrin, ed., *The Tanner lectures on human values.* New York: Cambridge University Press, 1981, 224–54.

"The subject and power: I. why study power? the question of the subject; II. how is power exercised?" in H. Dreyfus and P. Rabinow, *Michel Foucault: beyond structuralism and hermeneutics,* 2d ed. Chicago: University of Chicago Press, 1983, 208–226.

"Un cours inédit: Qu'est-ce que les Lumières?" (from a lecture given at the Collège de France, Jan. 5, 1983), *Magazine littéraire,* no. 207, 1984, 35–39. (Translated as "Kant on enlightenment and revolution" by C. Gordon, *Economy and Society,* 15 (1986), 88–96.)

"La vie: l'expérience et la science," *Revue de métaphysique et de morale* 90 (1985), 3–14. This is a slightly revised version of the Introduction to G. Canguilhem, *On the Normal and the Pathological,* translated by C. R. Fawcett. Reidel, 1978.

"What is Enlightenment?" translated by C. Porter, in P. Rabinow (ed.), *The Foucault reader.* New York: Pantheon, 1984. (Translation from an unpublished French original.)

5. *Selected interviews with Foucault (in chronological order)*

M. Chapsal, "Entretien: Michel Foucault," *Quinzaine littéraire,* May 15, 1966, 14–15.

R. Bellour, "Entretiens: Michel Foucault – *Les mots et les choses,*" *Lettres françaises,* Mar. 31, 1966, 3–4. Reprinted in R. Bellour, *Le livre des autres.* Paris: L'Herne, 1971, 135–144.

"Deuxième entretien avec Michel Foucault: sur les façons d'écrire l'histoire", *Lettres françaises,* June 15, 1967, 6–9. Reprinted in R. Bellour, *Le livre des autres.* Paris: L'Herne, 1971, 189–207.

J. P. El Kabbach, "Foucault repond à Sartre", *Quinzaine littéraire,* Mar. 1, 1968, 20–22. Cf. Foucault's objections to the publication of this interview: "Une mise au point de Michel Foucault," *Quinzaine littéraire,* Mar. 15, 1968, 2.

J.-J. Brochier, "Michel Foucault explique son dernier livre [*The archaeology of knowledge*]," *Magazine littéraire* 28 (1969), 23–25.

J-M. Palmier, "La naissance d'un monde," *Le Monde,* May 3, 1969, supplément, viii.

John Simon, "Interview with Michel Foucault," *Partisan Review* 38 (1971), 192–200.

Fons Elders, "Human Nature versus power," a discussion with Foucault and Noam Chomsky, in F. Elders, ed., *Reflexive water: the basic concerns of mankind.* London: Souvenir Press, 1974, 135–97.

B.-H. Lévy, "Non au sexe roi," *Nouvel observateur*, 12 mars, 1977, 92ff. ("Power and sex: an interview with Michel Foucault," translated by D. J. Parent, *Telos* 10 (1977), 152–61.)

G. Raulet, "Structuralism and post-structuralism," *Telos* 16 (1983), 195–211.

H. Dreyfus and P. Rabinow, "Afterword (1983): on the genealogy of ethics: an overview of work in progress," in H. Dreyfus and P. Rabinow, *Michel Foucault: beyond structuralism and hermeneutics*, 2d ed.. Chicago: University of Chicago Press, 1983, pp. 229–264.

M. Jay, L. Lowenthal, P. Rabinow, R. Rorty, C. Taylor, "Politics and Ethics: an Interview" (Apr., 1983), in P. Rabinow, *The Foucault reader*, New York: Pantheon, 1984, 373–380.

P. Rabinow, "Polemics, politics, and problemization," in P. Rabinow, ed., *The Foucault reader*. New York: Pantheon, 1984, 381–90.

R. Fornet-Betancourt, H. Becker, and A. Gomez-Müller, "L'éthique du souci de soi comme pratique de liberté (Jan. 20, 1984)," *Concordia*, 1984, 99–116. ("The ethics of care for the self as a practice of human freedom," translated by J. D. Gauthier, S.J., *Philosophy and Social Criticism* 12 [1987], 112–31.)

G. Barabedette and A. Scala, "Le retour de la morale," *Les Nouvelles*, June 28–July 5, 1984, 36–41. ("Final Interview," translated by T. Levin and I. Lorenz, *Rariton* 5 [1985], 1–13.)

6. Books about Foucault

Auzias, Jean-Marie, *Michel Foucault: Qui suis-je?* Lyon: La Manufacture, 1986.

Baudrillard, Jean, *Oublier Foucault*. Paris; Edition Galilée, 1977. ("Forgetting Foucault," translated by N. Dufresne, *Humanities in Society* 3 [1980], 87–111.)

Blanchot, Maurice, *Foucault/Blanchot*. New York: Zone Books, 1987. Contains translations of Foucault's essay on Blanchot, "La pensée du dehors," and of Blanchot's "Michel Foucault tel que je l'imagine."

Brede, Rüdinger, *Aussage und Discours: Untersuchungen zu Discours-Theorie bei Michel Foucault*. Frankfurt am Main: Peter Lang, 1985.

Cooper, Barry, *Michel Foucault: an introduction to his thought*. Toronto: Edwin Mellen, 1981.

Cousins, Mark, and Athar Hussain, *Michel Foucault*. London: Macmillan, 1984.

Deleuze, Gilles. *Foucault*. Paris: Les Editions de Minuit, 1986. (*Foucault*. Minneapolis: Minnesota University Press, 1988.)

Diamond, I., and L. Quinby, eds., *Feminism and Foucault: reflections on resistance*. Boston: Northeastern University Press, 1988.

Dreyfus, Hubert L., and Paul Rabinow, *Michel Foucault: beyond structural-*

ism and hermeneutics, 2d ed., Chicago: University of Chicago Press, 1983.

Gane, Mike, ed., *Towards a critique of Foucault*. London: Routledge and Kegan Paul, 1986.

Guédez, Annie, *Foucault*. Paris: Editions Universitaires, 1972.

Hoy, David, ed., *Foucault: a critical reader*. Oxford: Basil Blackwell, 1986.

Hug, J.-C., *Michel Foucault: une histoire de la verité/conception graphique*. Paris: Syros, 1985.

Kammler, Clemens, *Michel Foucault: Eine kritische Analyse seines Werke*. Bonn: Bouvier, 1986.

Kremer-Marietti, Angele, *Foucault et l'archéologie du savoir*. Paris: Seghers, 1974.

Michel Foucault: archéologie et genéalogie. Paris: Livre de Poche, 1985. Revised and expanded version of the preceding book.

Lemert, Charles C., and Garth Gillan, *Michel Foucault: social theory and transgression*. New York: Columbia University Press, 1982.

Lyantey, P., *Foucault*. Paris: Editions Universitaires, 1973.

Major-Poetzl, Pamela, *Michel Foucault's archaeology of western culture*. Chapel Hill, N.C.: University of North Carolina Press, 1983.

Merquior, J. G., *Foucault*. London: Fontana, 1985.

Perrot, Michel, ed., *L'impossible prison: recherches sur le système pénitentiaire au XIXe siecle. Débat avec Michel Foucault*. Paris: Seuil, 1980.

Poster, Mark, *Foucault, Marxism, and history*. Cambridge: Polity Press, 1984.

Racevskis, Karlis, *Michel Foucault and the subversion of the intellect*. Ithaca, N.Y.: Cornell University Press, 1983.

Rajchman, John, *Michel Foucault: the freedom of philosophy*. New York: Columbia University Press, 1985.

Russ, Jacqueline, *Histoire de la folie: Michel Foucault*. Paris: Hatier, 1979.

Sheridan, Alan, *Michel Foucault: the will to truth*. London: Tavistock, 1980.

Smart, Barry, *Foucault, Marxism, and critique*. London: Routledge and Kegan Paul, 1983.

Michel Foucault. London: Tavistock, 1985.

7. Issues of journals on Foucault

Evolution psychiatrique 36 (1971), 2: *La conception idéologique de l'Histoire de la Folie de Michel Foucault*.

Magazine littéraire 101 (1975).

Critique 31 (1975), 343: *A propos d'un livre de Michel Foucault [Surveiller et punir]*.

Humanities in Society 3 (Winter, 1980): *On Foucault*.

SCE Reports, Spring/Summer, 1982.

298

BIBLIOGRAPHY

Le débat 41 (Sept.–Nov., 1986).

Critique 42 (1986), 471–72: *Michel Foucault du monde entier.*

Philosophy and Social Criticism 12 (1987), n. 2–3: *The final Foucault: studies on Michel Foucault's last work.*

The Journal of Medicine and Philosophy 12 (Nov., 1987): *Michel Foucault and the philosophy of medicine.*

8. Selected articles and chapters on Foucault

Amiot, M., "Le relativisme culturaliste de Michel Foucault," *Temps modernes* 22 (1967), 1271–98.

Barthes, R., "Savoir et folie," *Critique* 17 (1961), 915–22. ("Taking sides," in R. Barthes, *Critical essays*, translated by R. Howard. Evanston, Ill.: Northwestern University Press, 1972, 163–70.)

Beyssade, J.-M., "Mais quoi ce sont le fous: sur un passage controversé de la 'Première meditation'," *Revue de métaphysique et de morale* 3 (1973), 273–94.

Canguilhem, G., "Mort de l'homme ou épuisement du cogito?" *Critique* 24 (1967), 599–618.

"Sur l'*Histoire de la folie* tant qu' événement," *Le Debat*, Sept.–Nov., 1986, 37–40.

Carroll, D., "The subject of archaeology or the sovereignty of the episteme," *MLN* 93 (1978), 695–722.

Casey, E. S., "The place of space in *The birth of the clinic*," *The Journal of Medicine and Philosophy* 12 (1987), 351–56.

Cohen, R., "Merleau-Ponty, the flesh, and Foucault," *Philosophy Today* 28 (1984), 329–38.

Corvez, M., "Le structuralisme de Michel Foucault," *Revue thomiste* 68 (1968), 101–24.

Cottier, G., "La mort de l'homme: une lecture de Michel Foucault," *Revue thomiste* 86 (1986), 269–82.

Dagognet, F., "Archéologie ou histoire de la medicine," *Critique* 21 (1965), 436–47.

Dallmayr, F. R., *Polis and praxis*, Cambridge, Mass.: MIT Press, 1984, Chapter 3.

Daumézon, G., "Lecture historique de *L'histoire de folie* de Michel Foucault," *Evolution psychiatrique* 36 (1971), 227–42.

Davidson, A., "Conceptual analysis and conceptual history: Foucault and philosophy," *Stanford French Review* 8 (1984), 105–22.

"Archaeology, genealogy, ethics," in D. Hoy, ed., *Foucault: a critical reader*. Oxford: Basil Blackwell, 1986, 221–34.

Deleuze, G., "Un nouvel archiviste," *Critique* 26 (1970), 195–209. A revised and expanded version appears as a chapter of *Foucault*.

"Ecrivain non: un nouveau cartographe," *Critique* 31 (1975), 1207–27. A revised and expanded version appears as a chapter of *Foucault*.

Derrida, J., "Cogito et l'histoire de la folie," *Revue de métaphysique et de morale* 3–4 (1964), 460–94. Reprinted in J. Derrida, *Ecriture et la différence*. Paris: Seuil, 1967. (Translated by Alan Bass as *Writing and difference*. Chicago: University of Chicago Press, 1978.)

Descombes, V., *Modern French philosophy*, translated by L. Scott-Fox and J. M. Harding. Cambridge: Cambridge University Press, 1980, Chapter 4.

Dews, P., *Logics of disintegration*. London: Verso, 1987, Chapters 5, 6, 7.

Dreyfus, H., "Beyond Hermeneutics," in G. Shapiro, ed., *Hermeneutics*. Amherst, Mass: University of Massachusetts Press, 1984, 66–83.

"Foucault's critique of psychiatric medicine," *The Journal of Medicine and Philosophy* 12 (1987), 311–34.

Dreyfus, H., and P. Rabinow, "What is maturity? Habermas and Foucault on 'What is enlightenment?'," in David Hoy, ed., *The Foucault reader*. Oxford: Basil Blackwell, 1986, 109–21.

El Kordi, M., "L'archéologie de la pensée classique selon Michel Foucault," *Revue d'histoire économique et sociale* 51 (1973), 309–35.

Ewald, F., "Anatomie et corps politiques," *Critique* 31 (1975), 1228–65.

Ey, H., "Commentaires critiques sur *L'histoire de la folie* de Michel Foucault," *Evolution psychiatrique* 36 (1971), 243–58.

Felman, S., "Madness and philosophy *or* literature's reason," *Yale French Studies* 52 (1975), 206–28.

Figlio, K., Review of *The birth of the clinic*, *British Journal for the History of Science* 10 (1977), 164–67.

Flaherty, P., "(Con)textual contest: Derrida and Foucault on madness and the Cartesian subject," *Philosophy of Social Science* 16 (1986), 157–75.

Flynn, B., "Michel Foucault and the Husserlian problematic of a transcendental philosophy of history," *Philosophy Today* 22 (1978), 224–38.

Frank, M., *Was ist Neostrukturalismus?* Frankfurt am Main: Suhrkamp, 1983, Chapters 7–12.

Fraser, N., "Foucault on modern power: empirical insights and normative confusions," *Praxis International* 1 (1981), 272–87.

"Foucault's body language: a post-humanist political rhetoric?" *Salmagundi* 61 (1983), 55–70.

"Michel Foucault: a young conservative?" *Ethics* 96 (1985), 165–84.

Gearhart, S., "Establishing rationality in the historical text: Foucault and the problem of unreason," in *The open boundary of history and fiction: a critical approach to the French Enlightenment*. Princeton, N.J.: Princeton University Press, 1984, 29–56.

Gordon, C., "Birth of the subject," *Radical Philosophy* 17 (1977), 15–25.

"Question, ethos, event: Foucault on Kant and enlightenment," *Economy and Society* 15 (1986), 71–87.

Greene, J., "Les mots et les choses," *Social Science Information* 6 (1967), 131–38.

Gutting, G., "Continental philosophy of science," in P. D. Asquith and
    H. E. Kyburg, eds., *Current research in philosophy of science.* East Lan-
    sing, Mich.: Philosophy of Science Association, 1979, 94–117.
"Michel Foucault and the history of reason," in Ernan McMullin, ed.,
    Construction and constraint: the shaping of scientific rationality, Notre
    Dame, Ind.: University of Notre Dame Press, 1988.
"Continental approaches to history and philosophy of science," in G.
    H. Cantor, et al., eds., *Companion to the history of modern science.*
    Chicago: University of Chicago Press, 1989.
Habermas, J., "Taking Aim at the Heart of the Present," *University
    Publishing* 13 (1984), 5–6. Reprinted in David Hoy, ed., *Foucault: a
    critical reader.*
"Genealogical writing of history: on some aporias in Foucault's theory
    of power," *Canadian Journal of Political and Social Theory* 10 (1986),
    1–9.
Der philosophische Diskurs der Moderne. Frankfurt am Main: Suhrkamp,
    1985, Chapters 9 and 10. (*The philosophical discourse of modernity,*
    translated by F. Lawrence. Cambridge, Mass.: MIT Press, 1987.)
Hacking, I., "Michel Foucault's immature science," *NOUS* 13 (1979),
    39–51.
"Biopower and the avalanche of printed numbers," *Humanities in Soci-
    ety,* 5 (1982), 279–95.
Hattiangadi, J. H., "Language philosophy: Hacking and Foucault," *Dia-
    logue* 17 (1978), 513–28.
Hiley, D. R., "Foucault and the question of enlightenment," *Philosophy
    and Social Criticism* 11 (1985), 63–83.
Hirst, P., and Woolley, P., *Social relations and human activities.* London:
    Tavistock, 1982, Chapter 9.
Honneth, A., *Kritik der Macht.* Frankfurt am Main: Suhrkamp, 1985,
    Chapters 4, 5, 6.
Huppert, George, "*Divinatio et eruditio:* thoughts on Foucault," *History
    and Theory* 13 (1974), 191–207.
Jay, M., "In the empire of the gaze: Foucault and the denigration of
    vision in twentieth-century French thought," in D. Hoy, ed., *Fou-
    cault: a critical reader.*
Kurzwill, E., "Michel Foucault: structuralism and structures of knowl-
    edge," in *The age of structuralism: Lévi-Strauss to Foucault.* New York:
    Columbia University Press, 1980, 193–226.
Lacharité, N., "Archéologie du savoir et structures du langage scienti-
    fique," *Dialogue* 9 (1970), 35–53.
Le Bon, S., "Un positiviste désespéré: Michel Foucault," *Temps modernes*
    22 (1967), 1299–1319.
Lecourt, D., "Sur l'archéologie et le savoir (à propos de Michel Fou-
    cault)," *Pensée* 152 (1970), 69–87. (Translated in D. Lecourt, *Marx-*

ism and epistemology: Bachelard, Canguilhem, Foucault, translated by Ben Brewster. London: NLB, 1975.)

Leland, D., "On reading and writing the world: Foucault's history of thought," *Clio* 4 (1975), 225–43.

Lévy, B.-H., "Le système Foucault," *Magazine littéraire* 101 (1975), 7–9.

Macherey, P., "Aux sources de 'L'histoire de la folie': une rectification et ses limites," *Critique* 43 (1986), 752–74.

Margolin, J.-C., "L'homme de Michel Foucault," *Revue des sciences humaines* 128 (1967), 497–522.

Maslin, M., "Foucault and pragmatism," *Raritan* 7 (1988), 94–114.

McDonnell, D. J., "On Foucault's philosophical method," *Canadian Journal of Philosophy* 7 (1977), 537–53.

Megill, A., "Foucault, structuralism, and the ends of history," *Journal of Modern History* 51 (1979), 451–503.

Prophets of extremity: Nietzsche, Heidegger, Foucault, Derrida. Berkeley, Calif.: California University Press, 1984.

Midelfort, H. C. Eric, "Madness and civilization in early modern Europe – a reappraisal of Michel Foucault," in B. C. Malament, ed., *After the Reformation, essays in honor of J. H. Hexter.* Philadelphia: University of Pennsylvania Press, 1980, 247–65.

Miel, J., "Ideas or epistemes: Hazard versus Foucault," *Yale French Studies* 49 (1973), 231–45.

Paden, R., "Locating Foucault – archaeology versus structuralism," *Philosophy and Social Criticism* 11 (1986), 19–37.

Piaget, J., *Le structuralisme.* Paris: PUF, 168, 108–15. (*Structuralism,* translated by C. Maschler. New York: Basic Books, 1970, 128–35).

Poynter, F. N. L., Review of *La naissance du clinique, History of Science* 3 (1964), 140–43.

Putnam, H., *Reason, truth, and history.* Cambridge: Cambridge University Press, 1981. Chapter 7, esp. 155–62.

Pratt, V., "Foucault and the history of classification theory," *Studies in History and Philosophy of Science* 8 (1977), 163–71.

Rajchman, J., "Nietzsche, Foucault, and the anarchism of power," *Semiotext(e),* 3 (1978), 96–107.

"Ethics after Foucault," *Social Text* 13/14 (1986), 165–83.

Reiser, S. J., Review of *The birth of the clinic, Social Science and Medicine* 10 (1976), 124.

Revel, J., and Bellour, R., "Foucault et les historiens," *Magazine littéraire* 101 (1975), 10–13.

Rorty, R., "Method, social science, and social hope," *Canadian Journal of Philosophy* 16 (1981), 569–88. Reprinted in *Consequences of pragmatism: essays 1972–1980,* Minneapolis: University of Minnesota Press, 1982, 191–210.

"Beyond Nietzsche and Marx," *London Review of Books* 3 (1981), 5–6.

"Foucault and epistemology," in David Hoy, ed., *Foucault: a critical reader*, 41–49.

Rouse, J., *Knowledge and power: toward a political philosophy of science.* Ithaca, N.Y.: Cornell University Press, 1987, especially Chapter 7.

Rousseau, G. S., "Whose enlightenment? not man's: the case of Michel Foucault," *Eighteenth-Century Studies* 6 (1972–73), 238–56.

Said, E., "*Abecedarium culturae*: structuralism, absence, writing," *Triquarterly* 20 (1971), 33–71. Reprinted in *Beginnings: intention and method.* New York: Basic Books, 1975.

"An ethics of language," *Diacritics* 4 (1974), 28–37.

"Linguistics and the archaeology of mind," *International Philosophical Quarterly* 11 (1971), 104–34.

"Michel Foucault as an intellectual imagination," *Boundary* 2 1 (1972), 1–36. Reprinted in *Beginnings: intention and method.* New York: Basic Books, 1975.

"The problem of textuality: two exemplary solutions," *Critical Inquiry* 4 (1978), 673–714.

"Travelling theory," *Raritan* 1 (1982), 41–67.

Sartre, J.-P., "Jean-Paul Sartre répond," *Arc* 30 (1966), 87–96.

Scott, C., "Foucault's practice of thinking," *Research in Phenomenology* 14 (1984), 75–85.

Serres, M., "Géométrie de l'incommunicable: La Folie" and "Le retour de la Nef" in Michel Serres, *Hermes I: La Communication.* Paris: Editions de Minuit, 1968, 167–90, 191–205.

Shaffer, E. S., "The archaeology of Michel Foucault," *Studies in History and Philosophy of Science* 7 (1976), 269–75.

Shapiro, M. J., "Michel Foucault and the analysis of discursive practice," in Michael J. Shapiro, *Language and political understanding: the politics of discursive practices.* New Haven, Conn.: Yale University Press, 1981, 127–64.

Shiner, L., "Foucault, phenomenology, and the question of origins," *Philosophy Today* 26 (1982), 312–21.

Silverman, H., "Jean-Paul Sartre versus Michel Foucault on civilizational study," *Philosophy and Social Criticism* 5 (1978), 161–71.

"Michel Foucault's nineteenth century system of thought and the anthropological sleep," *Seminar III*, 1979, 1–8.

Stone, L., "Madness," *New York Review of Books*, December 16, 1982, 36ff. Cf. also the subsequent "Exchange" between Foucault and Stone, *New York Review of Books*, March 31, 1983, 42–44.

Sztulman, H., "Folie ou maladie mentale? Etude critique, psychopathologique et épistémologique des conceptions de Michel Foucault," *Evolution psychiatrique* 36 (1971), 259–77.

Taylor, C., "Foucault on freedom and truth," *Political Theory* 12 (1984), 152–83. Reprinted in D. Hoy, ed., *Foucault: a critical reader.* Oxford: Basil Blackwell, 1986. Reprinted also in C. Taylor, *Philosophical papers, Vol.* 2. Cambridge: Cambridge University Press, 1985, 152–184. Cf. also the ensuing "Michel Foucault: an exchange," with W. E. Connolly, *Political Theory* 13 (1985), 365–85.

Valdinoci, S., "Les incertitudes de l'archéologie: arché et archive," *Revue de métaphysique et de morale* 83 (1978), 73–101.

Veyne, P., "Foucault revolutionne l'histoire," appendix to *Comment on écrit l'histoire,* 2d ed. Paris: Seuil, 1978.

Wahl, F., "Y a-t-il une episteme structuraliste? ou d'une philosophie en deça du structuralisme: Michel Foucault," in Ducrot, Oswald, et al., *Qu'est-ce que le structuralisme?* Paris: Seuil, 1968, 305–89.

Wartenberg, T. E., "Foucault's archaeological method: a response to Hacking and Rorty," *Philosophical Forum* (Boston) 15 (1984), 345–64.

Watson, S., "Merleau-Ponty and Foucault: de-aestheticization of the work of art," *Philosophy Today* 28 (1984), 148–66.

"Kant and Foucault: on the ends of man," *Tijdschrift voor Filosofie* 47 (1985), 71–102.

White, H., "Foucault decoded: notes from underground," *History and theory.* Reprinted in Hayden White, *Tropics of discourse: essays in cultural criticism.* Baltimore: Johns Hopkins University Press, 1978, 230–60.

"Power and the Word," *Canto* 2 (1978), 164–72.

"Foucault's discourse: the historiography of anti-humanism," in H. White, *The content of the form.* Baltimore: Johns Hopkins University Press, 1987.

INDEX

act, epistemological, 19
Aldrovandi, U., 144–5
Althusser, L., 13, 43
analytic of finitude, 200
animality, 75–6
Annales, 228, 229
a priori, historical, 242–3
archaeology of knowledge, 5, 198, 227–
9; in BC, 118, 134–6; of Classical madness, 80–5; in FD, 79–80, 88, 102–3;
and genealogy, 260, 270–2; and history of ideas, 244–9; and history of
science, 249–56; in OT, 163, 217–21
archive, 242–3
art, and madness, 98–9
Artaud, A., 99, 196
asylum, 91–5

Bachelard, G., ix–xii, 12–32, 33, 38, 40–
1, 45, 51–2, 229; relation to Foucault,
9–12, 52–3, 61, 62, 69, 111, 220–1,
253–6
Bataille, G., 3
Belon, P., 176
Bichat, F., 128–32
Binswanger, L., 58, 59–63
biology, 168–9, 190–3, 250
Bohr, N., 15–17
Boole, G., 196
Bopp, F., 193–4
Braudel, F., 248; *see also Annales*
breaks, epistemological, 14–16, 40, 69,
220
Broussais, F.-J., 46, 132–3
Buffon, G., 144–5
Burke, E., 83n

Cabanis, P., 43, 119
Canguilhem, G., 19, 20, 32–52, 67, 86,
229, 245; relation to Foucault, 9–12,
53–4, 100n, 101–2, 112, 117, 135–6,
137, 210, 218–21, 230, 231n, 253–6,
269–70
causality, in history of thought, 100–1,
249, 257, 271
Cavaillès, J., 5, 9–11
change, in history of thought, 246–9
Classical Age: episteme of, 146–7, 173–

5; view of knowledge, 147–
8, 155–6; view of language, 153–
5, 157–62; view of signs, 148–
55
clinic, *see* medicine, clinical
cogito, 203–5
commentary, 134, 145
Comte, A., 9, 37, 202
Condillac, E., 121–2, 170, 171
concepts, rules governing formation of,
235–7
confinement, 72–3, 83–4, 100–1
connaissance, 251–2, 253
continuity, 21–2, 40, 256–9
countersciences, 214–17, 223–4
Cuvier, G., 190–93, 195

Dagonet, F., 137n
Darwin, C., 167, 192–3
Derrida, J., 78n
Descartes, R., 13, 23–5, 28–9, 35–6, 73–
4, 80, 146, 151, 203
Destrutt de Tracy, 43, 170
Diderot, D., 39, 96, 167
Dijksterhuis, E., 37
Discipline and Punish, 6, 225
discontinuity, 246–9
discursive formation, 231–8
disease: anatomoclinical view of, 127–
33; Classical view of, 112–15; clinical
view of, 120–7
Doerner, K., 104
Don Quixote, 154
doublet, empirico-transcendental, 200–3
dreams, 59–60
Dreyfus, H., x, 241, 260, 267
Dumézil, G., 211, 266

economics, 186–90; *see also* wealth, analysis of
enlightenment, 11, 262; Foucault and,
1–2
enunciative modalities, 235–6
episteme, 140; Classical, 146–7, 173–5;
modern, 181–4; Renaissance, 140–6
ethnology, 214–16
evolution, 166–8
experience, 70, 103

formalization, 195–6; threshold of, 252–3
Frankfurt School, 11
Fraser, N., 281
Freud, S., 57, 59–60, 95, 196, 214
Freudianism, 10–11

genealogy, 6–7, 260, 270–2
general grammar, 157–62
Goya, F., 98, 264
Greene, J., 176n
Guéroult, M., 229
Gutting, G., 51n, 247n
Gymp, 22

Habermas, J., 257, 272, 277–8, 280n
Hacking, I., 179n, 247n
Hegel, G. W. F., 206
Heidegger, M., 59, 62, 63–4, 206, 223
Hertogh, C., 21n
Hexter, J. H., 179
histoire périmée vs. histoire sanctionnée, 19–20, 38, 40–1
history, 213–14; and archaeology, 27–9, 244–56; of concepts, 32–4, 101–2, 218–20; constructive, 175–9, 221; and the human subject, 228–31, 241–2; of science, 162–3; subject-centered, 228–31
History of Sexuality, 6–7, 225
Hölderlin, F., 196, 206
Hôpital Général, 69, 72
human sciences, 139–40, 208–17
Huppert, G., 176–7
Husserl, E., 9–10, 59, 202, 204, 223

ideologues, 43
ideology, 43–5, 258–9
imagination, 61–3, 156
internalist vs. externalist history of science, 37
interpretation, 196, 273–5

Jones, W., 193

Kant, I., 2–4, 13, 133, 182, 184–5, 198–201, 262, 275
Koyré, A., 9, 11
Kuhn, T., 16, 22, 33, 37, 50–2, 137, 247

labor, 186–90
Lacan, J., 10, 214, 266
Lafitte, P., 37
Lamarck, J.-B., 15, 167, 190, 192–3
language: Classical view of, 153–5, 157–62; and clinical medicine, 124–7; and the death of man, 207–8; modern

view of, 195–8; Renaissance view of, 144–5, 197; see also general grammar; linguistics; philology; signs
Las Meninas, 152–3
Lavoisier, A.-L., 15, 33
Lecourt, D., 12n
Lévi-Strauss, C., 215, 217, 266
life, see biology
linguistics, 216–17
Linnaeus, C., 78, 165
literary analysis, 209, 210, 211
literature, 196–7
Locke, J., 156
Lukàcs, G., 11, 229

Macherey, P., 66n
madness: and animality, 75–6; and art, 98–9; in the Classical Age, 69–70, 72–87, 250; consciousness of, Classical, 76–8; consciousness of, modern, 88–91, 95; Foucault's early work on, 55–69; in itself, 95–99; 263–5; and mental illness, 67–8, 85–7, 94–5; medical treatments of, 85–7; in the modern age, 87–95; in the Renaissance, 70–2, 104
Madness and Civilization, 70n
Maladie mentale et personnalité, 55–9, 64–6, 109, 249; differences from Maladie mentale et psychologie, 66–9
Mallarmé, S., 196, 197
man, 198–200; death of, 207–8, 224
Marx, K., 11, 43–4, 189–90, 192, 196, 202, 206
Marxism, 10–11, 64–7
mathesis, 155
Maupertuis, P., 44, 167
medicine: anatomo-clinical, 127–33; Classical, 112–15; clinical, 118–27; Foucault's critique of, 136–7; during the French Revolution, 115–19
Megill, A., 269n
mental illness, 67–8; Foucault's early work on, 55–66; and modern medicine, 94–5
Merleau-Ponty, M., 5, 9, 202, 204, 222–3
Merquior, J., 272
Midelfort, H. C. E., 104
Minkowski, E., 58
money, 169–71

Nagel, T., 222n
natural history, 162–9
Newton, I., 143
Nietzsche, F., 11, 71, 99, 196, 197, 206, 207, 208, 271, 277–8

nondiscursive practices, 256–60
norms, 21–2, 45–52, 254–6, 281–5

objectivity of science: Bachelard on, 25–7; Foucault on, 272–7
objects (of discursive formations), 234–5
obstacles, epistemological, 17–18, 41–2, 220–1
origin, retreat and return of, 205–7

Paracelsus, 143
Pavlov, I., 65
perception, in clinical medicine, 124–7
philosophy: Foucault's conception of, 284–7; modern, 184–6, 208–9
phenomenology, 202–3; Foucault and, 68–9, 222–3
philology, 193–5
Physiocrats, 171–3
Pinel, P., 91, 93–5
Porter, R., 104
positivism, 185–6
positivities, 242, 250
power, relation to knowledge, 275–7, 279–80
precursors, 39–40, 244–5
Priestley, J., 33
probability, in clinical medicine, 122–4
profile, epistemological, 17–18
psychoanalysis, 17n, 214–16; of reason (Bachelard), 17, 53; see also Freud
psychology, 209, 210, 211; Foucault's critique of, 105–9; and psychiatry, 65, 67–8, 97–8
Putnam, H., 272

Quine, W., 23

Rabinow, P., x, 241, 260, 267
Rajchman, J., x, 265n
Ramus, P., 176
realism, metaphysical, 29–32
realism, scientific, 27–32
referential, 240
reflex movement, 34–7
relativism, Foucault and, 272–8
Renaissance: episteme, 140–6; view of knowledge, 142–4; view of language, 144–5, 197; view of madness, 70–2, 104; view of wealth, 169
representation, 149–53, 174–5, 181–6, 199, 208–9
resemblance, 140–2, 155–6

Ricardo, D., 187–9, 192
Rousseau, G. S., 175, 177
Rothman, D., 104
rules, of discursive formations, 234–8
Russell, B., 196

Sade, Marquis de, 98, 264
Sartre, J.-P., 9–10, 61, 204, 229
Saussure, F. de., 239
savoir, 251–2, 253
Searle, J., 240–1
Sellars, W., 22, 29
Serres, M., 13, 229
Sheridan, A., x, 72
ship of fools, 72, 104
Schopenhauer, A., 185
signs: in Classical Age, 148–55; in clinical medicine, 120–2; see also language, philology
similarity, see resemblance
Smith, A., 186–7
Smith, R. C., 12n
social sciences, see human sciences
sociology, 209, 210, 211
spatialization, 112–15
speech-acts, 240–1
Spencer, H., 44
statements, 239–44
strategies, rules governing formation of, 237–8
strong program, 257
structuralism, 10; Foucault's relation to, 10–11, 111–12, 228, 266–70
Suarez, F., 177
subjective unities, 229–31

taxinomia, 155–6
Taylor, C., 272, 276–7, 280
thresholds, 252–3
Tiles, M., 12n, 21n, 23n
Tuke, S., 91–5

unreason (deraison), 73–5
unthought, 203–5
utilitarians, 171–3

Van Gogh, V., 71
Velasquez, D., 152–3
vitalism, 41–2

wealth, analysis of, 169–73; see also economics
Weber, M., 11
Willis, T., 36–7